TREVOR GRIFFITHS

Theatre Plays Two

Oi for England
Real Dreams
Piano
The Gulf Between Us
Thatcher's Children
Who Shall Be Happy ...?
Camel Station

SPOKESMAN

Also available from Spokesman

Sons and Lovers
Trevor Griffiths' screenplay
of the novel by D.H.Lawrence

These Are The Times
A Life of Thomas Paine
An original screenplay by Trevor Griffiths

Theatre Plays One –
The Wages of Thin
Sam, Sam
Occupations
Apricots
Thermidor
The Party
Comedians
The Cherry Orchard

First published in 2007 by Spokesman
Russell House, Bulwell Lane
Nottingham
NG6 0BT
Phone 0115 970 8318.   Fax 0115 942 0433
e-mail elfeuro@compuserve.com
www.spokesmanbooks.com

ISBN: 0 85124 721 0
ISBN-13: 978 085124 721 2
A CIP catalogue is available from the British Library

Printed by the Russell Press Ltd (phone 0115 978 4505).

For Gill

*Whose contribution has been immense
and whose commitment total*

Trevor Griffiths was born and educated in Manchester, and has been writing for theatre, television and cinema since the late 1960s.

The first volume of his collected theatre plays covers the period 1969 to 1980.

Volume two contains the plays written between 1981 and 2001.

His extensive work for the screen includes three major television series – *Bill Brand*, *Sons and Lovers*, and *The Last Place on Earth*; numerous single plays including *All Good Men* and *Through the Night*, and the television films *Country* and *Food for Ravens*. Many of his stage plays have also been produced on television.

For his film *Reds*, written with Warren Beatty, he received the Writers Guild of America Best Screenplay award and an Oscar nomination. Other films have included *Country*, directed by Richard Eyre, and *Fatherland*, directed by Ken Loach.

From the 1980s onwards he has also directed his own work both in theatre and on film. *Food for Ravens*, which he wrote and directed for BBC Wales, won both a Royal Television Society award and a Welsh BAFTA.

In 1982 Trevor Griffiths was given the BAFTA Writers Award.

CONTENTS

Oi for England   1

Real Dreams   25

Piano   69

The Gulf Between Us   115

Thatcher's Children   167

Who Shall Be Happy ... ?   229

Camel Station   259

OI FOR ENGLAND

Oi for England was first performed at the Royal Court Theatre Upstairs on 9th June 1982. The cast was as follows:

Swells   Peter Lovstrom

Finn   Paul McGann

Gloria   Beverley Martin

Landry   Dorian Healy

Napper   Robin Hayter

The Man   Paul Moriarty

Directed by   Antonia Bird

Musical Director   Andy Roberts

Designed by   Chris Townsend

Lighting by   Robin Myerscough-Walker

Sound by   Patrick Bridgeman

Oi for England

The main cellar room, brick and plaster, in basement of large Victorian house in Moss Side, Manchester. A door opens on to corridor and cramped wash and lavatory area. On the walls signs of fitful tenancy: pics, posters, badges, scrawls. The floor is cluttered with miscellaneous goods looted during riots. The names and logos of principal Manchester stores (Lewis's, Lillywhite's, Safeway's, etc.) are prominent on boxes, containers and carrier bags.

Three young skinheads are playing instruments and singing: **Landry** *(19) on drums,* **Swells** *(18) and* **Finn** *(17) on guitar. As they sing,* **Gloria** *(15), Manchester Jamaican in school uniform, can be seen at the half-open door, bobbing her head to the beat.*

Song

> In England's green and pleasant land
> There's them as sit and them as stand,
> There's some as eat and some as don't,
> And some who will and a few that won't.
>
> Oi, oi, join the few.
> Oi, oi, it's me and you.
> Oi, oi, what'll we do?
> Oi, oi, turn the screw.
>
> Sick of this, sick of all the shit,
> Sick of them as stand while the other lot sit,
> Sick of being treated like a useless tit,
> Sick of being shoved, sick of being HIT!
>
> Oi, oi, me and you,
> Oi, oi, coming through.
> Oi, oi, what'll we do?
> Oi, oi, turn the screw.
>
> Keep the light on, you in charge,
> You with the butter, us with the marge.
> Take extra precautions before you retire –
> This time a song, next time the FIRE!
>
> Oi, oi, coming through,
> Oi, oi, me and you,
> Oi, oi, more than a few,
> Oi, oi, turning the SCREW!

The song ends. An uneasy, frustrated silence, ruptured by the odd cough and twang. Landry, Swells and Finn stand or sit in separate silences. Landry tightens the skin on a side-drum. Swells plucks at a little chord that he's far from having mastered. Finn watches Swells' sullen efforts with distaste, anger and depression at work on the young face. Swells senses the unspoken criticism. He goes on practising. Ironic handclap from doorway. Swells' eyes snap at Gloria.

SWELLS: Piss off, chocolate drop. Black get.

Gloria laughs and sticks her middle finger in the air.

FINN: We're practisin'.

GLORIA: Yeah?

She laughs again. Finn grins a little, seeing some of his own joke.

FINN: What d'ya want?

GLORIA: Me dad says ... (*She rubs finger and thumb together*) ... eight quid owin'.

Finn looks briefly, bleakly, at Swells and Landry. Swells shakes his head. Landry doesn't even look up, still tautening skin on drum.

FINN: Tomorrer.

GLORIA: Said that last week.

Silence. Gloria studies the group: Finn and Swells study her. Landry drubs the side-drum with his fingers, sound growing, his ear close, attentive.

LANDRY: (*Cutting sound abruptly*) Tell 'im later tonight maybe.

Finn looks at Landry, who takes the look; looks at Swells, who looks at Gloria.

SWELLS: (*Hard, sudden*) Right?

GLORIA: (*Slow, unphased*) Who're you? Macho Man?

Swells swings his guitar off his shoulder, moving towards her. Gloria shifts almost invisibly into a taut, armoured, martial arts crouch. Swells stops

LANDRY: Give it a rest, creambun. (*Swells stares on at Gloria.*) Give it a REST.

Swells sniffs, spits very deliberately at Gloria's feet, turns to sit, legs spread, Martens rampant, in the old roundback that provides the room's seating.

SWELLS: A'm not 'anging around 'ere all night, right? Either we're doin' someat or we're not.

FINN: We're doin' someat. 'E'll be 'ere. (*To Gloria*) All right?

GLORIA: 'E needs it. The cash.

FINN: 'E'll have it.

GLORIA: You're Kath Finney's brother, aren't yer?

FINN: Yeah.

Swells snorts. Finn stares at him.

GLORIA: Saw 'er at the Caribbean, Sat'day. UB40 were on.

FINN: Aye?

SWELLS: (*Contemptuous*) UB40. (*Spits*)

GLORIA: What'll I tell 'im then?

Napper *in behind her, a plastic bag in hand.*

NAPPER: What'll you tell who, Topsy?

Gloria looks at him carefully. Napper is big, larded, denim jacket over braces and skin, MU scarf knotted round waist, blue neckchain tattoed on his right fist. He's high at something, pleased and nervy. Throws cans of Worthington E at the surprised three.

Friday. Rent Day. Right? Right.

He casually removes a brown packet from his jacket pocket, fiddles several notes from it. Gloria counts. He waits.

GLORIA: Eight.

Napper counts out two more, gives them to her.

NAPPER: Bye, Topsy. Say hello to Kunte Kinte, won't you?

GLORIA: (*Levelly*) Eat dick.

She turns. **The Man** *blocks the doorway. He stares at her, stone-eyed, then steps aside, giving Gloria half the doorway. Her face passes close to the Man's as she leaves. His nostrils flick.*

NAPPER: Hi. Come in. S'er old man's basement. S'where we work out.

The Man walks into the room. He's tallish, slim, calm, chill, about 40. He wears a long, unbuttoned leather overcoat in dark brown, a black round-necked wool sweater. Finn and Landry stare at him. He looks them over.

MAN: (*Quiet, almost pleasant*) I've got half an hour. Impress me.

FINN: Why? Who're you?

The Man frowns, looks at Napper.

LANDRY: What's goin' on Napper?

NAPPER: (*To the Man*) Eh, look, I'm sorry, 'aven't 'ad a chance t'ave a word ...

SWELLS: Are we doin' out or what?

NAPPER: Shurrit, will yer!

LANDRY: (*Big, raw, hard*) Never mind 'shurrit'. What's goin' ON? We said eight o'clock. You're a bleedin' hour late, Napper.

NAPPER: Right, right, I'm explainin', aren'ta?

FINN: Coulda fooled me, Napper.

MAN: (*Calmly, to Napper*) Sort it out, eh? I'll be in the van. Ten minutes?

He leaves, almost weightlessly.

NAPPER: (*Following him to doorway*) It'll be all right. Five minutes is plenty.

MAN: (*A shadow on stairway*) Good ...

He's gone. Napper turns back into the room.

NAPPER: You've no piggin' idea, you lot, 'ave you?

FINN: We don't bring people here, Napper. S'what we said ...

NAPPER: Oh, did we? An' who brought 'is soddin' sister here then?

LANDRY: Was different. Pigs were crackin' 'ead that night.

NAPPER: Landry, fer Christ's sake, give it a rest, will yer? I mean, this may be
   your scene, bangin' away in a cellar. I'm after someat better, you know?

*He's pacing. Reaches Swells' outstretched Martens. Looks at them. Swells moves
them, reluctantly. Napper walks another way, the dominance asserted, the ritual
barely visible.*

FINN: Like what?

NAPPER: Oh, like PLAYING, you know? Like at a gig, you know? Fer money,
   with an audience, like. Ye've 'earda that, 'ave yer? People DO do it ... out
   THERE.

LANDRY: Stop wankin' off, Napper.

NAPPER: (*Fierce*) Look, Landry, when you can find eight green 'uns for this 'ole,
   you can call me a wanker, all right?

He smiles a bit, pulling it back. Landry smiles.

SWELLS: Yeah, where'dya gerrit?

Pause

NAPPER: (*Sniffs*) Gorrit from 'im.

SWELLS: What, is 'e a puff?

Landry laughs. Finn smiles. Napper comes down.

NAPPER: You're a NIT, you. Wharrayer?

SWELLS: (*Giggling*) I'm a nit. (*He puts his hard, knuckled hands out in front of
   him. Napper places his own quite carefully against them. There's dried blood
   on Napper's left hand.*) S'that?

NAPPER: 'Ad a brush. Wi' one of our little brown brothers. Bugger bit me.

Shows him. They laugh, remove their hands, the ritual dissolved.

FINN: What is 'e then?

NAPPER: Oh, not much. 'E's just a feller lookin' for a skinband for a carnival he's
   puttin' on in Platt Fields, sixth o' next month. (*He sniffs, opens another
   Worthington E, studies his impact.*) London band's let 'im down ...

SWELLS: Yer kiddin'.

NAPPER: Pillock.

LANDRY: What, fer money?

NAPPER: Thirty quid. (*Pause. Searches for clinching inspiration. Pats pocket.*) Ten up front. (*He grins, clenches his fist, smacks the air with it, the ball in the back of the net. Swells stamps his Martens, happy. Landry looks at Finn, shrugs his shoulders to say 'Sounds good?' Slinging his guitar*) Ladies and gentlemen, bit of order for a new band from Moss Side, making a long overdue first public appearance today. Let's hear it for ... WHITE AMMUNITION! (*The crowd goes rapturous in the back of his throat. He belts out several chords.*) What do yer say? 'E's outside in 'is van. 'E wants to 'ear us play. I rest me case. (*He winks at Swells. Swells pecks his nose with his thumb, happy.*) Do I ask 'im or what?

He's a step to the door, unhooking his guitar.

FINN: Who is 'e?

NAPPER: Who is 'e? He's The Man.

FINN: 'S'is name?

NAPPER: Landry, can you explain to Finney 'ere what's goin' on?

FINN: 'S'is NAME?

NAPPER: (*Blowing*) I don't bloody KNOW 'is name, prick. They call 'im The Man.

FINN: 'Kind of a name's that?

NAPPER: What kind of a name's NAPPER? S'a name. Ask 'im.

FINN: Where'd yer meet 'im?

SWELLS: Oh, come on, Finn, soddin' nora, what's it matter where 'e fuckin' met 'im?

FINN: I wanna know who I'm dealin' with.

NAPPER: Listen, sunshine, you're not dealin' with anyone. 'E's dealin' with US.

SWELLS: Fuckin' A.

NAPPER: (*Suddenly*) Look, I'm fetchin 'im down.

LANDRY: (*Up from drums and down the room*) 'Old it Nap. 'E's not goin' anywhere. (*Napper turns back again. Stands in doorway, tense, angry.*) What's the rush?

NAPPER: (*Deliberate*) No rush, Landry. Let the bugger go. The offers WE'VE had, we should worry. Let 'im join the queue.

LANDRY: (*Even*) Not sayin' that, Napper. Just give us the story. We bin waitin' over an hour right? We were meant to be practisin'.

NAPPER: All right, all right, all right. I'm late, I'm sorry. Someat cropped up. Burra met this guy, right? An' 'e's serious.

FINN: Where?

NAPPER: What?

FINN: Where d'ya meet 'im?

NAPPER: Where'da meet 'im? Met 'im in a pub.

Silence. They eye each other. A police siren flirts to life a quarter of a mile away. A second joins in.

FINN: What pub?

NAPPER: Skin pub, off the Oldham Road.

FINN: What's it called?

NAPPER: Don't remember. Prince of someat.

FINN: Princea Wales?

NAPPER: Coulda bin. Yeah.

The sirens die. The name hangs. Finn looks at Landry. Walks back down room. Squats against side wall, arms on knees.

SWELLS: Princea Wales. Our Rit's husband used to use it. S'all right.

Landry looks at Napper. Shakes his head. Looks at Finn, who's withdrawn.

NAPPER: What the fuck's wrong NOW?

SWELLS: (*Shrugs*) Search me.

FINN: I'm English. I don't wear a swastika for nobody.

Silence.

NAPPER: What's 'e on about? (*Down room*) What you on about, you?

FINN: (*Disengaged, deliberate*) Princea Wales. 'Itler's bunker. NF, BM, the lot.

NAPPER: Oh, Christ, 'ere we go. (*Striding, puffing*) When're you gonna grow up, eh? T'man's offerin' WORK. 'Eard of it? That thing people used to do quite a lot of, once. Listen, you wanna spend t'rest of yer life knockin' corner shops off an' singin' tough in a cellar, that's your look-out. I wanna DO someat. (*Pause. Indicates the room.*) I thought that's what this was about. (*Pause.*) I'll play in a long white frock if I 'ave ter.

SWELLS: You'd look nice in a frock, Nap.

Silence again. Finn sits tight-lipped, withdrawn. Swells looks at Landry, who's undecided and fulcral. Napper's quite taut, unable to push further.

SWELLS: (*Up room, at Finn*) Anyway, you're not fuckin' English, you're fuckin' Irish.

FINN: (*Deliberate*) I'm English.

SWELLS: You're fuckin' Irish.

NAPPER: 'E's English. It's 'is grandad who's Irish (*To Landry, conciliatory*) 'E's not one of them nutters.

FINN: 'E's a nutter.

NAPPER: 'E'da said, wunne?

FINN: They don't SAY. You find out.

NAPPER: Finn, they put concerts on. MMI, they're called. I've seen tickets. Bona fide. On the level. Dead straight. (*To Landry*) What do you think, Lan?

LANDRY: I don't mind. (*To Finn*) What d'ya think? (*Finn says nothing.*) Do no 'arm t'play fer 'im, anyroad.

FINN: (*Sharp*) We're called AMMUNITION, Napper.

NAPPER: (*Sullen*) Yeah, whatever you say, Finney.

SWELLS: (*Slow*) What's wrong wi' callin' usselves white?

NAPPER: Ammunition's fine. All right.

Finn looks at Landry, then stands and gathers his guitar.

LANDRY: Best get your man.

Napper nods, elated. Legs it up the stairs. Swells gathers his guitar. Landry returns to his kit.

SWELLS: (*As if it had never stopped*) Your Kath reckons she's Irish.

FINN: She is.

LANDRY: What we gonna play?

SWELLS: Yeah, come on, Finn.

FINN: (*Casual*) I couldn't give a shit.

SWELLS: You're the music man.

FINN: Doesn't matter. The Man's not 'ere for music,

LANDRY: (*Hardening a touch*) You don't KNOW that, Finn.

FINN: (*Bleak*) Yeah, well, I 'ope I'm wrong. I do. 'Cos I'm sicker doin' nowt. Drive yer daft. Eat, sleep, sit, stand.

LANDRY: (*A touch tougher*) Yeah, well, why don't we stop pullin' our plonkers an' get someat worked out, all right? (*Pause. Finn nods eventually.*) Right. Now it dunt matter what we play s'far as 'e's concerned (*Nods in Swells' direction*), 'cos 'e can put 'is two chords anywhere. What d'ya reckon we do best, Finn? S'down ter you, son. (*He's distracted by two fire engines racing through streets close by. Napper in the doorway.*) Wharappened?

NAPPER: No sign of 'im. Pissed off waitin', I suppose. (*He kicks a box, quite viciously.*) Sick o' this.

SWELLS: Did you look?

NAPPER: 'Course I fuckin' looked! You think I went up there and closed me fuckin' eyes? You henry.

Silence. He prods a carton with his boot.

SWELLS: (*Defending the question, surly*) Coulda bin parked in t'next street.

NAPPER: 'E DROPPED me 'ere, 'im and 'is mate, pillock. I know where he was parked. 'Es gone. Scarpered. Whoosh. I'm sick as a pig.

Silence.

FINN: So. We got ten quid for nowt. Easy money, eh, Napper?

Napper finds this not funny. A moment.

LANDRY: (*Beating air above drum skin with manic speed*) Let's DO someat. (*He belts a cymbal, wild, energy rushing from him, anger cording arms, jaws. He stills the brass eventually, levels out slowly. Calm*) I don't wanna spend the night arguin' wi' me mates.

FINN: I say we practise.

He looks at Swells. Swells looks across to Napper, who's reached the grid window, below pavement level, behind the drum kit. Napper broods. Swells shrugs indifference, compliance.

What you say, Nap?

NAPPER: (*His back to the others, quiet*) I say fuck this, Finn. It's a waster time.

Silence.

FINN: (*As quiet*) No, it aint. (*Napper makes no answer.*) We've bin arrit six months, less. Took us over a month to loot the gear. Two afternoons a week, you an' Swells from scratch. We'll get a gig when we're ready.

NAPPER: (*Turning*) We got a gig. You pissed on it. A job. (*Snapping slightly*) Who do you think you bloody ARE, anyway?

LANDRY: I'm askin' one more time ...

NAPPER: (*Abrupt*) I say we go an' do a few shops. Could be another big 'un, by the sound of it. All right, Swells?

SWELLS: Yeah.

NAPPER: Lan?

Landry lays his sticks down. Shrugs, lifeless.

What you say? Get on the street? Bit o' fun. Kick some head. (*He runs at the room, delivers a terrifying box-kick in the air. Ends up with his back to doorway.*) Come on, Finn. Let's do it. I promised me Auntie Winnie I'd try and gerrera micro-wave.

The Man is in the doorway. He stands in silence. Napper has become aware of him through their stares.

Thought you'd gone ...

MAN: (*Quiet, simple*) I'm 'ere. Ready to impress me?

He scans them.

NAPPER: Er, yeah. Yeah, sure.

Napper looks at the others. Eyes move to Finn. He waits, then slings his guitar across his shoulder and begins the set-up. They join him. The Man sits on the roundback half-way down the room. He's taken a walkie-talkie receiver from his coat pocket. He places it on his knee. They're about ready, up the room.

MAN: (*Reminding himself*) What you call yourselves?

FINN: Ammunition.

MAN: White Ammunition, right?

Finn looks at Napper. The Man watches Finn's look.

LANDRY: (*Quiet*) 'S it gonna be, Finn?

Finn plays a sudden strong introductory sequence. The others get ready.

FINN: (*On brink of their entry*) ... Sod the Lord – pass the ammunition ...

And they're away.

> There's gonna be a death,
> Gonna to be a killing.
> Someone up there's gonna cop it one day,
> God and weather willing.
> Law and order, up your arse.
> The orders are yours and the law's a farce.
> Watch out for the crash, the course is collision.
> Sod the Lord – pass the AMMUNITION!

They play with verve. A colossal noise. Swells plays well above himself. Napper begins to relax. Landry's hard and subtle Charlie Watts. Finn is the music, and good.

> There's blood on the wall.
> It's a quid to a shilling
> Someone up there's gonna measure his length,
> God and weather willing.

The Man is listening. The tranceiver's still on his knee. His fingers are on the volume control, adjusting it. The police radio frequency can be heard. Outside, the action building.

> Law and order, up your arse.
> The orders are yours and the law's a farce.
> Watch out for the crash, the course is collision.
> Sod the Lord – pass the AMMUNITION!

The song deafens. Their involvement and passion are touchable: energy and spirit collect, cohere in performance.

> There's gas on the streets;
> It's not for a filling.
> Someone up there nearly wasn't tonight,
> God and weather willing.
> Law and order, up your arse.
> The orders are yours and the law's a farce.
> Watch out for the crash, the course is collision.
> Sod the Lord – pass the ammunition.

They repeat the chorus a last time; it's shouted, handclapped, terrace-chanted, driven on Landry's drum.

> Law and ORDER, up your ARSE!
> The orders are YOURS and the law's a FARCE!
> Watch out for the CRASH, the course is COLLISION.
> Sod the LORD – pass the AMMUNITION!

Chordflare, cymbals. Silence. They stand for moments, triumphantly dazed at having heard themselves heard and high on that energy, the Man down the room barely remembered. It's some while before they hear and react to the closer and more clamant sound of the clashes taking place in neighbouring streets, which the end of the music has uncovered.

SWELLS: (*Moving to grid window*) Shaggin' nora, listen to that lot.

LANDRY: (*Head turned*) Close. C'be a big 'un.

Napper, still in the music, catches Finn's eye.

NAPPER: (*Small grin, touching guitar*) Good eh?

FINN: (*Smiling*) Fair.

In a sudden short lull in the street noise, their attention is pulled to the broken sound of the Man's voice down the room. He stands with his back to them, foot up on chair seat, murmuring into the tranceiver. He is talking to Roy, a contact in a van parked outside. Roy is in touch by CB with other vans and bases in the south of the city. It's a simple but effective system for deploying and mobilizing active cadres, particularly on riot nights. The Man bleeds information on black and police movements from Roy, feeds back instructions.

MAN: Tell Willie sit still, we'll call him; tell Mac t'get down to the Barley Mow an' see if Watt's lot're about ...

It's casual, quite practised, not self-dramatizing.

Din rises from nearby streets again, surging, ebbing, but the four lads continue to watch the Man. They hear next to nothing of the exchange, but sense connection with the action on the streets. When they speak, it's sotto, among themselves.

SWELLS: S'e up to?

LANDRY: Prob'ly ord'rin' curry 'n chips at t'Dakker.

NAPPER: 'Ushitup, 'e'll 'ear yer.

SWELLS: 'Ey, 'e's norra blueboy, is 'e? Looka this soddin' STUFF.

Surveys the room's loot. Cupboards bulge.

NAPPER: Dickhead. Think I'd bring a bleedin' rozzer 'ere?

SWELLS: Yer fuckin' daft enough.

NAPPER: Hunh.

FINN: (*Deliberate*) 'E's no blueboy.

Napper looks at Finn sharply, expecting trouble. Finn stands by the grid-window, listening to the disturbance slip towards riot.

    (*Bleak*) 'Eavy shit.

He looks at Landry.

LANDRY: Me mam's down t'Troc. Bingo.

NAPPER: (*Sharp sotto*) 'Ey up.

The Man's almost with them, silently claiming the space. The open tranceiver bubbles and spurts on the chair he's left it on. The lads wait in silence: Napper and Swells expectant, alert; Landry quiet, impassive; Finn remote, at the window. The Man stops some paces from them, says nothing, lips pursed as if in thought.

MAN: Listen to it. Listen to England. Listen.

Some looks pass between Napper, Landry and Swells. Finn has resumed his retracted squat by the wall.

NAPPER: (*Uneasy*) What'dya think ter music?

MAN: (*Deadpan*) Was a riot.

Nothing. The Man is a heavy presence. Eating space, doing nothing. Feet shift. Finn watches through hooped hands.

NAPPER: (*Nervy*) Warrabout t'job?

MAN: It's possible. Do you want the job?

NAPPER: You kiddin'? 'Course we want the job.

The Man scans them. Questions Finn silently. Finn remains still.

LANDRY: (*Quietly*) What IS the job?

A sputter down the room. The Man listens. It passes.

MAN: Free concert, Platt Fields, May the 6th. Skinfest. Truckin' a lotta people in. Fifteen, twenty thousand mebbe. Heavy. London band – Shed Brigade? – 've given back word.

SWELLS: Chelseaboys. Ffff.

Pause.

MAN: Might be a bit grown-up fer you lads.

A sudden thrash of police trucks at top of street as they charge a crowd. Screams, oaths, thuds, cries, running feet, the pop of shattering missiles, a gleam of petrol bombs. They listen.

SWELLS: KGB's busy. Bastards.

The noise recedes, their street not chosen.

NAPPER: (*Annoyed by the distraction*) What the FUCK'S going ON out there?

Landry shrugs ignorance. Swells is definitely 'search me'.

MAN: (*Almost casual*) Know the Union Jack Club?

NAPPER: Raby Street? Just round t'corner.

MAN: Crowda kids trapped inside.

SWELLS: What, coppers got 'em, you mean?

MAN: (*Shakes head*) Blacks. (*Silence.*) Hundreds of 'em. (*Silence.*) Anderton's Puffballs're tryin' ter scatter 'em. No go. (*Pause.*) Those lads need help. They're gonna burn.

Napper looks around the room, gauging temperature.

NAPPER: Mebbe we'll go down there, eh? (*Waits.*) See what's goin' on.

SWELLS: (*Shrugs*) Sure.

LANDRY: (*Shrugs*) Why?

Finn stays still. The Man studies them.

MAN: Gonna tek a chance and book you. Don't let me down. Platt Fields, May the 6th. Get there for five. I'll want four numbers. It's thirty quid in green uns on the night, nothin' up front. That's the deal.

NAPPER: Great.

SWELLS: Great.

MAN: You GOT four numbers?

NAPPER: (*Fractional check*) ... Sure. Yeah.

LANDRY: D'you say nothing up front?

MAN: (*Calm*) On the night. That's the deal.

Landry looks at Finn. Finn looks at Napper. Napper refuses contact.

SWELLS: (*Innocently*) Who do we ask fer? When we get there?

MAN: Just ask for The Man. They'll know. (*On his way*) Got any questions, ask 'em now. I'm due elsewhere.

He's down by the chair and indicating his movements to Roy in the van. Napper's elated, jabs Swells on the biceps. Swells grins, picks out 'James Bond' theme on guitar, wafting it subtly towards the Man on the tranceiver. Landry watches Finn guardedly. Finn stands abruptly, one movement from hunkers to upright. The Man begins closing aerial, pocketing set. Two fire engines slither past the top of the street, brief instants down the night's long and slippery pole. The Man turns in the doorway.

MAN: OK?

FINN: (*Very simple*) I gotta question.

NAPPER: Man's on his way, Finn boy.

Napper and the Man exchange brief looks, a thin hint of obscure collusion somewhere, but a long way from the nose.

FINN: (*Moving forward a little*) S'about the songs.

MAN: Yeah?

NAPPER: Knock it off, Finn, WE can sort that out.

MAN: Leave 'im be. (*To Finn*) What about the songs, son?

FINN: S'just workin' out what sort o' stuff you'll be needin' in Platt Fields on local election night ... (*It lies a moment between them, not visibly remarked by either.*) We've got all sortsa stuff ...

MAN: Like what?

FINN: (*Simply, as if summoning them*) Oh... 'Black and white, unite unite', that's one. 'The Nazis are coming, they've been before', 'Adolf didn't do it, it's all a packer lies', 'There's a jackboot where my brain used to be'. All sorts.

MAN: (*Deadpan, undrawn*) Ahunh. Interesting titles.

FINN: It'd 'elp if you could tell us where you're comin' from, wi' this concert. (*Nothing.*) You know, the politics ...

MAN: Politics? Why're you raisin' politics? S'a concert.

FINN: Yeah, only it's a free un, innit? An' if there's no dough on t'door ...

He leaves the meaning to complete itself.

MAN: (*Calm, unhelpful*) Yeah? What?

Finn looks at Landry, as if wondering how much more he can say.

FINN: OK, I'll be straight wi' yer, mister. I know yer wanna gerroff... (*Looks at Napper, whose eyes are large with anxious anger.*) ... I made them song titles up. We don't sing that kinda SHIT, all right? We call ourselves Ammunition 'cos we're ready for firin', but not against our own. So if you're from that anti-Nazi league or any o' them other black-'n-white-unite freaks, it's no deal. We're not interested. You might as well sling yer 'ook. Right, you 'ave it.

Finn breathes deep, thrusts hands in pockets, looks briefly at the others, as if pleased with himself for having got it off their chests. Napper's stony, powerless now to intervene; Swells strokes his scalp with the palm of his hand, trying to fathom it; Landry's twigged, likes Finn's style.

MAN: (*Eventually*) You'll be Finn, right? (*Finn nods.*) Napper mentioned you might be trouble. (*The Man walks back into the room, undoes his coat, takes out his cigarettes, lights one, offers. Swells and Napper take.*) So. You guys got me down fer a nigger's man, that right?

He scans them swiftly. Swells shakes his head with alacrity.

NAPPER: (*Miserable*) Not me, mister. Listen, you get off. WE can sort this out.

MAN: Get off? Ha. (*The laugh is short, one chill sound.*) Somebody's gotta put this boy RIGHT. (*He says this with sudden energy. Landry gets up from the drums, eases towards the arena.*) Hear this. On the night of May the 6ᵗʰ – local election night, as you point out – Moss Side will see its biggest concert ever. Half a dozen bands, twenty thousand kids from all over the area, bussed and trucked from Liverpool, Widnes, Runcorn, Preston, Chorley, Bolton, Bury, Rochdale, Oldham, Ashton, Stockport, Salford ... Doleboys like yourselves, school over years back, job not yet begun. English. Working-class. White. (*THEM, his hand indicates*) Sicker bein' kicked around, ignored, shat on, pushed to the bottom of the midden, up to their necks in brown scum, the diarrhoea their rulers have seen fit to flood this England with. (*He indicates the street outside. The din has receded but remains, even at a distance, intense, bitter.*) Their England. Made on the backs, made by the sweat and bone of the white working class, generation after generation. This England, run BY foreigners, FOR foreigners. Jews, Arabs, coons, Pakis, wogs from all corners of the earth. Chocolate England. (*Long pause.*) Now. Anyone plays black-'n-white-unite-unite at THAT concert better have a pretty fat club book, 'cos they're liable to get their throats ripped out before they reach the first chorus. Here ... (*He's fiddled a block of tickets from his coat pocket, hands Finn one, then the others.*) 'MMI presents', see it?

SWELLS: (*Seeing it*) Oh, yeah.

MAN: Movement Music Inc. Movement. (*One hand*) Music. (*The other*) Incorporated. (*The hands join*) Concerts, music: politics by other means. All clear?

He looks at Finn.

FINN: Yeah. As a bell. Thanks fer tekin' t'trouble.

MAN: No trouble. (*Smiles*) I'm glad to say. See you on the night?

FINN: You bet.

MAN: (*Into tranceiver*) Comin' up, Roy. Out. (*To them*) Ammunition. All right.

He leaves, like air. They stand in silence, listening for the sound of the front door pulling to.

NAPPER: (*Toneless*) Great.

They break up, a bit aimless, deflated. Some stains of anger and tiredness in the air.

SWELLS: What's goin' on? (*He's pretty well ignored.*) I don't gerrit. (*Nothing.*) Bleedin' 'ell ... (*Finn squats against the wall. Landry lies flat on an old mattress. Napper cases his guitar, then hunches down on the chair, a copy of* The Sun *between his feet, open at page three. He stares at the picture expressionlessly.*) You're a load o' wankers, you lot, do you know? Are we doin' it or what, Nap? (*Napper's eyes remain on the page.*) Wharrabout it, Lan? (*Landry stares at the ceiling. Swells switches to Finn.*) You reckon the man's a nutter, do you?

FINN: What do YOU think?

SWELLS: (*Frowns, thinks*) I dunno. 'Ow d'yer tell? Seemed all right ter me.

FINN: E's a Nazi

SWELLS: Yeah? 'Ow d'yer mean?

FINN: Gas chambers. Concentration camps. Dictators.

Swells copes with this.

SWELLS: Oh. (*Strokes head*) 'E sounded all right to me. (*Looks round at others*) So we're not doin' it? (*Landry and Napper give him nothing, remote in their respective spaces.*) Fuck.

He sits on Landry's drum stool, pissed off, miserable. Silence. Distant din from streets, rising, falling. Swells looks towards Napper, wants him to argue for playing the gig. Napper sucks his damaged hand, stares on at the pic.

SWELLS: Anyroad, the man thinks we're turnin' up. Somebody's gonna have ter give back word. Bloody ain't gonna be me, I'll tell yer. He looks a mean bleeder.

NAPPER: (*Without looking*) Finn'll tell 'im. Won't you Finn?

FINN: You tell 'im, Napper. You know 'im better.

Napper looks up, takes Finn's look. A loveless moment.

LANDRY: (*From nowhere, not moving*) Time you reckon it is?

FINN: (*They're all watchless*) Nine?

SWELLS: (*Eventually, worrying on*) Thing I don't get, if 'e said there were nowt up front, 'ow come 'e gives yer ten quid advance? Nap?

Napper, back to The Sun, *looks up briefly.*

NAPPER: 'E didn't.

SWELLS: Yer a lyin' bugger, aren't yer? (*Thinks*) So where'd it come from?

NAPPER: (*Simply*) I thieved it.

SWELLS: Yeah? Where from?

Napper thinks for a moment, then stands up and crosses the room to enter their space.

NAPPER: Where from? From a feller. (*Pause*) Wanna know 'is name?

SWELLS: What yer talkin' about?

NAPPER: 'Ang on. (*He searches in his top pocket, draws out a brown envelope. Several bank notes overlap its edge. Reads.*) Mr ... Jarwah ... lal ... Chor ... jewry.

SWELLS: S'that?

NAPPER: S'is wage packet.

SWELLS: (*Laughing*) Yer kiddin'.

NAPPER: Straight up.

SWELLS: 'Ow'd yer gerrit?

NAPPER: Owda gerrit? I battered the fucker 'an took it off 'im.(*He stares at Finn, then Landry, then Finn again.Vicious*) Paid the fuckin' RENT, right?

FINN: 'Ard, aren't yer?

NAPPER: 'Ard enough.

LANDRY: (*Remote*) 'Ard as a bucketa tripe.

NAPPER: 'Ard enough.

FINN: Work 'im over, did yer?

NAPPER: 'Im an me. One on one.

FINN: Bet 'e was real big, right?

NAPPER: Big enough.

FINN: Yeah. Indians. Huge. (*Pause.*) What you do, jump 'im?

NAPPER: I asked 'im fer a light. I'd left me matches in the Prince o' Wales. I was waitin' for a 93 outside Pailin's Mill. This feller walks past. I asked 'im fer a light. He's countin 'is fuckin wages. 'E walks right past me, couldn't give a toss, little black bastard's countin 'is wages. I'm eighteen an' I've never 'ad a job in me fuckin' life! So I blobbed 'im one an' took the lot. Fifty-eight quid. Serves the fucker right.(*Beat.*) I'll tell yer someat else, smartarse, while we're at it. I'm WHITE. I'm proud of it. I think it's the best thing ter be. I agree with the man. I ain't tekin' second place to no niggers 'n' Yids in me own country. If 'e's a Nazi, so am I. I just think I'm English. What're you? Fuckin' MICK, that's what you are. What d'you fuckin' know? Listen to that lot! (*The din has flared again. Windows implode; the dull plug of gas canisters hitting air four streets away.*) It could be us lot down there tonight at the Union Jack. Gettin' our 'eads kicked.

SWELLS: Not me. S'a lousy pint.

NAPPER: (*Withering him*) I'm just SAYING. Twat. (*To Finn*) I just don't get you. I don't. I don't know where yer comin' from. I don't know what yer about.

FINN: (*Slowly, distinctly*) Yeah, well, that's maybe 'cos you're THICK, Napper.

Silence. Napper seems to swell. Finn gets tighter, tauter.

NAPPER: Callin' me thick?

Finn stands slowly, takes a half-pace forward, to free himself of the wall.

FINN: Just acknowledgin' a fact, Napper.

Landry gets up, quite quick and lithe. Places himself easily between them.

LANDRY: Cool down.

NAPPER: Stay out, Landry.

LANDRY: Cool DOWN. (*He stares hard at each in turn*) Not tekin' sides. You wanter fight, do it on t'street. Chances are you won't even be noticed. (*Waves at window*) Not down here. We need this place. The old bugger upstairs'll throw us out.

Napper stares on for several moments, then makes for a cupboard. Takes two packs of Players No. 3 from a carton and stuffs them in his pockets.

NAPPER: YOU may need this place, Landry. Personally, I couldn't give a SHITE. Personally, I think it's about washed out. (*To Swells*) I'm gonna do a coupla shops, if there's any goin'. Whadderyer think?

SWELLS: (*Sniffs*) Yeah. I don't mind.

NAPPER: (*To Finn*) I'll see if I can pick yer someat up on me travels. Golliwog, mebbe.

He leaves, Swells in tow. Finn follows them to the doorway. Landry looks for his jacket. Finn comes back towards him.

LANDRY: Gotta go. See if I can see me mam. This lot'll scare 'er ter death.

FINN: You played good.

LANDRY: Enjoyed it.

FINN: Best.

LANDRY: Think 'e means it? Napper?

FINN: (*Nodding*) Good riddance.

LANDRY: Nap's all right. Bit nervous.

FINN: Thought I'd 'ave a word wi' Tomo. 'E plays a bit.

LANDRY: Yeah? Any good?

FINN: (*Smiling*) Good as Napper.

Landry chuckles. Finn chuckles

LANDRY: Why not? (*On move*) See yer t'morra?

FINN: Yeah.

Landry stops, turns.

LANDRY: Wanna come?

FINN: No, it's all right.

LANDRY: 'Ya gonna do?

FINN: Mooch. Nowt.

LANDRY: Story of our lives.

FINN: Yeah.

LANDRY: Tekin' yer word for it, Finn. (*Simple*) I'da played. I don't really give a shite. I just wanna play. I just wanna DO someat, get outa the pighole. (*Stubs the floor with his boot, no speaker but needing to speak*) Don't really understand the rest of it. Politics 'n' that. Never really bothered. Look after me own business. (*Thinks*) 'Cos no bugger else will. (*Waits for something. Nothing*) I tell yer SOMeat better 'appen. I'm sicka this lot. I am. (*Finn nods. Landry zips his jacket, one motion.*) Anyroad ... takin' your word for it, Michael. See yer on the ice.

Landry leaves.

FINN: (*To empty room*) Yeah. See yer on the ice.

A police truck thrashes into the street outside, screaks past the window in pursuit. Petrol bombs flare in its path. Finn crosses to watch the night. Shouts, screams, some pain and fear. The din moves on again. He listens, watches.

Footsteps on the stairway beyond the door. He hears them, tenses slightly, doesn't turn. The lights are switched out. The footsteps recede, then approach again. He turns. Gloria stands in doorway.

GLORIA: (*Hand to switch*) Sorry. Thought I heard you go.

FINN: Leave 'em. Just off.

They look at each other bleakly across the darkened room. Gloria is in streetgear: jeans, bomber, basketball shoes, wool hat, a heavy metal torch hooked round her wrist. She's hard, energized.

GLORIA: Stay 'ere a bit. Do yourself a favour.

FINN: 'Ow d'yer mean?

GLORIA: Asians're on the rampage. Crackin' eads. SKIN'eads mainly.

FINN: I got no quarrel.

GLORIA: How will they know?

Finn ponders it. Moves a few steps into the room. Sits at Landry's drums.

FINN: 'S'it about?

GLORIA: Old Asian guy got 'is faced kicked. Your lot. (*She touches her head, signifying skins.*) They don't like it. They're gettin' it together. Gorra gang of 'em caught down t'Union Jack on Raby Street. (*Pauses and laughs oddly.*) They're burnin' it down, man. Asians. Gettin' angry! 'Ad enough. All right! (*She eyes him, curious. He sits impassive, eyes on drumskin.*) Me dad's bin jumpin' up 'n' down in fronter t'telly. 'E were gonna come down 'n throw y'all out. (*Laughs again*) Voted Conservative at t'last election. (*Finn laughs a little in the darkness, a sad sound.*) Where's yer mates? (*He shrugs*) 'S'e a mater yours? (*He looks. She chills into the Man's posture. He shakes his head.*) What'd'e want?

FINN: Ammunition. (*She waits*) Lookin' for a band. For a gig.

GLORIA: Yeah? (*Pause*) 'D'e get one?

Finn doesn't answer at once. A rubbish skip burns in the street outside. Flamelight washes and tumbles across the room. Finn shakes his head eventually.

FINN: 'E offered.

GLORIA: You turn 'im down?

FINN: Yeah.

GLORIA: Gerraway. Why?

FINN: Di'n't like 'is style. Di'n't like the deal. Why d'y ask?

GLORIA: (*Sniffs*) Smelt 'im a mile off. Real white man.

FINN: (*Quiet*) I'm a white man.

Gloria swings the torch in her hand, beams it on his face, scrutinizes it.

GLORIA: Yeah, I guess y'are.

Surge of noise in adjoining street. The repeated splat of windows being crumpled by pick-helves one after another.

I gorra go.

FINN: (*Standing*) Down there?

GLORIA: Might 'ave a look.

FINN: Wait.

He walks to a tall cupboard, opens it, waves her to join him. She comes, reluctant and curious. She cannot read his mood. He stands inspecting the cupboard's contents. It is bursting with lifted miscellanea: hardware, electrical goods, sports gear, canned food, cigarettes, toothbrushes, shampoo, Chinese slippers, seed packets, soap powder, spring water, writing pads, Mothercare items, cutlery, chocolate bars, books. All in enormous quantities, grabbed at random.

GLORIA: Bin busy.

FINN: Mmmm. (*He's sifting, searching, occasionally locating.*) You'll need some things. Night like this. Could catch yer death. (*He looks at her. She hasn't understood, wants to understand. The stare is frank between them, grows almost intimate.*) Here. (*He hands her things to hold, items of sportswear, two of most things.*) Tek 'old.

GLORIA: (*Muted*) Wharrathey?

FINN: I'll show yer.

Finn takes a boxer's training cap from the gear she holds, straps it on to his head, draws a black balaclava over his head, to hide it: nods to Gloria to do the same. They begin to prepare themselves, as if ritually, yet with a faint sense of mockery at the conceit they're inventing. They smile occasionally, helping each other with occasional items – Batsman's chest-protectors, hidden under jackets, shin pads, thick elasticated elbow pads, a cricket box for Finn. Gloria's eyes are demurely held down. During their gladiatorial transformation they speak very occasionally, small familiar sounds in the shadowed silence.

FINN: Be. Prepared. They are.

GLORIA: 'S your first name?

FINN: Michael.

GLORIA: Michael Finney. That English?

FINN: (*Thinking a little*) Irish.

GLORIA: Mine's Gloria.

FINN: That English?

GLORIA: Yeah.

Pause.

Why'd yer see that feller off?

FINN: 'E was a Nazi.

GLORIA: 'S that to you?

FINN: Me grandad used ter tell us about 'em. He were in Germany in t'war. Showed us a picture 'e took, in a concentration camp. I lived with 'im when I were little. (*Pause*) A lot o' bodies. A lot. Like celery. Sticks. (*Pause*) Fuck THAT. (*Pause*) Me grandad says: if you're not a human, what are yer?

GLORIA: A Nazi.

FINN: Right.

They smile, quite dry. They're about finished. Changed, odd, like children, overgrown.

GLORIA: Listen. Don't you come. No place for honkeys tonight, Moss Side.

FINN: I'll 'ave YOU, right? No sweat. Give us a coupla minutes. I've gorra few
     things,

GLORIA: I've gorra get Pearl from across t'road. See yer on t'corner. (*She sweeps
     the torch into her two hands like a baseball bat, poised for the pitch, grins.*) All
     right!

*She leaves, high, lively. Finn takes a Sharp radio cassette and some tapes from
the cupboard, closes the doors, carries the radio to Landry's drums, places it
down there, selects and inserts a tape. He begins cleaning up, casing guitars,
collecting cigarette butts, beer cans, papers ... The music sneaks into the room,
follows him round it: 'As I roved out'. The song slows him, snares him, little by
little, until he stands, guitar in hand, to focus on its dense, sad, very Irish sound.
Without warning, he swings the guitar, smashes the radio from the drum and on to
the floor, where it lies dead. He returns to trance for a moment. Draws deep
breaths. Smashes the drums with a colossal clatter and deadly force.
Systematically, he destroys drums, guitars, speakers, chair, surface contents in a
deadly, speechless fury. He stops eventually. Stands with a guitar stock in his
hand. He lays it quietly down. Studies himself carefully in a wall mirror. His face
is calm, young, neat. His hands approach the mouth, insert a boxer's gumshield.
The boy leaves the face. What's left is hard, barely recognizable. Suddenly, music
starts up again in the room.*

> And I wish the Queen would call home her army
> From the West Indies, Americay and Spain,
> And every man to his wedded woman,
> In hopes that you and I would meet again.

END

REAL DREAMS

based on *Revolution in Cleveland,*
a short story by Jeremy Pikser

The text published here represents the best version of the play I can at present write. It incorporates in different layers several distinct critical inputs: the first production in Williamstown; a sustained and comradely critical discourse on the text with members of the Eureka Theatre Collective in San Francisco; and the second production in London. A theatre piece takes a long time to be 'finished', leavable; and I'm clear there's more to be done.

Real Dreams is respectfully dedicated to those many Americans who continue to struggle for justice and equality against all the odds in a land, long mad, whose Dream has by now become, almost literally, the rest of the world's nightmare; and if to one in particular, to Jeremy Pikser, the friend, comrade and writer of promise who gave me his story. Write on.

Trevor Griffiths
1987

Real Dreams was first performed at the Williamstown Theatre Festival on 8th August 1984. The cast was as follows:

B.T. Dylan Baker

Karen Robin Bartlett

Arons Nina Bernstein

Ringo Nick Brooks

Sandler Scott Burkholder

Portia Sonia Jaeger

Sally Lucinda Jenney

Yancy Charles McCaughan

Ramon Jose Santana

Jack Kevin Spacey

Knobby Jon Tenney

Bob Ashton Wise

Directed by Trevor Griffiths

Designed by Jon Hutman

A mute black and white video monitor, slung high in the set, carries images of late-sixties American political struggle intercut with a chronicle of Vietnam. The monitor is on before the audience arrives and remains on until it has left. Each production will decide for itself how and when to use the monitor during the action of the play.

Real Dreams

ACT ONE
SCENE ONE: THE SET-UP

Black.

*Lights up on yard of clapboard and brick house in poor working-class
neighbourhood, West-of-the-flats, Cleveland. The light is thick, heavy, high
summer pre-storm; air dense, barely breathable.*

*Two women, four men lie around the scrub of dirt and grass, stilled by the heat. A
dog barks, streets off; stops. Thunder, a way away. A half-gallon jug of red wine
snails hand-to-mouth among them, motion slowed on the wet air: through* **Yancy,**
27, tough, wiry, who stands gazing towards the city and the advancing storm;
B.T., *20, large in cowboy hat, leather boots, denim, slumped against a box;*
Portia, *22, long frizzy hair, prone on the dirt; by* **Sally,** *20, jeans and ribbed
sweater, who drinks from a can of Stroh's and passes it up; by* **Bob,** *30, hillbilly
from West Virginia, in Hawaiian shirt, who shares Sally's box and beer; to* **Ringo,**
19, thin, scruffy, book-ending B.T. across the yard.

B.T.: *(to air, soft)* Ho Ho Ho Chi Minh ...

RINGO: *(eventually; a slow chime)* Dare to struggle, dare to win.

Silence. Thunder, closing. Crossfade to:

Kitchen, overlooking yard, street. Unreal light, half electric, half day. **Sandler,**
*19, short, thickset, stands at a work surface before the window, peppermill in
hands, staring at the street.*

SANDLER: Summer of '69. Kids off the campuses. Fanning out across the country.
Bringing the war home. Building the Revolution. We're in Cleveland. Paulette?
Paulette isn't.

*Thunder. The voice of a woman, metallic, whiney, drifts up at him from
somewhere. Sandler takes a swig on a bottle of red wine, eyes fixed on outside.*
Karen *appears, a china dish in her hand, from the cupboard below the work
surface. She's 28, tall, heavyish, lipstick, shadow. Onions have rawn her eyes.*

KAREN: Fuckin' onions. Goddam, Sandler, you're not even listening ...

SANDLER: *(not)* Listening? Sure I'm listening. You're telling me about your ex ...

KAREN: ... I'm *telling* you about the formation of political consciousness in a
woman ...

SANDLER: OK. That's cool.

*She resumes the preparation of the beefburgers; considers continuing the treatise.
He waits till she's almost there.*

Let me know when we get to the part where I say, 'Couldn't agree more, or as
Marx would have it, when the pain ceases to be a pleasure it's time to haul

some ass, baby' and you say, 'Fuck you, Sandler', will you? (*Karen's work slows in the silence. Thunder, closer, not yet theirs.*) 'S that Jack?

It isn't. Someone begins tuning a guitar in a nearby room.

KAREN: *(quiet)* Fuck you, Sandler. You're so fucking scared of your feelings, man ... (*Sandler takes another slug of wine.*) ... 'Where's Jack?' ''S that Jack?' 'Hope Jack don't get caught in this motherfucker' ... you wanna know if *Paulette* was there, at the meeting, with *Reiner* ... Fact is, you're a bigger mess than me. So tell me. I understand; who else? You already peppered that ...

He stops the peppering he's just resumed. Puts the china bowl of potato salad below the work surface, heads slowly for the back door to the yard. Introductory chords of 'Sacco and Vanzetti' in next room.

SANDLER: It's Independence Day. I'm for gettin' drunk.

KAREN: Sure. (*Reaches for the wine.*) Sure. Get your act together.

Crossfade to:

Living room. **Arons**, *21, small, thin, mild, sits on the stool, guitar on thighs, in a soft spot; unreal light; sings first verse of 'Sacco and Vanzetti', quite loud, rambunctious:*

> Say there, did you hear the news,
> Sacco worked at trimmin' shoes,
> Vanzetti was a peddlin' man,
> Pushed his pushcart with his hands.
>
> *Chorus:*
>
> Two good men a long time gone,
> Sacco and Vanzetti are gone.
> Two good men a long time gone,
> Left me here to sing this song.

Crossfade to:

Yard. The almost-frieze almost as before. Arons, unseen, moves into the chorus, the sound lower, perspectived by wall and window. Sandler arrives, barefoot. Searches out a spot in the frieze of bodies in the immediate path of the jug. Hands sift dirt, pull at grass, pick toes.

B.T.: *(faint contempt)* Hey, it's Sandler.

SANDLER: *(to audience)* 'The Set-Up.'

RINGO: *(B.T.'s echo)* Yeah. How ya doin, man?

SANDLER: *(slumping down; discomforted)* OK. OK, comrade.

YANCY: *(stormwatch)* This is one motherfucker.

B.T.: *(from below hat)* How's it lookin', Yance?

YANCY: Just hittin' Cleveland Heights. Then it's Case Western, down Superior and Chester and Euclid, across the flats and.

No one speaks.

B.T.: 'S hope it drowns a few pigs on the way.

RINGO: Yeah. What you say, Sandler?

SANDLER: *(still waiting to)* Sure. I'd drink to that.

B.T. makes no move to release the jug. Sandler looks at Sally, who has the Stroh's to her lips. Sees Bob next to her.

(offering hand) Hi, Bob, didn't see you there, how's it going, pal?

BOB: *(taking it)* Good, thank you, neighbour, just dropped by to shoot the breeze … Drink a beer?

He indicates the can in Sally's hand. Sandler waits for her to offer it. She stands, eases damp cloth gathered between buttocks and under arms with unselfconscious fingers; resumes her seat. Arons has stopped the song to retune a string.

SANDLER: Guess I'll stick to the wine, thanks, Bob …

B.T.: *(calling to the house)* Arons.

ARONS: *(unseen)* What?

B.T.: Will you shut the fuck up with that hootenanny liberal crap …

RINGO: We had a meetin' about that …

The retuning stops. Silence.

SALLY: *(from nowhere)* Let's hear it for male supremacy.

B.T.: Bullshit.

PORTIA: *(honest, friendly)* It's a perfectly valid point Sally's raising, B.T. …

B.T.: Bullshit.

PORTIA: *(patient)* The meeting didn't say Arons couldn't sing, the meeting decided we weren't interested in a sing-along.

RINGO: Bullshit.

YANCY: Bullshit nothing. *(Looks at Ringo hard, though the voice is soft. At B.T.)* The women're right. You guys're outa line. *(Thunder bangs and rumbles, almost theirs. Yancy swings to look at it.)* Jesus, it's comin' in fast.

Air cools at speed. People grow sharper, in the expectant freshness. The light is dark; violet. **Ramon** *has arrived unseen with the thunder: neat in shirt, slacks, shoes. When he speaks, it's as if out of shot.*

RAMON: I lookin' for Jack. He here?

People find him, startled; greet him with warmth: 'Hey Ramon, good to see you, man', 'Happy 4th', etc.

B.T.: He ain't back yet, man. Got a meeting across …

YANCY: ... You're a mite early for supper, Ramon. You got a problem ...?

Ramon scans them a moment in silence.

RAMON: No. I got no problem. I wait inside.

Thunder, fast, close. They swing to look at the sky. Ramon's gone. Yancy returns to his street vigil.

SANDLER: Jesus, what's with Ramon? (*People shrug, uncertain.*) Any signa Jack, Yance?

YANCY: Uhunh.

PORTIA: *(fingers in hair)* That was *so* scary.

YANCY: Feel it?

They feel it, some fear at the edges.

BOB: Big as a mountain. Oh boy.

YANCY: Feel it. This one's all the way from Hanoi.

B.T.: *(across the yard)* Sounds like old man Anderson humping his wife back at fuckin' Kent State, don't it, Ringo?

Bob covers his mouth at the language, chuckling.

B.T.: I bet Anderson's old lady's pubes're like Brillo, man.

RINGO: No, man. SOS, man. Dig? SOS?

They chortle, embracing a past they didn't actually share.

SANDLER: *(tentative, desperate)* You finished with that thing, B.T.?

He points to the jug. Thunder whacks above them. Soft splashes of rain, early spillage.

YANCY: *(looking up, arms out)* Hey.

SANDLER: Shit.

B.T.: Yahoo.

The rain arrives in hoppers. They take it open-mouthed, on faces, shoulders, bellies, as the sky debouches. Without warning, Yancy rockets his hard body through a series of perfect gymfreak flips. They cheer, applaud, excited, released. B.T. stands, half in macho response, half self-parody, tries the same series, lands ludicrously on his arse first time of asking. Ringo follows; others, Portia, earnest, Sally, clean, easy; Bob claps his hands repeatedly, as if to music, hooping and yipping; Sandler, a gentle declension to earlier compulsions; children of the storm. Begin slow crossfade to:

Kitchen.

KAREN: *(through window))* Are you guys crazy'r what? Get the fuck in here will you ...

They troop off for the house, laughing, hugging, joshing as they leave the light. Karen gathers towels and paper rolls, ready to repel. Rain pounds the house, almost drowning the trail of their loony laughter as they round it.

Fade in yard area, now the living room. Emblematic images of revolutionary summer, 1969, define the space. Arons sits at the window watching the storm. Ramon stands, remote, swaying, watching her. People begin to pile up in the kitchen doorway.

KAREN: Keep those feet outa this goddam kitchen. Get. Get.

She throws the towels and rolls, bars the way with a broom. They stream into the living room, spraying water from heads and limbs as they go. Karen watches through her wide window-hatch, envying the fun she's missed. Yancy crosses to her, the only one allowed in; gives her a hug.

RINGO: Hey, Yance, man, where the fuck'd you learna do those fuckin' flips, man?

YANCY: *(through hatch; Gable smile under Gable moustache)* Did gymnastics in the marines, it's nothing man. What d'you say, Bob?

BOB: *(opening six-pack)* Looked pretty neat to me, pal.

Sally and Portia towel each other down. Sandler watches Sally, Portia mutters something, Sally laughs, Sandler looks away, crosses to Arons in the window. Stands behind her, looking out.

B.T.: *(jug still in hand)* Fuck, see that? Flat on my fuckin' ass.

RINGO: Great.

The high's already fading. Karen comes in from the kitchen, unclipping her hair; short skirt and top. Yancy follows.

KAREN: Oh shit, just look at this place, will you?

PORTIA: You wanna dance, Karen?

KAREN: I don't care. I guess this takes care of the goddam barbecue …You gonna stand holding that thing all night, B.T.?

B.T. hands her the jug, a touch offended. She drinks, while Portia sorts 'The way you do the things you do' on to the Motorola. Lightning, long moments of it.

ARONS: God, this is really going crazy, Geoff.

SANDLER: Fuckin' storm, man.

The Temptations' Greatest Hits *gets under way. Karen and Portia funk around, best friends, rarely more than adjacent to the music. People lounge to watch, clapping the floor. Sally joins them, after a moment, effortless and faultless Beaver Falls; slowly takes the stage. Sandler looks in, drawn by the wet grace and power of the movement. Ramon edges in, eyes agleam. Portia and Karen sing along, arm in arm. B.T. and Ringo yeahyeah her on. Thunder, lightning, fast, devastating. Room lights go, come back, several times. The stylus stops, slides, starts, slides again. Karen crosses to lift the arm, the only one to move.*

YANCY: (*father*) 'S OK. 'S OK. Just a good old Cleveland lightning-ball.

KAREN: Holy shit.

YANCY: I seen worse. You all's living in a mean town.

ARONS: (*at window, quiet*) Holy shit's right. It's Jack. That crazy boy.

People crowd over to look, lifted by the news. Ramon drifts towards the jug, collars it, retreats to a wall.

YANCY: Jesus.

B.T.: Hey, Arons, your aunt's VW looks like a fucking U-boat …

RINGO: No, man, a submarine.

B.T.: Whadda you think a fuckin' U-boat is … ?

RINGO: I dunno, man …

YANCY: Goddam, the man's gonna drown out there …

B.T.: It's a fuckin' submarine …

RINGO: So I was agreein' …

YANCY: Get the door, somebody.

Sally's almost there. Calls to Jack up the path. People shift to greet him, Arons to the fore.

ARONS: Hey, Jack.

Jack's in, poncho gleaming. He's tall, messy, not shaped; 24; stands, shaking water, as he scans the room.

PORTIA: God, you're really *wet*.

Jack ducks for Portia to help him off with the poncho.

B.T.: Hey, Jack, how was the meeting, man?

JACK: (*half-crouched*) Everything all right here? (*Nobody follows.*) Tremont's got no phone or electricity. The storm is kicking the shit outa this city. The radio said four people killed already …

A bubble of 'Holy Shits'. and 'Jesus Fucking Christs' around the room.

YANCY: We got no problems, Jack.

Jack claps his hands, exuberant now.

JACK: Outta sight. (*Strides in, hand extended to Ramon.*) Hey, Ramon, man, good to see you. How's it going, man?

RAMON: (*nothing*) OK, man, OK.

JACK: Hope I'm not too late to eat. I'm fuckin' starved.

B.T.: (*insistent for attention*) Hey, man, what about the meeting?

A small silence. Jack looks at him levelly for a moment.

JACK: *(flat)* Meeting was outta sight. *(up again)* What about dinner? You gonna take a bite with us, Bob?

BOB: I gotta eat later, Jack …

JACK: We got enough, Karen?

KAREN: Well, we were hoping to grill the burgers outside … But I decided to put hot dogs on the stove, and there's salad and stuff …

JACK: *(bellow)* Fuckin' right on! The correct line on dinner is definitely dogs, salad and stuff …

He strides for the kitchen, sucking Karen, Sandler and Arons in his tailstream. The room's minimally reordered for eating: B.T., Ringo, Bob. In the kitchen, Jack doles out dogs and salad on to the china Karen provides, Sandler cuts a French roll, sticks a slice on each plate, Portia brings salt, pepper, mustard, paper cups and red wine to the cleared space. Yancy and Sally take laden plates, two at a time, from hatch to people or places in the room. They work fluently, easy, absorbed; little chat.

KAREN: Go easy on the china, B.T.

B.T.: That still the line on the china, Jack?

JACK: Never mind the fucking china, B.T. Why's everybody so goddam wet?

B.T.: We bin doin' flips and fuck knows what in the yard, man. You missed something, man. I fell on my fuckin' ass.

JACK: *(a critical look at Yancy)* Fourtha July, hunh?

Yancy keeps his eyes steadily down on the plates in his hands. Thunder. The lights bobble again, settle down.

(advancing back into the room) Let's do some eatin'. While we can see. Come and eat, Ramon, you're the guest of honour …

They settle on the floor, a rough circle, to eat and drink.

Ramon perches on a box, outside the group, drinks deep, picks at the plate of food.

PORTIA: Fourtha July.

RINGO: Right.

They eat.

YANCY: *(mouth full)* Hey, Sandler, you make this potato salad?

SANDLER: *(tense)* Yeah, I made it, Yance.

YANCY: This fuckin' potato salad is insane, man. *Insane.*

PORTIA: It's really *good,* Geoff.

Sandler basks a little in the gathering praise.

KAREN: Sandler's an excellent cook.

JACK: Great salad, Geoff.

SANDLER: Well, if you must know, the real credit goes to Arons, who ripped the bacon off of Fisher Fazio's … It's bullshit without the bacon.

JACK: Then I guess we'd better raise a glass to Arons …

Cartons are refilled. 'Arons, for the bacon' is toasted. Thunder, already someone else's.

ARONS: *(a shrimp)* I got the jug, too.

JACK: *(holding it)* You got the jug?

ARONS: Sure. And a carton of Kools.

B.T.: Yeah, but they're non-filters. Like smokin' a fuckin' blowtorch.

JACK: You'll smoke them anyway, B.T. Nice work, Arons. Fish in the sea.

KAREN: Anyone got views on the macaroni salad, I made that.

SANDLER: Perfect.

YANCY: Absolutely.

KAREN: Yeah.

JACK: How's the family, Bob?

BOB: Kids're fine. Just too many of 'em …

Laughter. A stool crashes to the floor, as Ramon struggles upright. He takes a few rubbery steps, to free himself, stands with the china plate in his hand, food slipping and sliding from it. People spread out a little, out of his path.

RAMON: I got an announcement. *(He sees the food fall, tries to rectify, almost drops the plate.)*

KAREN: Hey, Ramon, watch the china, man …

He stares at them, broods from face to face.

RAMON: Tonight. You gonna off the A. & P.

Silence. Nobody knows much what to say.

RINGO: *(low)* What'd he say?

YANCY: Take it easy, Ramon …

JACK: *(quick)* Leave it, Yance. OK? *(slow, clear)* What d'you mean, man?

RAMON: I mean, man, you gonna rip off the A. & P. tonight. It's orders from the S.P.I.C.s. To you. *(Wobbles. Sits on a box.)* A. & P. got to burn tonight.

They look at each other. B.T. sits upright, chuckling to himself. Eyes turn to Jack. Jack sits, head in hands, as if weighing things.

PORTIA: *(sotto)* This guy is really drunk …

Jack's head flicks up, silences her.

JACK: The Spanish People in Cleveland organization told you this in person, Ramon?

RAMON: *(punching himself)* Ramon, me, right.

JACK: Fine. We've got to talk about it, man.

RAMON: You've got to talk about it? You bin talkin' for weeks, man. 'S all you people ever do …

Ramon jerks upright, grabs a wall to stay on his feet.

JACK: Hey, Ramon, cool it, man, OK?

RAMON: *(slow)* OK. I be back in a while give you the rest of the orders. I gotta go get cigarettes.

He leaves; gathers himself by the back door for the prolonged walk; is gone. Thunder, receded. They look at Jack. Jack sits on, in thought.

SANDLER: *(low)* What's goin' on, Jack? This for real?

Jack lifts his head; reads his company.

BOB: *(out of it, can to lips)* That guy's crazy. What the hell's he talknabout anyways? The S.P.I.C.s're crowda Spanish kids kickin' butt on Detroit Avenue … They're younger'n you people …

He laughs, drinks, at ease. Jack finds the moment.

JACK: *(gentle; simple)* Listen, Bob. We're gonna hafta talk … among ourselves, you know?

BOB: Hey, listen, sure thing. Denise an' the kids'll be waitin' supper anyways …Thankye all kindly for the … eats …

YANCY: *(an excess of empathy)* You wanna look in later, you're welcome, Bob …

BOB: Sure thing.

JACK: *(quick)* Better still, Bob, we finish our business, we'll give you a call.

BOB: Couldn't be better. Thank you all kindly

He leaves by the kitchen door; a decent, courteous man. People begin to gather inwards for the talk.

KNOBBY: *(off; in side path)* Hey, cousin, I just lef' your place, Denise's hollerin' like a mountain cat …

Bob starts talking to him off, explaining. **Knobby** *claims he's expected, it's OK.*

JACK: *(on his feet, the move)* What the fuck's goin' on here? *(Turns on them; hard suddenly.)* Who invited Knobby?

KAREN: *(remembering, in panic)* Oh my God. I promised him a reading lesson tonight.

JACK: Great. Outta sight, Karen. The day of the regional meeting with national leadership? Pretty unlikely we'd have anything to talk about, even in the normal run of things ... Where's your *head* at, Karen? (*She's withered. He glares on at her. People are scared of his mouth, like this.*) Listen ...

Three bangs on the door and Knobby's in, a book in one hand, a parcel in the other. He's short, well muscled, a touch flash-macho, ducktail haircut.

KNOBBY: Happy Fourth, ever'body.

B.T.: Hi, Knobby, how's it goin', man?

KNOBBY: Quite nicely, thank yer. (*Karen moves to remove him. He deflects her with the parcel.*) Brought these, I thought they'd look nice in the house

KAREN: What are they?

KNOBBY: Flowers. (*She inspects the parcel for the breathing hole; finds none. He takes it from her.*) I'll do that, why don't you get a vase or sumpn?

Karen looks for help, finds none, heads for the kitchen. Jack joins her there. Knobby unwraps the heap of sodden flowers — lilies, gladioli, dahlias, the odd rose —from the brown paper.

KNOBBY: Some fuckin' storm, eh? Morgan's Flower Market got washed clean out ... Fuckin' flowers everywhere, man ...

He shows the draggled swatch of ex-blooms. Some pallid nods and smiles around the group. Holds them out for Sally to smell.

SALLY: Great.

SANDLER: What's the book, Knob?

KNOBBY: (*checking reading*) It's er ... On ... New ... Democracy. By Mao Tse-tung. 'S in English, course ...

SANDLER: Sure.

Silence. He stands with book and flowers. Jack's muttered critique of Karen in the kitchen carries through the window-hatch, indistinct but unavoidable.

KNOBBY: (*polite*) 'M I interruptin' sumpn?

KAREN: (*decisive, from hatch, showing vase*) Bring the goddam flowers, will you, we'll work upstairs tonight ...

KNOBBY: Sure will, miss ... (*He smiles at the group, winks, leaves for the stairs by the front door.*)

B.T.: You have yourself a good time, Knobby ...

RINGO: (*leering*) Yeah.

PORTIA: (*defensive*) What's that supposed to mean?

Jack returns to the main room. They take their places to face him. He stands for a moment, quiet, quite bleak.

JACK: Arons?

ARONS: Yes, Jack?

JACK: What do you think?

She sits, a shrimp in the spotlight, unexpectedly on the line.

ARONS: I don't know, Jack. I mean, I know the S.P.I.C.s've bin asking supermarkets to honour the Farm Workers' boycott of Californian grapes … an' I know for a fact the A. & P. haven't agreed, cos the one I ripped off yesterday were Grade A Delano … I don't know. Doesn't it seem kinda sudden?

Jack waits, impassive, but she's finished.

JACK: Portia?

PORTIA: *(stickling)* I just don't think we should let Ramon'r anyone else … hand out orders like that, Jack. I mean, to me it sorta sets a bad precedent.

YANCY: Too fuckin' right it does. I mean Ramon's an outta sight motherfucker — dig? — but comin' in here givin' us fuckin' orders? *(Holds his hand out flat, miming the anger he's controlling.)* No fuckin' way, man. No way.

PORTIA: Exactly.

ARONS: I'll go with that.

Jack looks towards Sally, who shrugs, unfussed. At Sandler, who says nothing.

JACK: Everybody see it like that?

B.T.: *(sudden, standing)* I fuckin' don't. I ain't no chickenshit and I ain't scareda trashin' no fuckin' A. & P. and I don't want no fuckin' Ramon sayin' I am, man.

RINGO: Right on.

PORTIA: B.T., man, you're so damn tough. Who're you trying to impress …

JACK: *(quiet, depressed)* B.T.'s right. (*Silence. A thin film of dread begins to settle on the room. Sandler has it on his palms. Furtively tries to dispose of it. Fails.*) What the fuck are we here for? Mm? Anyone remember? This is the S.P.I.C.s' turf. They live here; they've *been* living here. This shit is *their* shit. We come in off our campuses, setting up our … SDS collective … right? … on our fuckin' summer programme … trying to organize city kids for the National Action in Chicago in the fall, right? … and fulla shit about how we're willing to put ourselves at the disposal of black and brown leadership, and the first order we get, what do we do? We say no, we'll follow black and brown leadership when we feel like it. What the fuck are they gonna think of us? . We've got four hundred years of white imperialism to lick before they're gonna trust us and this is the first shit we pull? For weeks we've been pushin' Ramon to get 'em to meet with us face to face; this is recognition they're offering. OK, I don't like the action, I don't like the timing, not one fuckin' bit, but we can't just say no. If Ramon tells them we're bullshit, you'd better believe it, we *are* bullshit. And we'll have nothing. Not a single fuckin' contact. That's it. *(Watches them carefully, gauging where they are.)* Leadership made it clear in the meeting this afternoon, the National Action in Chicago takes priority over everything, study programmes, cadre development, learning from the people, whatever. They see 50,000 working-class kids out there in Lincoln Park, bringing the war home. Leadership wants action, dig? *(Fixes on them again.)* So maybe it's time we started earning a bit of *respect* around here. Read me?

B.T.: I fuckin' read you, man. What d'you say, Ringo?

RINGO: Let's fucking do it, man.

JACK: Sally?

SALLY: *(cool)* It's cool.

Jack nods, looks at Yancy.

YANCY: I got no problems *doin'* it, I don't like the relationship …

JACK: *(nodding)* Sandler? *(Sandler's arrested, half-way to the kitchen, glass in hand. Gentle, devastating)* You wanna give us the benefit of your doubts, man, while you're around …?

SANDLER: Mouth's kinda dry, Jack.

B.T.: *(scorn in the grin)* 'S only fear, man. Passes.

SANDLER: *(quiet)* OK. I think this is fucked up.

JACK: Tell us.

SANDLER: I got no problems trashin' the fuckin' A. & P., OK? Clearly, black, brown and poor white people get trashed by the A. & P. every day of their fuckin' lives with the lousy habit-forming overpriced fuckin' 'food products' they dump on 'em. And there's nothing wrong with the S.P.I.C.s tellin' us to do it, Yance … I mean, that's what following black and brown leadership's gotta mean. I can dig on that. When and how is the fuckin' issue. Let's say we got an alliance goin' with the S.P.I.C.s, OK? They come to us and say, 'Blow up the fuckin' A. & P.', we say, 'Outta sight, let's plan it together; What night, who goes, what we use.' This shit has got to be planned. Not on a couple hours' notice after we're all fuckin' drunk, for Christ's sake, including Ramon. And I don't see why this can't be laid out to Ramon, Jack. 'The action's cool, but not tonight. Let's plan the fucker.'

SALLY: *(in the silence)* Dig.

She looks at Sandler; he looks away, pleasured by the favour. Arons, Portia, Karen agree.

B.T.: Dig shit. What's the fuckin' big deal on trashin' a fuckin' A. & P.? You gotta be sober to mix up a few fuckin' molotovs, for Christ's sake …

JACK: *(flat)* Who's drunk here? *(Hands go up, Jack's included. Sandler's goes up, then comes down.)* You drunk or what?

SANDLER: I drank. I'm not drunk.

JACK: *(sitting down)* OK. We do it Sandler's way. But we can't lose Ramon. I just hope to fuck I can convince the motherfucker.

Air is released from taut lungs, as they absorb the decision. Above, the sound of bedsprings, under use: echt whambam thankyou ma'am.

SALLY: *(deadpan)* On New Democracy.

They relax into chuckles, bits of laughter.

B.T.: *(to ceiling, mock loud)* Watch the fuckin' china.

A few choked-back calls of tense joy from Karen. Silence.

PORTIA: *(serious, concerned)* Oh God, here we go again …

JACK: *(eventually standing)* I'll be on the stoop. Waitin' for Ramon. We need to talk about the meeting later …

He leaves by the back door, Arons in his wake.

YANCY: Who's on KP?

B.T.: Yeah.

RINGO: Yeah.

YANCY: Tell you what, you bring the stuff through, I'll start in on the washin' up …

B.T.: Dig it, comrade.

They begin clearing up. Yancy goes to the kitchen, stands framed in the hatch rolling up his sleeves. Sally finishes her can of beer. Looks at Sandler briefly, expressionless; leaves by the back door. Sandler stands on, as the lights crossfade to:

Stoop. Faded light; haze and vapour over the street. Kids play the firecrackers at the far end of the block: cannons in a faraway war. Jack sits on a box, staring at his feet. Arons squats on a step, below him, chin on knees.

ARONS: How'd those people die, Jack? In the storm?

JACK: *(grave, remote)* Three in boats out on the lake, one hit by lightning over near Lorain.

ARONS: *(catching his tone)* God. *(Jack says nothing.)* Don't you love that smell? *(He says nothing, plays with a pebble between his shoes.)* Reminds me of my grandmother.

JACK: *(flat, retruded)* Brian Jones offed himself. Did you hear? Yesterday. In his pool.

ARONS: God.

Sally comes round the side of the house. Approaches slowly, sits on the steps by Arons. Leans back, breathing, eyes closed. Jack watches her a moment.

JACK: You fitting in OK here, Sally?

SALLY: Sure.

ARONS: *(hugging her, kissing her cheek, fond)* She's fitting in fine. Doesn't miss Penn State hardly at all.

SALLY: What do *you* think?

JACK: I think you're doin' OK. I think you should start sayin' more.

SALLY: *(finally; unmoving)* OK. (*Sandler arrives, lacks confidence to rupture their circle, stands by a box on the edge, scans the street.*) You want to talk about that?

SANDLER: Maybe he won't even come back. Could be in his bed on Detroit right now, sleeping it off ... We gotta get a new line on this cheap red wine ...

ARONS: He's such a gentle man. I hated seeing him drunk like that ...

JACK: *(back with his pebble)* I just hope to fuck we covered all the bases back there ...

A firework rocket erupts from the street, trails weird light across their space.

SANDLER: *(to Jack; carefully)* So, who was at the meeting, man? Reiner show ... ?

ARONS: *(undeflectable)* You know, I just remembered ... he quoted Che to me the other day. *(finding it)* 'Riesgo de ponerme en ridiculopero, un revolucionario verdaero es dirigido por sentimientos de amor.' 'At the risk of sounding ridiculous, a true revolutionary is guided by feelings of love.'

A shout in Spanish, loud, challenging, from down the street: 'Compañeros'.

SANDLER: Shit. He's back.

Jack stands, stares down the street.

JACK: What's he doin'?

SANDLER: I don't know. He fell down.

SALLY: Jesus.

More shouting in Spanish. Knobby and Karen appear at the front door. Approach the stoop.

RAMON: Vamonos.

KNOBBY: You people need anything, I'll be next door at cousin Bob's ...

JACK: Thanks. Knobby. It's under control.

KNOBBY: Ain't afeareda no fuckin' spics, no sir.

KAREN: Just go, will you ... and watch your mouth.

KNOBBY: I'll see you later, sweet potater. *(book in left hand, raised)* Thanks for the er ...

He shades off into the near dark, whistling a hillbilly tune. Another shout, closer.

KAREN: *(standing a moment)* The things we do for the revolution … *(Makes her way back in.)* I'll put the coffee on. Doubtless you'll fill me in when you have a moment.

JACK: 'S he coming?

SANDLER: He appears to have lost his way.

JACK: Call him.

Sandler looks at Jack carefully.

SANDLER: Ramon! Over here, man.

JACK: We'll get this over with. *(Ramon arrives, several drinks down the road. They think he might speak. All his energy appears to be needed to control the movement of his body. Eventually)* Hi, Ramon.

RAMON: You people ready for your orders?

JACK: Have a seat, man. *(Ramon sits, frowning.)* Listen, we think it's outta sight the S.P.I.C.s want us to off the A. & P., really outta sight … *(Ramon says nothing, lifts his head a little, focusing.)* But shit like this gotta be planned, man. Together, you know what I mean …? We'd like a meeting with these guys, talk it out with 'em …

Ramon squints at Jack, careful, dangerous.

RAMON: What you sayin' here …?

JACK: I'm saying the action's cool, comrade …

RAMON: OK, let's do it.

JACK: But not tonight, man. You talk to the S.P.I.C.s, you tell 'em we want a meeting …

Ramon stares at Jack, the others.

RAMON: You goddam fuckin' *pussies* is what you is. You fuckers. Pussy faggots. You wan' me to talk to the S.P.I.C.s, I talkin' to the S.P.I.C.s and then you fuckin' *dead.*

He goes wild, sudden, frightening. Tears stream down his cheeks and nose, spitballs dance from his mouth. The people on the stoop are very still, paralysed by the scale of his anger and humiliation.

RAMON: *(demonic)* Coño. God damn you fuckin' pussy faggots. I put my ass on the line for you with these people, you pussies. Some fuckin' revolutionaries. You comin' in here … An' we supposer *trus'* you? My word is my life, you faggots. Chickenshit.

He swings off into darkness, slashing the air with his arms, coils of heavy Spanish unwinding behind him.

JACK: Ramon, come back here, man … (*Rafts of Spanish scream in from the dark. Looking hard at Sandler*) Oh boy, have we fucked this one up … (*Sandler looks down at his feet, appalled.*) We're goin' down the tubes, children …

Ramon returns, pursued by new furies; picks up a box and smashes it against a wall, yelling at the top of his voice. They scatter, save Sally, who stands motionless, watching.

JACK: (*mad*) Ramon, goddam it, come back here, man, you'll raise the whole fuckin' street …

Ramon's stumbling off; falls to his knees, mutters and whimpers, almost weeping. Sally approaches the kneeling figure; stands behind him.

SALLY: Ramon. This is Sally. Please just shut the fuck up and listen to what Jack has to say, will you?

Yancy and Karen arrive from the house. Jack waves them still. Joins Sally. Looks down at Ramon.

JACK: (*distinct, depressed*) Ramon, you're right. It's OK, man. We'll do it.

Ramon looks at him, then eyes the rest of them. They're busy eyeing each other.

Give us half an hour. It'll be all the way dark. We'll move then, OK?

Ramon nods, takes Sally's hand to get to his feet, wipes his face with the insides of his sleeves.

RAMON: Whasse call, him next door?

JACK: Bob.

RAMON: I sit over there.

B.T. and Ringo round the house. B.T. has a stave in his hand.

PORTIA: (*watching Ramon leave*) Jesus.

B.T.: Where's the fuckin' action, man?

JACK: (*marshalling them*) OK. We're gonna do it.

SANDLER: (*off the mark fast*) Lay it out, Jack.

KAREN: (*scared, working at it*) Could I ask how this decision was reached?

YANCY: (*tough*) 'S not material, Karen. Discussion's over.

JACK: (*soft, steady*) Yance, take the van and fill it up. (*Throws him the keys.*) You'll need money …

YANCY: (*on the move, tapping his back pocket*) Did two days for Manpower this week, I have it. (*Stops, turns.*) You want me along on the action?

JACK: You'll look after things here. (*Yancy nods, the discipline holding, heads off down the street.*) You made that coffee, Karen?

KAREN: It's brewin'.

JACK: B.T., Sandler, Sally and me'll do it. OK?

Sandler nods, stiffly. Sally nods.

B.T.: You bet.

RINGO: (*sitting on it*) Aw shit, man.

JACK: We'll use Aron's VW. Questions?

KAREN: I'd like to go, Jack.

RINGO: Come off it, Kushner, that's the stupidest thing I ever heard.

KAREN: Fuck you, Ringo, you're just mad cos B.T.'s going and you're not. I've got to get into heavy shit some time. I'm 27, I've never even bin fuckin' busted …

JACK: Karen. (*She shuts up at once.*) Another time, cool. This action's our first and it's not exactly overplanned. Another time. Cool?

KAREN: Sure, Jack. Just thought I should raise it.

JACK: Appreciate it. See everybody gets coffee. Ringo, help her. (*They leave for the house.*) Arons, check the plugs on the car, I don't want the fucker stallin' on us … (*Arons leaves at once, the discipline tight and holding.*) B.T., you and Portia organize Coke bottles, half a dozen, a funnel, a lengtha rubber tube, what else … ?

B.T.: Rags, man, we'll need some fuckin' rags (*He's gone.*)

JACK: (*calling*) Five minutes. We gotta plan this fucker. (*Looks at Sandler. At Sally. Quiet*) This OK for you?

SALLY: No sweat.

JACK: (*to air*) Pure fuckin' farce.

Arons tries starting up the VW; it draws, starts, putters out.

SANDLER: (*soft*) Read it wrong, Jack. Sorry.

JACK: (*flat*) *I* read it wrong. It was a collective decision. You ain't responsible.

BOB: (*approaching, from next door; Knobby in tow, slipping into his jacket*) Jack. We're goin' with ya.

JACK: Bullshit, Bob.

KNOBBY: Bullshit, bullshit, why not?

JACK: (*lifting slightly*) 'Cause you're not involved, fuckhead. Forget it. Who told you about this anyway?

KNOBBY: Hey, waita minute, feller …

BOB: (*slow, decent*) We don't know what'n hell this's all about but if y'all're gettin' into sumpin' this dangerous, we're goin' with ya. That crazy Puerto Rican you all's lettin' order you aroun' tole us, man.

JACK: Look, you guys, thanks, we dig it, truly man, you wannin' to help, but this thing's fucked up an' you've got a *family,* Bob, are you crazy?

BOB: *(grinning)* No crazier than you all.

JACK: *(moved)* Forget it, OK? Really.

Bob offers his hand. Jack takes it.

BOB: Awright, Jack. But we don't like it. You watch out now.

JACK: Sure.

KNOBBY: Change your mind, let us know. I'll go crazy with anyone …

They wave, drift back to their house. Arons starts the car up again. It runs. Ringo arrives, mugs of coffee on a breadboard, hands them round in the near-darkness of the stoop. From indoors, the sound of Tracy Nelson, 'I just can't find another man to take your place', on the turntable.

SANDLER: Can somebody get my sneakers? They're in the living room.

JACK: *(to no one)* Whereof one cannot speak, thereof one must be silent. *Tractatus Logico Philosophicus.* And other inerasably bourgeois bullshit.

The song indoors gathers, grows more intense in its despair.

RAMON: *(off, calling)* What you waitin' for, man? Let's go.

He crashes around in Bob's strip of garden.

JACK: *(tired)* We were gonna wait for it to get darker, man, remember?

RAMON: *(stumbling around)* It's dark, man, it's fuckin' dark, you wanna wait till fuckin' midnight or somethin'?

JACK: Yancy's not back, he's getting gas for the cocktails.

RAMON: We don't wait, we get gas on the way. Let's go.

JACK: *(sudden, shouting to the house)* B.T.! Get out here, will you. *(A call from within, a door slams, Jack lets air out slowly through tight teeth.)* Pure fuckin' farce. *(calling)* OK, Ramon. You're callin' the shots.

RAMON: That's right man, that's fuckin' right.

JACK: Get in the car. *(B.T., Ringo and Karen arrive. B.T. wears a black balaclava, fatigue jacket, basketball shoes, carries a heavy torch and a bin-liner, bottles clinking inside.)* You got what we need? *(B.T. clanks the bag, Ringo throws a pair of sneakers at Sandler's bare feet.)* Tell Yancy what happened. He's in charge. Let's go.

He leaves, B.T. and Sally behind him. Sandler runs after them, one sneaker on, another in his hand. Ringo follows, to see them off. Portia and Karen draw close, arms round each other, watching from the stoop. The car starts first time. Car doors slam.

JACK: *(off; patient, dangerous)* Will you get in the car, Ramon? Get in the fuckin' car, will you, man. *This* car, Ramon. Fuckin' Jesus.

A car door slams. The car's in gear and away down the block. The music reasserts.

KAREN: *(finally)* No one ever says goodbye. You noticed that?

Slow fade to black.

SCENE TWO: THE ACTION

In the blackness, the fast crump of a roller-door opening. A flashing neon light on the rear wall proclaims the A.& P. Slow, edgy, arrhythmic lighting dimly reveals the side of the building and the spare lot. At the base of the wall, beyond the raised roller-door, a '64 Chevy, a FOR SALE sign: $800, parked under a lamp. Two street lights, left and right, define the parking lot.

Over this, from inside the cruising car:

SALLY: We still ain't got the gas, Jack.

SANDLER: Want me to ask Wittgenstein back there what we should do?

JACK: *(Over shoulder)* We're fuckin' there, Ramon. Where d'you suggest we get the gas?

RAMON: Pull over. *(Brakes; handbrake; engine.)* Over there. We get some gas.

SANDLER: Fuck it, Jack, you could take photographs in that fuckin' light …

RAMON: *(lifting)* I give the orders, I say we get the gas over there …

JACK: *(desperate)* OK, OK. Over there it is.

Car doors bang. Traffic, street sounds, a block away. The four appear out of the dark, crouch in the shadows, stare at the building and the Chevy.

RAMON: *(from the car, distressingly loud)* Less go, less go.

They cringe tighter to the floor.

SANDLER: *(nervy)* This is our leader? Vay ist mir.

JACK: *(sotto)* OK, I'll take a look … *(He moves forward a couple of crouching steps. Stops. To audience)* 'The Action.'

SANDLER: Jack, I hatea say this …

JACK: *(fast, hissy)* Then don't, OK? *(flattening)* Don't make me have to deal with your defeatism, Geoff, 's that OK? Not at the moment. Would you stand up and look natural, for Christ's sake? *(He moves forward, is lost in shadow.)*

B.T.: *(tough, hoarse)* Just shut the fuck up, Sandler. This's a fuckin' *action* man. You're on active service. In the People's War, man. Keep it shut. Jack wants your thoughts, he'll ask you for 'em.

B.T.'s eyes never leave the building, the car. He's coiled like a spring, alive and arrested in the moment; filled by purpose. Sandler looks at Sally, who faces out, covering their rear, some distance away.

SANDLER: *(tense)* B.T., believe me, man, I accept every damn word you say, I was genuinely offerin' sympathy ...

B.T.: *(terse; handrolled cupped in his hands)* He don't need your fucking sympathy right now, just get in line.

SANDLER: *(angering, against his instinct)* I'm in line, I'm in line, man, give me a break, will you ...

SALLY: *(fast)* Shuddup. *(They freeze. Car headlamps play momentarily across them, curve left and cruise away.)* Clear.

Jack's returned. Squats to one knee to confer.

JACK: We're gonna have to lob stuff through windows, this place is built like a brick shithouse.

SALLY: *(clear, across the distance)* Jack.

JACK: Yeah, Sal?

SALLY: We gotta cover the corners. There's a lotta stuff around.

JACK: Sandler, stay back here with Sally, anyone enters the street I wanna know about it. B.T. you got the stuff? *(B.T. clanks the bag.)* Er ... everybody know the procedure for if you get busted ... *(They do.)* Who's on charges here? *(They all show hands.)* O.K. You gonna put that fuckin' thing out, B.T.? *(B.T. stubs the handrolled under his shoe, apologizes.)* Let's get the gas.

Jack and B.T. approach the building, disappear into shadow, reappear eventually by the Chevy through the arch. Throughout what follows, they are seen at work trying to siphon gas into Coke bottles. Sandler watches a moment, then spreads towards the uncovered corner. Cars slide wetly by, a block away, in the silence. The two stand quite still, on the edge of their street lamps, silvery outlines in the haze of light. Sandler takes a pace or two forward, absorbs the light, mainly in his face. When he speaks, he's on radio mic., relayed, flexible acoustic.

SANDLER: *(remote, high-school debating voice)* To be or not to be never was, isn't now, and never could be the question. To those who see history scientifically, we on this side of the argument – 'commie bastards' was the charming allusion bestowed on us by my learned opponent – to those who see history as substantially a history of class struggle, the critical question has never been be or not be but do or not do. We must always first and foremost deal with questions of power, not questions of mere existence. Let me spend a little time illustrating our thesis. Take, for example, the aggressive military presence of American imperialism in Vietnam ... *(His voice breaks in on itself, inward now, flaky under pressure. Off mic.)* Fuck it, Paulette, I *need* you, I need you a lot, when you needed me, last fall, I was there, remember? I mean, sure we agreed we each had the right to decide our own futures, but when did I abrogate the right to be consulted? I'm bleeding, Paulette. Can't stop it. Thirteen fuckin' months of mutuality, respect and trust down the tubes for what? For Reiner? For a guy who's known movement-wide for nothing, for *nothing,* hear me?, except the size of his prick and his extreme readiness to give it employment ... (*Begins to step from the light. Stops, spectral. Speaks in own voice.*) Maybe this, after all, is what revolution, war, history is like: unlikely people doing things they're afraid to do and maybe don't want to do in the first place. We wade in gasoline, who knows which match will send it up? One. Galvanizing. Symbol. What difference will it make then that Ramon was drunk and Sandler was scared and spoke against the action? (*A bottle smashes under the archway. Jack curses, a single expletive, Sandler and Sally look inwards to check, turn back, look at each other across the dark, resume watch. Sandler picks a stone from his foot. He has only one sneaker.*) Seen anything of Ramon?

SALLY: Still in the car. Maybe he's asleep.

SANDLER: You OK?

SALLY: Sure.

SANDLER: I hope you hear by my voice that I ain't pulling no male chauvinist shit on you.

SALLY: Yeah, you're scared.

SANDLER: You got it. Aren't you?

SALLY: Some.

SANDLER: You're unreal.

SALLY: Why'd you take your hand down?

SANDLER: I dunno. It sorta came down.

SALLY: Crap, man. You wanted to come.

SANDLER: How else do I lick it? Or anybody? Do it.

SALLY: (*after pause*) Shit, Sandler.

SANDLER: What?

SALLY: I'm 20, I never even tasted Chinese food, Sandler.

He begins to chuckle.

B.T.: (*from arch, calling*) Sandler. Get the fuck down here fast.

Sandler begins to scutter towards the arch, gets caught at once in the headlamps of a car approaching the intersection 30 yards away. Brakes, a sense of scouting, the lights advance, as the car cruises circumspectly forward.

SALLY: (*strong deadpan call*) One guy, on his own, headed straight at us.

Brakes again. The car's quite close. More scrutiny. They stay quite still, rabbits on the highway. In the silence, Ramon staggers on, sodden with booze. Stares blindly at the lights. From behind the headlamps, the voice of a 50-year-old law-abiding Clevelander, a prototypical good German.

VOICE: *(high Ohio tenor)* Hey. I seen what you're doing. And you better stop stealing that fella's gas, because I'm calling the police …

RAMON: *(a sudden scream)* Why don' you mind your own fuckin' business, you little fuck? I gonna kill you fuckin' ass. I kill you fuckin' ass … *(He goes up a couple of gears, faster in Spanish, as he lunges out in the direction of the lights.)* Singao de mierda. Pon tu coche mierdero en el culo grosero, hijo de mamalon. Que haces por aquí. Debes etar in casa, mirando su maldita tele …

The car crashes into reverse and creeps rapidly backwards, brakes, crashes into first.

VOICE: I'm gettin' the police. You'll see.

He drives off, at his version of a lick. Ramon sits down on the fringe of the car park; whistles fragments of 'America' from West Side Story. *Jack and B.T. are back with the others. Jack has a rag wrapped round a bad, bloody gash on the palm of his right hand. Nobody marks it.*

JACK: *(bleak)* Fuckin' Feydeau, man. Get Ramon in the car, we're goin' … Sally!

They try to get Ramon to his feet. He's all but out; gives minimal and unreliable help.

B.T.: You callin' the action off, Jack?

JACK: *(struggling with Ramon)* This action is postponed, while we get the fuck outta here before the pigs arrive and start plastering us into that wall over there …

B.T.: *(arm around Ramon's waist)* Dig it. We do it later, Yancy'll have the gas, pigs'll go back to the trough.

SANDLER: *(helping where he can)* This thing needs talkin' over again, Jack. That guy was really close. Something happens here, he'll be around to identify us.

RAMON: Where we goin'?

They ignore him. Help him off. They become voices.

B.T.: Look, Sandler, so we get busted, there's some actions worth gettin' busted for.

SANDLER: *(retreating)* OK. I just think we oughta talk it over, that's all.

B.T.: *(bleak)* That's all you ever wanta do, Sandler.

Sally has remained, scouring the terrain for evidence of their occupation. Picks something up. Brings it under the street light. Inspects the sneaker in her hand. She leaves. Car doors slam. The car drives away. Slow fade. Towards the end, the sound of a patrol-car siren, blocks away, answering a call. On black, a sudden brilliant explosion of festive fireworks throws lurid flickery red light over the A.& P. For a moment, it burns. Dies to black again.

ACT TWO

THE LESSON

Black.

Sounds of police siren, fire engine, en route.

Living room. Karen, Portia, Arons and Ringo stand motionless staring out. A fierce, deep red glow lights their faces. They're held; silent. Dull sucks and rumbles, as fire eats air. A slow, iconic moment. Behind them, room and kitchen area are sparely lit by storm lamps and candles. There's a sofa in the room, handsome, proudly set.

Fire engine gets closer, a block away. Arrives, settles down at once.

Jack, Sandler, B.T., Sally in fast by kitchen door, unseen and unheard by the watching group.

JACK: Anyone mind telling me what the fuck's goin' on here? Shit. (*He's thudded against the sofa.*)

KAREN: Oh, Jesus, Jack, I'm sorry, it's my sofa. Larry brought it over, he was looking after it for me …

JACK: Later, Karen, OK …

YANCY: (*fast, in through the back door*) Pigs. Get away from those fuckin' windows, how many more times have I gotta tell you, you assholes.

Portia, Arons and Ringo move back fast into the shadows, as the patrol car screams in and stops across the road. Doors slam, some shouts, some shouted replies. The fire's already ebbing away, under control. Yancy crawls into the room.

JACK: (*desperate suddenly, hoarse*) Yancy, who the fuck sent for the pigs? Are we being set up or what, man?

YANCY: (*across the darkness, patient, patently more in control*) Someone set that old DeSoto parked in front of Gordon's front yard on fire. I don't know who sent for the pigs, Jack. We bin right here, all of us, as ordered. I've been out back hidin' stuff. They coulda bin comin' here, after you …

Silence. The cops stand by the patrol car, radioing a preliminary report on the fire. On the response, it's mainly static.

PORTIA: (*from darkness*) You hurt your hand, Jack?

JACK: (*flat*) It's OK.

YANCY: (*deliberately*) So what happened, man? You get hit? Let's hear …

JACK: (*fast*) 'S Ramon here? (*He's not.*) Sandler?

SANDLER: (*tense, from shadow*) I left him in the yard, Jack. Said he wanted to take a piss.

JACK: *(in a scathe of air)* You left him out *there?* With the place swarmin' with fire pigs and fuck knows what? I don't believe this is happening ...

Silence. Sandler bites his lip, chidden. They sit or crouch in the shadows, barely there. The red orange of the fire has all but gone. In the dark, the storm lamps gradually assert themselves, beacons against the night.

SANDLER: Want me to go look for him, Jack?

JACK: *(slow, tired; slumping on Karen's sofa)* No. Leave him where he is. Maybe he went home. *(Beat.)* OK, listen, people. We fucked up. Some asshole good citizen saw us syphoning gas and we split.

It's depressing news. They search out each other's faces in the gloom.

RINGO: So what you sayin', man, it's over?

Jack doesn't answer. Doors slam, an engine starts, the patrol-car siren starts up.

RAMON: *(off; on the stoop)* Hey. You hear me in there?

JACK: Jesus fucking God. *(Banging on the door, loud, mad. Lifting; fierce)* Ramon, this place is crawlin' with pigs, what the fuck d'ya want?

RAMON: *(eventually; reasonable)* I splittin'.

JACK: *(controlled; weary)* Why not wait till the pigs split, man?

RAMON: *(fast, up)* I splittin' now. *(Pause.)* Action cancel.

The fire engine leaves. Karen gets up, crosses the room raising lampwicks and lighting more candles.

B.T.: What's the fuckin' line on the candles?

KAREN: In case you think I thought this one up, my idea of some fuckin' bistro in the Village, we had a power failure, Jack. It's the best I could do in the fucking circumstances. Phone's still workin'.

Jack has his head in his hand; collecting his thoughts. People have relaxed, begin little wanders, move bits and pieces here and there. Begin to feel perhaps they have come through.

JACK: *(collected)* OK. *(Stands.)* Listen up a minute. *(They gather.)* Make sure you're around tomorrow. All day. I wanna discuss our meeting with national leadership first thing. And I'm calling a criticism/self-criticism session for the rest of the day. Which I will lead. For tonight, we lock the doors, stay inside, get some sleep. We're in one piece. Next time we'll be better. Right, Ringo?

RINGO: *(not wholly gung-ho)* You bet, Jack.

JACK: B.T.?

B.T.: Yeah, you bet, Jack.

Jack walks towards the staircase by the front door.

ARONS: I'll get some stuff up, clean that hand ...

JACK: *(not looking)* Thanks, Arons. I'd appreciate it.

He leaves. Arons has gone to the kitchen, puts water in a bowl, finds cotton wool and iodine. Karen joins her. Eventually sends her on her way. Looks exchanged, as Jack leaves; worried, concerned, a touch embarrassed. Portia hovers by Yancy. Sandler and Sally squat crosslegged on the floor, each in the other's eyeline.

RINGO: I shoulda gone, B.T. I fuckin' offered, man.

B.T.: *(flat on the floor, eyes closed)* Wouldn'ta made no difference, Ringo. It was a fucked-up action.

RINGO: Yeah?

B.T.: Never had a chance.

RINGO: Yeah? So why the fuck'd we go on it?

No one speaks for a while.

B.T.: *(as if tranced)* Fourtha July, man.

Silence again.

YANCY: *(on duty still)* I was plannin' on crashin' out, but if you guys're startin' in on tomorrow's criticism session, maybe I'll join you.

RINGO: Hell no, Yance, we weren't doin' that …

YANCY: Good. Jack'll appreciate that. *(he picks up a storm lamp.)* You comin' up, Porsh?

PORTIA: I need to talk with Karen.

YANCY: OK.

He leaves. Portia joins Karen in the kitchen.

RINGO: Fourtha fuckin' July.

B.T.: *(flat again)* Fuckin' fourtha July.

RINGO: Fuckin' July fourth.

B.T.: July fuckin' fourth.

RINGO: Fourth Ju-fuckin'-ly.

B.T.: *(stumped)* Inde-fuckin'-pendence Day. *(They're amused.)* That's all she fucking wrote.

He gets up, waves, leaves for the stairs. Ringo waits, checks the room for askers, finds none, follows.

KAREN: *(through hatch)* You people want anything? Arons got some nice Earl Grey … *(The phone on the window-hatch ledge begins ringing.)* 'S OK, it's probably my ex about the fuckin' sofa, let it ring …

SANDLER: *(to Sally)* Tea? (*She shakes her head. Earl Grey has been a foreign language.*) One tea. *(serious)* You're a fuckin' security risk, Karen, givin' the fuckin' number out like that, you know that?

KAREN: *(waitress)* One tea. (*The phone stops. She gives Sandler a finger. Watches him covertly eyeing Sally.*) Did you ask Jack yet whether Paulette was at the meeting, Sandler? (*Sandler squirms, deflated. Karen chuckles. The phone rings again.*) This bastard's gonna wake the whole house ... (*Picks up the phone; in improbable ansaphone voice.*) The number you have called has been temporarily disconnect ... What? *(Listens, stopped.)* Er sure. Hold on a minute, will ya, I'll go get him ... (*Lays the receiver down, crosses from kitchen to front-door area. Urgent; calm*) Jack. Could you come to the phone, please? I think it's the S.P.I.C.s.

Jack comes in quickly, shirtsleeves, heads for the phone, picks it up from the room side of the hatch. Yancy appears, without shirt, lamp in hand; B.T. and Ringo, shorts, undershirts, socks; Ringo has their lamp.

JACK: Yeah, this is Jack. (*Listens.*) What? (*Listens, cuts in.*) Listen, who is this, is Ramon there? Lemme call you back, what's your number . . . OK, OK, OK, you call back in five minutes. Right. (*Replaces the receiver slowly, turns to face them. To ceiling; controlled call*) Arons?

ARONS: *(on the move)* Here, Jack. On my way. (*She arrives from upstairs, bowl in hand, towel over shoulder.*)

JACK: You use the phone tonight?

ARONS: Yeah.

JACK: Who'd you call?

ARONS: My aunt. Why?

JACK: *(dead)* Your aunt. Why'd you call your aunt, Arons?

Arons looks around the uncomprehending room for help.

ARONS: I was nervous. About the action, I guess. She's a good person. I just wanted to talk to her.

JACK: Did you tell your aunt about the action, Arons?

A mutter of 'What's', exhalations of bafflement.

ARONS: No. Are you crazy? Acourse not, Jack, Jesus.

JACK: Are you sure? You didn't say anything about the car?

ARONS: Jack. Stop it.

JACK: *(rubbing his face)* I don't even know what the fuck we're talking about. They didn't even say anything about your goddamned aunt. Did you call the Fire Department?

ARONS: *(disbelief crescent)* You're asking me if I called the fire pigs?

JACK: *(lifting)* Did *anybody* call the fuckin' fire pigs, I gotta know, people. I wanna know. I swear this has gotta be on the fuckin' line. *(Stares at them.)* Did anyone?

No one speaks.

YANCY: *(gentle)* Cut the mystery shit, Jack. What the fuck is this about?

JACK: *(slow)* The S.P.I.C.s say Arons called the fire pigs. The little chick is what they said. And they wanna know how come? And I'm goin' fuckin' nuts or somethin' cos I don't fuckin' get it. They say they saw her and they heard her. I don't know how they achieved this. Maybe they had someone out back watching saw her on the phone and just assumed she was talkin' to the fire pigs, I don't *know,* I don't fuckin' know.

KAREN: They sure sounded mad.

SALLY: This is bullshit. What's the deal, Jack?

The phone rings. They listen.

JACK: *(remote)* They're calling back, Sal. *(Crosses, picks up the receiver.)* Yeah, this is Jack. Listen, comrade, you got it all wrong … *(Listens, for some time, stopped cold.)* No, hey, hold it, man … *(They've hung up. He drops the receiver on its stand. Picks it up again. Dials a number, fast, urgent. Waits.)* Come on, Ramon, man. Be home. *(Waits, then in a voice barely more than a murmur.)* They want us to turn Arons over for interrogation by midnight. Cornera 25ᵗʰ and Detroit.

YANCY: *(dazed)* Fuck *them.*

JACK: *(same level)* Or they say they're coming over to kill us.

He gives up on the phone. People absorb what they've heard.

YANCY: Fuck them.

Silence again.

JACK: *(drained)* What time is it?

YANCY: Eleven. Minute after.

JACK: Lock the doors, Yance. I gotta check something out.

He leaves for upstairs. Yancy starts locking doors.

ARONS: Maybe I should try to talk to them.

SALLY: *(distinct, decisive)* Forget it. No way.

B.T.: *(mainly shielding Jack's leadership)* Yeah? Who fuckin' died around here? This ain't gonna be no fuckin' joy ride, these fucks don't piss around …

SALLY: *(into light, hard, direct)* We don't piss around either, B.T. No way. I've seen shit as heavy's anythin' you've seen, only I got no balls to rattle, so maybe you think I know nothing, and maybe I don't know much at that, but I learned some things that can't be otherwise: like, if we don't defend each other, who defends us? No way Arons goes outta that door. I say so. You got it?

RINGO: Fuck, Sally. B.T. wasn't sayin' that ...

Jack's back in the room, an address book in hand, watching.

SALLY: *(back in the shadow again)* Fine, Ringo.

JACK: O.K. Here's what we do. I found another number for Ramon he's sometimes at, we keep trying both till we get him, we've got about an hour, we get him over here and work this thing out. In the meantime ... *(he looks at Yancy.)*

ARONS: Jack, we were discussing if I should try and talk with them ...

JACK: *(simple, dismissed)* Forget it. OK *(on)* In the meantime, we get our shit together. Yance?

YANCY: *(on the move)* Two minutes.

JACK: B.T., Ringo, give him a hand.

They leave, quickish. Jack crosses to the phone, begins dialling. Gets no answer. Tries the second number. Sandler, Sally, Portia, Karen scan the street outside the front windows. Arons follows Jack to the phone, continues bathing and cleaning the wound.

PORTIA: This is really awful.

KAREN: It'll be OK, baby. We'll get it together. Jack'll sort things out ...

Silence. Jack curses at the back of the room. The four peer on.

PORTIA: Fourtha July.

KAREN: We're still gonna smash the fuckin' state.

SANDLER: Onea these days.

KAREN: *(quiet)* Fuck you, Sandler.

SALLY: Nice couch, Karen.

KAREN: You like it?

SALLY: 'S nice.

KAREN: It was my mother's, she gave it me when I got married. Never move without it. 'S Louis-seize or something.

Sally looks briefly at it over her shoulder.

SALLY: 'Louie says'?

KAREN: 'S what they say.

The back door bangs. Yancy, B.T. and Ringo in quickly, laden. Yancy lays down his load to relock the door. B.T. and Ringo lay down the heavyish boxes they carry in the centre of the room. Yancy carries his heavy sacking over, lays it down between the boxes with a clunk. They gather round, silent. Jack puts the phone down, approaches the rough circle of people. Arons tags along behind. Jack goes on one knee, flips open the box lids, then lays bare the contents of the sacking: five guns – an M-3 carbine, an M-1, two .22 rifles, a shotgun. Looks up at them carefully.

JACK: Anyone got anything to say, say it now.

He waits. No one speaks.

YANCY: *(soft)* Ten after, Jack.

Jack nods. He's calm; deathly.

JACK: It's possible nonea this is real; the S.P.I.C.s won't show. Ramon'll talk with them and straighten them out about us, maybe they're testin' us out or somethin', maybe the whole fuckin' evenin's bin a test ... An' it's possible they're comin' to off us. Figurin' we're a buncha pussy faggots in the paya of the fuckin' FBI. So. We gotta be as heavy as the traffic. An' I'm not talkin' about bein' discredited, I'm talkin' about being wiped out. *(Looks around, suddenly boyish. Grins.)* Nobody said learnin' to live the life of the people was gonna be easy.

People smile, work on the rigor in their cheeks.

B.T.: *(half self-parody)* Gimme the fuckin' shotgun. Nobody calls me a pussy faggot and lives.

Tension eases a touch. People smile at B.T., warmed a bit. Jack watches them; loves them all.

RINGO: Fuckin' A. Goes for me too, man.

They look at him; pale, neglected, unlovely, trapped inside his acne and his asthma; are saddened back into the present.

JACK: Yance, lay out how you think we do this, will ya, I gotta try ... (*The phone rings. Jack's there fast.*) Hello, yeah ... No. No, she ain't. No, she ain't expected back tonight, she's er ... she's spending a few days with her mother. Her father then. What can I say, she ain't here. Terry called, I'll give her the message. OK. (*He puts the phone down. Stares down the room at Karen. She goes to speak, gets smart, lowers her eyes.*) Let's do it, Yancy. I'll try Ramon.

YANCY: Right. B.T., you used anya this shit?

B.T.: *(defensive)* Sure. I handled stuff. Sure.

YANCY: Take the M-1. Back bedroom. (*B.T. takes it; fishes in a box of clips, begins filling his cowboy hat.*) Anyone else? (*They shake their heads.*) OK, I take the big feller upstairs, rest don't matter so much anyway, so long as whoever's got the shotgun got good nerves. It's gotta be point-blank range.

He scans them. Sandler tries to look tough; fails. Karen passes: no question. He holds on Sally.

SALLY: Cool. *(She dips for the gun, puts cartridges in a china bowl.)*

YANCY: Kitchen.

RINGO: *(off the hook)* Fuck it, man, I ain't scareda no fuckin' shotgun, man ...

YANCY: *(on)* Sandler, take a .22. Living room.

Sandler dips for his.

Ringo, B.T.'ll need you upstairs for back-up, the M-1's a motherfucker.

Jack's given up on the phone. They know it.

You used anya this, Jack?

Jack shakes his head, headed back.

Karen, you spell Sandler down here; Arons, with Sally … Portia, you're with me.

PORTIA: Fine, Yance.

YANCY: *(handing him a .22)* I figure you should move around, Jack …

JACK: You gonna show us how to use these things?

YANCY: I'll do that when we got people in position, Jack, we gotta get a move on.

JACK: OK. Here's what we do. Only shoot if you *see* someone shoot first, or getting ready to throw a cocktail. *See.* Dig? Anybody rushin' the house without a cocktail or a gun firin', just holler out. I fuckin' don't want anyone shot unless it's absolutely necessary. If they try to come in the door without shooting, we'll take care of them inside. And nobody needs to go freakin' out, all we're doing is bein' prepared. Let's go.

Jack rounds the room, dowsing the candles. Ends up at the phone, dialling Ramon. Pairs move off to their assigned posts. Sally and Arons move to the kitchen; we lose them. Sandler and Karen move the sofa closer to the windows. Sandler draws the bolt of the .22 experimentally, fiddles a 9mm. from his pocket, slides it in, closes the bolt. Fear edges the movements; makes them sharp, arrhythmic. Karen sits on the couch.

KAREN: I've bin hoping against hope we're gonna get outa this in one piece, but watchin' you with that fuckin' thing, Sandler, I know we're in deep trouble.

SANDLER: *(grim)* Shut the fuck up, Karen, would you?

KAREN: Why'd they wanna kill us, tell me that, they never even fuckin' met us. *(He says nothing. She watches his tense frame by the window, gun clutched to his chest like a teddy.)* Was it bad tonight, down the A. & P.?

SANDLER: Karen. Compared to this. It was fun.

KAREN: Shit. You think we're going to die?

SANDLER: If I thought it mattered, I'd give you an answer,

KAREN: What does that mean?

SANDLER: I don't know. I just thought it sounded good. Give me a break, will ya?

KAREN: *(sad)* Poor Sandler.

Silence. She watches him watch the street. An owl hoots, end of street; a second. Jack puts down the phone; listens. Nothing. He takes a window, book-ending Sandler. Karen's face is a dim glimmer behind and between them.

JACK: *(sotto)* Fuckin' owls already.

SANDLER: So how was the meeting, man?

JACK: The meeting. *(blank)* Heavy. Still lotsa trouble with the Running Dogs about the National Action. They've still got this United Front bullshit stuck up their ass. Katzen says they're actually talkin' to the Mobe-Fucks about a fuckin' peace march in Washington. Walker thinks they're ready to split.

SANDLER: Jesus. I hate splits.

KAREN: Let 'em split. Dahlberg an' Alman're shits. I hate 'em.

SANDLER: *(dogged)* So who was there anyway? Barry and Hamer from Columbus?

JACK: Linda came instead of Hamer. God, she's getting heavy. She fuckin' creamed Reiner around women's militia. It was outasight.

SANDLER: *(casual)* Reiner was there, hunh?

JACK: Ahunh.

SANDLER: Anyone else from Akron?

JACK: Doug and Sue.

KAREN: *(great timing)* I think Geoff wants to know if Paulette was there, Jack.

JACK: Oh Jesus. Sandler … We're sittin' here with fuckin' guns in our laps praying to Christ the fuckin' comrades don't blow us away by sun up and you're worried about fuckin' *Paulette? (Pause.)* She's in San Francisco, Alan took her with him to meet with the Panthers.

KAREN: What?

JACK: I'm checkin' upstairs. Keep an eye on the fuckin' street, OK?

He leaves. Sandler takes it in image by image, bowels burning, brain aghast.

KAREN: *(at his shadow)* Fucking San Francisco. Jesus.

An owl hoot, close; another; silence. Metallic sounds of B.T. and Ringo upstairs being put through gun drill by Yancy; they dismantle, reassemble and load the M-1.

JACK: *(from the darkness)* Fuck. Anybody remember to turn the light switches to off?

ARONS: *(from darkness)* It's done, Jack.

JACK: Thanks, Arons.

RINGO: *(puzzled)* Lights *are* off, Jack.

JACK: *(deadpan)* Thanks, Ringo.

Clicking upstairs, the snap of a clip. Karen watches Sandler's trembling frame in the gloom.

KAREN: *(soft)* Geoff?

SANDLER: What?

KAREN: Let her go. Can't you see that staying with you was just holding her back? Geoff?

SANDLER: Fine, Karen. Fine.

KAREN: This personal shit holds us all back, Geoff. We've got more important things to deal with. The Man wants us hung up in love and romance so we won't fight him.

SANDLER: *(not wanting this)* Listen …

KAREN: I'm not like somea the others. I understand love. You know, after Leroy – the sax player usedta beat me up all the time? – *I* was destroyed, you know. And I thought Harold would pull me together. Because he loved me. That's why I married him. But my alienation was too heavy … I don't know. I tried to die. Something went. It was Yancy and Portia helped me through. The movement gave me something to live for again.

SANDLER: Let's do our job, Karen.

KAREN: Men hold women back, Geoff. That's how it is.

SANDLER: Listen, when I met Paulette at counter-orientation at Oberlin, she had the politics of fuckin' Bambi. She didn't know Stalin from Trotsky, she didn't even know Snic from Core. I *made* her, Karen … And now she's fuckin' her way to the top …

A slow volley of hoots rings the house, very close. Another, returning down the loop.

JACK: *(off)* Great. They can't even wait till fuckin' midnight. You see anything up there?

Bring up upper-right bedroom. Yancy, with gun, and Portia.

YANCY: Nothing, Jack.

JACK: *(off)* B.T.?

Bring up upper-left bedroom. B.T. with M-1 and Ringo.

B.T.: Not a thing, Jack.

JACK: Anything, Sal?

Bring up kitchen-door area: Sally, with shotgun, and Arons.

SALLY: Nothing.

The four dim images of the defence of the collective hold for some moments. More hooting, sudden, encroaching. All lights cut, save Sandler's.

SANDLER: *(on radio mic)* So this is what happens when you leave me, hunh? You go to San Francisco with the most famous and sexiest man in the whole revolutionary movement to meet with the Panthers. While the rest of us are stuck in Akron, Columbus, Cleveland …

KAREN: *(hoarse, from the darkness)* What do you think they're gonna do, Jack?

JACK: *(hoarse, from dark)* Karen, how the fuck am *I* supposed to know?

SANDLER: *(on)* Those of us who prefer to deal with history scientifically might want to account for Paulette's political development somewhat differently. A year before she met me she was getting herself gassed at the Pentagon. Gassed and cut. Barbed wire. I saw the scars. Later, through sheer black tights. As it happens, I was there too. But I turned back. On the Memorial Bridge. It was getting late and the Pentagon was still fuckin' miles away and my aunt had a special dinner waiting for me over in Chevy Chase. *(Trembles slightly, living this present and that past together.)* I didn't *make* her. I held her back.

Owl hoots. Silence. Hoots and stick-clicks.

KAREN: *(from the dark; sotto; an attempt at scorn)* This is so fuckin' corny, you know, I saw Randolph fuckin' Scott in this movie, who're they tryin' to scare?

Upper right. Yancy, gun, window. Portia crouched behind.

YANCY: *(blank)* 'Weapons are an important factor but not the decisive factor in war. People, not material, form the decisive factor. War cannot be divorced from politics for a single moment.'

PORTIA: *(blank)* 'The people are like water, the revolutionary army are like fish.'

Hooting, fast, penetrating. Jackal calls; answers. Crossfade to:

Upper left. B.T., gun ready, Ringo behind.

RINGO: *(as if Joplin)* 'It's all the same fuckin' day, man.'

B.T.: *(sings, as if Dylan, stone-faced; gun-guitar)*
                    Gas in the streets
                    Napalm in the park
                    Bombs in the airways
                    Turning day into dark.
                    And there's blood on the moon.
                    Going underground. Underground bound.
                    Got a message for the man
                    With the shadow on his jaw:
                    America ain't my fatherland
                    And the president ain't my pa.
                    Blood and bone. Gonna sink like a stone.
                    Hanoi lovers sitting out in the park
                    Making love and revolution in the noontime dark
                    Feel a dripping on their shoulders
                    Feel a trickle on their hair:
                    Blood on the moon.
                    Going underground. Turn my heart to stone.
                    Underground. Gonna bring the war home.

Take out B.T. light. Black. A flurry of hoots, circling the house. Bring up:

Sally and Arons, dimly framed in kitchen window. Sally has the gun. Arons is quite scared.

ARONS: Oh God, here we go.

SALLY: 'S OK. These fucks're havin' themselves a good time just *scarin'* us to death, they won't need to come in.

ARONS: You think so? *(Works it out.)* I guess this is the first time I realized dying's a part of it.

SALLY: Yeah.

ARONS: An' I was sort of wonderin' if it ever happened in my parents' lives.

SALLY: I sorta knew in Chicago.

ARONS: Oh sure, pigs, the State, I guess I knew that. I mean, now it's ... we're anybody's, anybody could just ... rub us out, you know, like even the people we're solid with, I mean, the people. I mean, we're waiting here with shotguns and fuck knows what to kill our brown brothers who're out there somewhere planning how to off *us,* it's a fuckin' unfunny joke ...

SALLY: We got no *choice,* Arons. We put choice behind us when we started this thing. All we gotta do now is what's necessary. Maybe this is the people's first lesson for us: respect grows from the barrel of a gun.

ARONS: Oh shit. I wish you hadn't said that. And I absolutely know it's true. *(Take out light. Owl calls, dispersed, slightly less close. They continue in black.)* Where you from, Sal?

SALLY: Beaver Falls.

ARONS: Where's that?

SALLY: Nowhere.

Owl hoots, less threatening, spaced.

Lights on, upper right. Yancy, on a box, gun cradled. Portia sleeps, next to him.

YANCY: *(listening, then interrupting)* ... Listen, man, you don't believe it, you've spent twenty-seven years on a Ford assembly line, getting broken down to what you are now, deaf, lame, arthritic and goddam nowhere, man, I know it, man, I lived through it, I watched it growin' up, gave me my first politics, watchin' what capitalism did to its people. This is a pig society: we behave and think and feel like pigs. So why should we behave any different in South-East Asia? I've been *in* the fuckin' military, for Chrissake, I know what it's like and what it's for, and I'm telling you, its sole purpose is to enforce White Racist America's foreign policy, which is to reconstruct the world in its own fuckin' image. Pig world. A worlda pigs, snuffin' at the trough. *(Pauses. Grins, softens.)* Didn't go down too good at my court martial, that speech ... but er ... as it was my whole line of defence ... I had no choice. Listen, Dad, you look a lot better, stronger, than you did last week, how're they treatin' you in here? *(Listens. Pulls out a pack of Camels.)* Fuck it, Dad, you just had a lung removed, you're asking for cigarettes, are you crazy're what?

He chuckles, fond. Crossfade to:

Karen on couch. Tracy Nelson again: 'I'll never find another man to take your place'. Karen joins the song briefly, as if in her sleep. Crossfade to:

Kitchen. Sally in special, gun vertical, check on barrel.

SALLY: *(interior letter-voice)* 'Camp Superior, Ohio, 4th July.

Dear Mom, Your letter arrived the day I left Ohio State for the summer-camp job and I've been worked off my feet since I got here. Thank Pop for the 25 dollars and tell him I'll write when I get a chance – it's appreciated. By the way, I wrote Grandma but got no answer – is she OK? She sent me a Navajo bracelet, coral and silver, for my birthday: beautiful.

'Mom, you don't say it, but I sense you're still upset I'm not coming with you and Pop on the camping trip this year. Don't be. It's only that I need to spend the time working out what I want to do with my life, now my teens are behind me. It doesn't mean I don't love you both, really. And how long is it since you and Pop spent free time together, away from the store and all that goes with it? You owe it to each other. Oh yes, I'm short on shirts, pants, T-shirts and sneakers – could you raid my bedroom and see what's there? And could you send them to me care of Karen Kushner, 10 Michigan Avenue, West-of-the-flats, Cleveland. We've been told not to use the camp address until the leader finds out which hut's intercepting the mailman and pocketing the goodies. Karen's a friend who comes out waitressing weekends and she'll see I get them.

'OK. I'm due at the pool in five minutes – life-saving drill. Tomorrow canoeing. Otherwise, I'm fit, well and pretty happy. A kiss for Pop, a tickle for Brandy and a special hug for you. Sal.'

Crossfade to:

Upper right. Yancy at window, gun slung across shoulder. Portia sits watching him, awake again, a blanket round her shoulders.

PORTIA: Hi. What time is it?

YANCY: Three. Sleep.

PORTIA: Oh God. Is everything still as awful?

YANCY: No, they've quieted down. They ain't gone.

PORTIA: Did I tell you Jack's wife called?

YANCY: No.

PORTIA: She's in Pittsburgh.

YANCY: Still in the movement?

PORTIA: Stronger than ever. And having a really good time.

YANCY: Ahunh.

PORTIA: Anyway. It set me to thinking maybe we should have that talk you said we should have about us as a couple an' things.

YANCY: *(a beat)* OK.

PORTIA: I sense a lotta resentment from the others, us bein' the only ones an' everything .

YANCY: Yeah?

PORTIA: An' I think, like, ideologically it's a bit suspect, you know what I mean?

YANCY: I can dig that.

PORTIA: Anyway. Jack asked me a couplea days ago if I'd be interested in goin' over to Akron, they're openin' up another house ...

YANCY: Yeah? What'd you say?

PORTIA: I said I'd like to. I think I have to. What do you think?

YANCY: Do it.

PORTIA: Yeah?

YANCY: Sure. Any move that frees you as a woman for the revolution gotta be objectively correct. Your voice ain't heard here.

PORTIA: That's right. You speak for both of us, even when you don't.

YANCY: OK. You tell Karen yet? *(She shakes her head.)* She'll be a problem. *(Portia grunts, relaxing back towards sleep.)* I'll miss you.

PORTIA: It's crazy. Why would anyone wanta leave a guy as OK as you?

YANCY: That's the fuckin' dialectic, baby.

She laughs. He puts an arm around her. They cuddle. Lights out. Black. Owl hoots still there, dispersed: a fainter presence, but not lost.

Special up on Jack, living room, behind the sofa, gun in one hand, a crumpled page of type in the other. He scans the page briefly, looks at his audience.

JACK: 'Report on West-of-the-flats Collective to National Leadership. Comrades. The collective – then five men and three women – set up base here June 5th. A fourth woman joined us last week. All nine have committed to the programme until the fall.

'Internal Development: In four weeks, the gains have been few and painstakingly gathered. Daily criticism self-criticism sessions have raised awareness on aims and objectives, strengthened collective discipline, shaped chains of responsibility and established lines of command and generally increased our cohesion as a group. On the down side, the assault on cultural and psychic formations in group members has met with very limited results (see attached reports on individual members). Realistically speaking, the smashing of the liberal under the skin is likely to take some time. The key-text reading programme helps, though the shortage of copies (two Mao, one Fanon, three Lenin) slows us down.

'Outreach: Significant gains here have yet to be made. We have established a relatively unquestioned presence in the neighbourhood. Contact with working-class youth has been so far confined to recruitment drives at schoolyards, playgrounds, parks and beaches, with as yet little tangible yield. But though this is clearly not good, a recent strong contact with a member of the Puerto Rican Socialist Party holds realistic possibilities for a significant advance in this field. The man in question spends a good deal of time in the house, accepts our programme and is currently negotiating a meeting with the area's most militant youth section (S.P.I.C. – see note attached).

'Personal Comments: *(Long pause.)* None. Yours in struggle, Jack Stone. July 3rd, 1969.'

Upper left. Ringo dreams of food. B.T. listens, impassive.

RINGO: Hostess Twinkies, Cheeseburger-Deluxe with onions, a chocolate milk shake, right, a T-bone steak with mushrooms, yeah, and a Big Mac, French fries and a peanut-butter and jelly sandwich, yeah, and some flapjacks with real maple syrup and Frosted Flakes and yeah a fucking great Pepperoni pizza … oh and hold it, how about a …

Very slow crossfade to:

Living room. Pre-dawn, dark, dank. Karen sleeps on her matrimonial sofa, body as untidy as sacking, mini-skirt rucked and rumpled. Her glasses hang from her face. Sandler sits on a box, gun still in hands. A single owl hoot. A second, much later. Sandler pays no heed. Sound of water-closet being flushed. Jack appears. Sandler starts.

JACK: 'S Jack. 'S OK. (*He draws up a box to join Sandler, looks briefly at Karen. Then stares at floor. Sandler watches him. Jack becomes aware of the gaze. Looks up.*) How're you doin'?

SANDLER: OK. How 'bout you?

Jack puts his head down, looks at his boots.

JACK: (*serious enough to cry*) Sandler. I'm goin' outa my fuckin' head, man. (*Sandler says nothing, disturbed, embarrassed a little.*) I mean, what the fuck is happening, man? This is fuckin' *Wagon Train.* (*Looks up.*) I shouldn't be talkin' like this … I don't know why I'm fuckin' tellin' you … Probably cos you're an asshole intellectual. Like I used to be. Regression in the face of crisis. (*Sandler tries to smile; can't.*) Here we are, man, what are we doin'. We're protecting our goddam womenfolk. From the savages. Only what we're supposed to be doin' is *joinin'* the savages. It wasn't supposed to turn out like this. For Christ's sake, Sandler. (*almost at a whisper*) It wasn't supposed to turn out like this … What was I supposed to do? Maybe I shoulda told Ramon to fuck off in the first place … but what would that have done? I mean … (*Stops; can't find what he means.*)

SANDLER: There was nothing you could do, man. Except what we're doing.

JACK: *(bitter, not looking)* Don't give me that shit, Sandler, just look at the fuckin' mess we're in, we're supposed to be forming an alliance wi' these people ...

SANDLER: *(fast)* What the fuck *are* we, man? We're just fuckin' kids. Doin' the best we can with what we've got, which ain't that much ...

JACK: *(harder, more desperate)* We're supposed to have a theory, a strategy and a tactic, Sandler. We're supposed to know what we're doing. 'Do the best we can'? This isn't the Oberlin-Kenyon homecoming game ...

SANDLER: *(sudden)* Wait one fucking minute, man. Who in hell *ever* knew what was goin' on and what the fuck to do about it? Lenin? After twenty years of practice underground, overground and all around town and the greatest fuckin' genius political mind of all time he got shit right mebbe two out of three times. Unless you listen to Rosa Luxemburg, in which case it was a lot less than that. *(Gathering)* Leadership ain't about gettin' it right every time, it's about gettin' it right more often than most. *(Pauses.)* What do you expect from us, Jack? Sure it ain't no fuckin' football game, but we're still fuckin' college kids ... All we can do is try, and fuck it, we're trying. Just like Ramon. He ain't no Fidel, man: let's face it. Who knows what crazy shit's goin' on with them out there ... maybe they're doing us a big favour, teachin' us what it feels like to play for keeps ... Maybe they just don't like us honkeys and want to mind-fuck us a little. Maybe they want an excuse to kill our asses. We've gotta take it as it comes and right now it comes like Ramon. But there *is* a revolution goin' on out there, and there's not a part of the world can't feel it. We didn't start it, we're not gonna finish it, and we're not gonna have a lot to say about what happens in between. But we know what it's for and what it's against. And we know who's gonna win. All we can do is push. In whatever direction looks like the right one. Hard, and as long as we can. And we are, man. We are. (*He gets up, walks over to Karen, props his rifle on the couch, gentles her hair with his fingers.*) All of us, man. And if we fuck up all summer long, no one's gonna tell me Dahlberg or the Mobe or PL or any other buncha white commie college kids is gonna do any better either. And no one's gonna tell me there's anything better to *be* in this pig world than what we're tryin' to become. After we're all dead, maybe someone will know if any of us were worth anything ... What we've gotta worry about now is *not* doing it. All the shit that holds us back and fucks us up — the personal, the comfortable, the safe, the neurotic, the racist — you know, everything that feels natural — well, that shit's there, it's gonna fuck us up, but we gotta make sure it doesn't stop us, man, drive us back to bein' good citizens or hippies or junkies or pigs. I know what *I'm* workin' on ... It's a list as long as your arm, man ... But we're only gonna get as far as we get, man.

Jack gets up. Sways a little, adjusting.

JACK: *(ironic)* Thanks, Geoff, I needed that. Now let's see if you can explain all that to the Comrades.

SANDLER: Comrades're gone, Jack.

They listen to the silence. Faint dawn light deepens the room. A dog barks. Jack stifflegs slowly off into shadow.

JACK: *(yawning)* National leadership need to know by next week whether you agree to leave Oberlin and work for us full time … If the answer's yes, they wanna put you in a leadership cadre …

Sandler's left. The question hangs. He kneels, buttocks on heels, begins to strip down to a sort of white judo suit, the loose jacket tied at the waist. Dawn light continues to grow.

SANDLER: Ramon called next day to say things were cool and offered no explanation. We didn't press. We figured it must've bin some sort of test. Four weeks later, after a few dozen failed attempts to recruit a single working-class kid to the National Action, and half a dozen reports of Paulette going round the country with different members of the leadership, I left the collective. For New York. Where with the help of some Lebanese hash and amphetamines, an empty apartment belonging to a friend of my sister, and the three all-night TV stations, I set a personal record for uninterrupted television watching: eighty-three hours. *(Begins tying a red sash round his forehead.)* But these are dreams that will not go away. These are real dreams.

The others – all eleven – have emerged, in the judo garb and the red head-sash, from the gloom. Arons carries a huge, fine NLF flag, which she waves menacingly, side to side. They walk on their bare heels, arms in karate state of preparedness; but the pace is slow, dreamlike. They form a knot of bodies, looking out, nuclear, unified. Light brightens, whitens, dreamlike (Bergman's Dream). Their movements soften into slow early morning Tai-Chi, disciplined, graceful. Cohere, eventually, into a group, a collective unity, in the bright unreal light.

ARONS: 'Prison Poem': Ho Chi Minh.

They deliver, a phrase each, with perfect timing, tone and meaning, Ho's poem written in prison.

> The wheel of the law turns
> without pause.
>
> After rain, good weather.
> In the wink of an eye.
>
> The world throws off
> Its muddy clothes.
>
> For ten thousand miles
> the land
>
> spreads out like a brocade
> Light breezes. Smiling flowers.
>
> High in the trees, amongst
> the brilliant leaves
>
> all the birds sing at once.
> Men and animals rise up reborn.

They stop. Arons salutes the auditorium with the flag. Raises it again.

RAMON: What could be more natural? After sorrow, happiness

Fade down to flag; a single image: it's now Sandinista.

Above it, the TV monitor's alive with images of victory.

END

PIANO

An original play based on the film
Unfinished Piece for Mechanical Piano
by
A. Adabashyan and N. Mikhalkov
Subtitle translation by
Peter Seward and Lydia Seward

The text that follows is a theatrical mediation of Adabashyan and Mikhalkov's remarkable *Unfinished Piece for Mechanical Piano* (1980), itself an imaginative filmic reworking of themes from Chekhov's plays (most notably *Platonov)* and his short fiction. The Russian film-makers, whether out of respect or simple unconcern, have allowed me to plunder their own piece in order to find my own; and I'm truly grateful for the generous space they've afforded me.

If I call *Piano* a new play, then, it is in part because I have no right to saddle them (or indeed Chekhov) with the piece I've finally fashioned. For while in respect of character, relationship, incident and dramatic terrain, *Piano* draws heavily on these several ur-works, there is yet within it, at the level of tone, language, form, means and intentions, something other than what they have sought to say, for which I must both claim and accept full responsibility.

As to what exactly that something other is and where precisely it might be found upon the tragicomic map of the human project, I can at this stage, a month ahead of the play's first rehearsal, usefully say nothing. So let me instead offer a context for a possible reading of the piece with a passage from the late and deeply missed Raymond Williams:

'The condition of realism in the nineteenth century was in fact an assumption of a total world. In the great realists, there was no separation in kind between public and private facts, or between public and private experience. This was not, as it may easily appear in retrospect, a wilful joining of disparate things. Rather, it was a way of seeing the world in which it was possible to experience the quality of a whole way of life through the qualities of individual men and women. Thus, a personal breakdown was a genuinely social fact, and a social breakdown was lived and known in direct personal experience. Chekhov is the realist of breakdown, on a significantly total scale.'

Modern Tragedy, 1966

Should *Piano* prove to be about anything at all, I suspect it may prove, like its illustrious forebears, to be about just this felt sense of breakdown and deadlock; and thus perhaps, in a nicely perverse irony, about what it's like to be living in our own post-capitalist, post-socialist, post-realist, post-modern times.

Trevor Griffiths
Boston Spa
24 May 1990

Piano was first performed at the Cottesloe Theatre, London, on 8th August 1990.

The cast was as follows:

Radish   Keith Bartlett

Zakhar   Kevin O'Donohoe

Triletski   Oliver Cotton

Anna   Penelope Wilton

Porfiry   Geoffrey Palmer

Sergei   Duncan Bell

Yasha   Peter Caffrey

Petrin   Stephen Moore

Platonov   Stephen Rea

Sashenka   Julia Ford

Colonel   Basil Henson

Sophia   Suzanne Burden

Shcherbuk   Philip Voss

Petya   Robbie Engels

Gorokhov   Michael O'Connor

Director   Howard Davies

Designer   Ashley Martin-Davis

Lighting   Chris Parry

Music   Dominic Muldowney

Dance   Jane Gibson

A southern province of Russia in the early summer of 1904.
The garden, terrace and veranda of the late General Voynitsev's estate.

Piano

ACT ONE

Black.

RADISH: *(From above, unseen.)* It's *all* right, little peasant. We can do it, we can get it over. Everything's possible.

Bring up shadowy unreal light. Two men hump a large, heavy object wrapped in cowhide across a high narrow plank bridge. The work is hard, precarious; the men sweat, strain, their progress bruisingly slow. **Radish,** *the older of the two, gaunt and cropped, guides the younger.*

Left. Straight. Easy. *(They inch precariously out on to the planks. Eventually:)* Rest, Zakhar.

The load's lowered. **Zakhar,** *young and dreamy, sucks for air. Radish edges round the load to test the planking ahead. Zakhar slumps to a sit, stares down into the drop below.*

ZAKHAR: Let's find another way, Radish. It's too risky, this. Radish?

RADISH: *(Mind on problem)* There is no other way. If there's another way, what are we doing here?

He walks carefully back to the load, studies its shape and outline, scrutinizes the labels stuck on to the hide.

ZAKHAR: What is it? Does it say?

RADISH: *(Face to wrapping)* This? Cowhide. *(He looks at the youth, grins weirdly.)* Says it's a machine. Come from Moscow. Two thousand roubles.

Silence. Zakhar deals with the unimaginable.

ZAKHAR: Don't, Radish. You're tickling me again.

RADISH: *(Finger to label:)* Two thousand roubles. See for yourself.

ZAKHAR: Is it possible?

Radish chuckles, an odd growling sound. Sits to rest.

RADISH: Anything's possible.

ZAKHAR: *(Serious; after thought)* Zzish. No wonder it's so heavy. *(They sit in silence, staring out. Bleed in birdsong, breeze in trees, running water below; the sound is hollow, alienated, as unreal as the light.)* My Aunt Katya says if you look up at the heavens without blinking you can see the angels. *(Silence. Zakhar stares upward.)* Tiny little angels on high, flapping their wings and going zzihzzih like mosquitoes. Read me some more of your story, eh?

RADISH: What for? You've heard it a hundred times.

ZAKHAR: It's a fine tale.

RADISH: It's not a tale. It's my life. *(He takes out a grubby note-book from his pocket, thumbs pages.)* Where was I?

ZAKHAR: Moscow.

RADISH: *(Eventually)* 'Moscow. Everything seemed possible. He had found work as a house painter, learned roofing and glazing, and landed a contract to work on the building of a new railway station in the suburbs. Twelve men he paid from his own pocket, a peasant from Zukhovo, son of serfs.' *(Long silence.)* 'The second winter it rained fifty-nine days in a row. The men were laid off, he made do with odd jobs in the city, painting, papering walls. But rain or shine, the police were round to his lodgings every week for their bribe money. The last job he took was in a gentlemen's club, papering the reading room. He'd agreed seven kopecks a roll with the committee, but when he came to get paid the steward told him to sign for twelve. Perhaps he had a cold or a toothache, it wasn't the first time he had been asked to fiddle an employer's books, but he refused. The steward called the chairman, a handsome, cultured gentleman with gold-rimmed spectacles, who listened carefully to the steward's account, then handed our hero the pen and said: "One more word from you, you miserable bag of snot, and I'll smash your face in".'

Silence. Zakhar gives him a look.

ZAKHAR: What did he do?

RADISH: *(Resuming:)* 'He said "With respect, sir ..." And the gentleman smashed his face in. Next day the police took him in, the gents club had charged him with fraud and extortion. When the case came to court, the very policeman he'd been paying bribe money to for a year and more testified he had left his village of Zukhovo without a permit and that was that. Four years in Siberia. Penal settlement.'

Silence. Radish strokes his cropped head. Zakhar watches.

ZAKHAR: Sometimes, Radish, I think the Lord does not like the peasant.

Radish looks at the blond dreamy youth for a moment, pockets his book, smiles.

RADISH: It's possible, Zakhar.

ZAKHAR: That's where you met the General, mm?

RADISH: Mm. Among others. So many strange folk there. Some who would eat only vegetables, mm? *(Zakhar shakes his head, bewildered.)* Some who believed the Lord God would come again amongst us to bring down the corrupt and the powerful. Still others who believed it was the peasants themselves who would rise up and smite the oppressor. *(Zakhar purses his lips, shakes his head.)* I learned reading there. And writing. And thinking.

ZAKHAR: All men think, Radish.

RADISH: All men have thoughts, maybe. Thinking's different. Thinking has to be learned. Like making bombs. And laying them.

Silence, a voice calls from the distance: Zakhar. Zakhar. Zakhar. *The men ignore it.*

ZAKHAR: You learned those things there?

Radish nods. Zakhar shakes his head. The call again. Radish levers himself upright, begins imaging the journey across the planks.

RADISH: Yasha

ZAKHAR: Yasha.

Radish tests the planks again with his foot. Zakhar takes out a small mouth organ, begins a low, haunting melody. Radish listens a moment, a smile on his lips.

RADISH: Will we go?

ZAKHAR: Tell me about the bird.

RADISH: Again? *(Zakhar grins.)* And *then* we go? *(Zakhar nods, swivels to watch him out on the planks.)* All right. About a year into my sentence, I was detailed to restore the icons in the Regimental Chapel. When the General saw what I could do, he put me to work at the big house on his wife's holy pictures. His first wife, yes? Not this ... pretty one. She was sick, well she was dying, there was nothing he would not do to ease her going ... He even came home one day with a big green parrot, for company while he was away. Some days before she left this world, she asked to see her dearest icons. I'd been working flat out on them for months to have them ready. I took them into her chamber and held them up in turn for her. Our Lady of Khazan. Our Lady of Smolensk. Our Lady of the Three Arms. Her eyes filled with tears when she saw them. She muttered something, I stooped to catch her words. *(Dark, hoarse, unreal voice.)* 'Do me one last kindness, my man, that I might go to my grave in peace.' *(His hand stretches out across the room he's back in. Zakhar stares slack-mouthed, deep in the performance.)* 'Kill that bloody parrot. I cannot get a wink of sleep for it.'

Zakhar laughs, claps his hands. Radish bows ironically.

ZAKHAR: Is there anything at all you believe in, Radish?

RADISH: Believe in, maybe not. But there are things I know.

ZAKHAR: What things?

RADISH: Grass dies. Iron rusts. Lies eat the soul. Everything's possible.

The voice calls Zakhar again. Radish takes his place at the rear of the load, Zakhar at the front. They suck air, dip, lift, totter forward.

Slow crossfade to **Yasha,** *in butler's tails and tie, trying to disengage a lady's corset from the branch of a garden tree with a long pole. He calls from time to time:* Zakhar. Zakhar. Zakhar. *Curses. Resumes his task.*

Voices, laughter from behind him.

Fade up: A samovar, steaming gently. Near by, **Triletski** *and* **Anna** *play chess at a garden table.* **Petrin** *sits in a deckchair some distance away, his back to them, reading a newspaper. Further off a slung hammock, empty.*

TRILETSKI: *(Off laughter.)* ... It's true. Right there in the orangery. *(Anna looks up, smiles faintly, returns to the game, cigarette in mouth.)* Then there was the case of the Kalitins' daughter ... remember the Kalitins? Kalusha? *(Anna nods vaguely.)* Built like a goose. Of course, I was a younger man then, and still a touch shy. What a time I had with their Kalusha, I was never off the premises, her father had to take out a bank loan to pay for the coffee I drank ...

ANNA: Sh. You stop me thinking.

TRILETSKI: *(A look, a move.)* Check. *(He carries his cup to the samovar, shortens a little to check teeth and hair in the steel reflection.)* Well, I was staying over one weekend, it's two in the morning, I'm all tucked up in my little monk's bed there when ... click ... the door opens ... *(He looks across at Anna, pleased to have her attention.)* and ... my heart was pounding like a cannon, you can imagine.

ANNA: I can imagine. Get to the point.

TRILETSKI: It's too humiliating.

ANNA: An illicit visit from your little goose. How?

TRILETSKI: *(Refilling cup.)* It wasn't her. It was the old maid servant, eighty at least, deaf as a bell, with an enema bottle in her hand, mm? And, if you'll pardon the indelicacy, insisting on giving me one. *(Anna laughs. He returns to the table, pleased.)* I raised no objection. I never argue with the deaf. In any case, I thought it might be a custom in the house. Next day it turned out she'd come into the wrong room. But it put an end to the romance, I'll tell you ... Funny, eh?

ANNA: *(Laughing.)* No. Vulgar. Here.

She holds a cigarette out for him. He leans forward to take it in his lips. Sounds of people approach off.

TRILETSKI: Merci, mon ange.

ANNA: Pas du tout.

TRILETSKI: Je brûle pour une cigarette.

ANNA: Ah oui?

She gives him a dark, smoldery look. He takes it for a moment, at length is happy to escape to the safety of the approaching voices. Yasha, pole still up, stops mid-probe to check arrivals.

PORFIRY: *(Off)* Like that. Hunh? Like that. D'ye see? Like that.

Porfiry – *shy, gentle, late fifties; a landowner – enters, in full calling gear save a coat, scythe in his hands, demonstrating a mowing movement on the still air for someone behind him not yet visible. He turns, as* **Sergei**, *small dog under one arm and Porfiry's jacket over the other, shepherds on a young* **Peasant**, *the object of the exercise.*

PORFIRY: You understand? (*He demonstrates the movement again. The peasant nods sourly, cap in hand.*) Here, take it.

The young peasant takes the scythe. Sergei – thirty, in fine linen peasant smock – waves him away.

SERGEI: ... Nevertheless, Porfiry Semyonovich, it is in such pure and simple-hearted peasants that our country's moral strength resides.

He hands Porfiry his jacket, helps him with it.

PORFIRY: Perhaps it *is,* perhaps it isn't, dear Sergei, but where will any of us be if they can't use a scythe properly? In my day, we held quite different beliefs. Our moral strength was based on chivalry. It was woman *we* worshipped. We put her on a different plane, as the better being, the salvation of the species. *(Looks shyly across at Anna.)* And so she is still.

ANNA: How did this pawn get here?

TRILETSKI: *(Glancing at board:)* Which?

ANNA: This one. Who put it there?

TRILETSKI: You did.

ANNA: Ridiculous.

TRILETSKI: You did. Are you suggesting ...?

ANNA: Oh yes. *(Laughs.)* Pardon, monsieur.

They laugh, close, intimate. Porfiry turns away, heads for the samovar, Sergei in tow.

PORFIRY: In my day, one went through fire for one's loved ones. Nowadays ...

SERGEI: ... Nowadays we have the fire brigade. (*He laughs brayingly at his own joke. Porfiry sniffs, debating tea. Anna and Triletski exchange a dry look.*) Jokes on one side, I must pursue my theme. The common folk are, in the view of many of us, as rain clouds hovering over the fields of humanity, in which the seeds of our future are already sown and waiting ... (*Anna begins to whistle 'The Marseillaise' very badly. Sergei bobs closer to Porfiry.*) Mama doesn't like this kind of talk, of course. Poor Russia. Come on, Voltaire.

He lays the dog down, walks away toward the hammock, clicking his fingers. The dog watches him, Sergei stops, remonstrates in dumb show, fingers clicking. The dog looks away, uninterested.

TRILETSKI: You are an amazing woman. *(Anna stops whistling, looks up at him inquiringly.)* You whistle just like a navvy. Your move.

ANNA: I'm bored. (*She looks at Porfiry, who bows, eager to serve; smiles; looks. at Petrin, head in paper.*) Read me something, Gerasim. *(Petrin grunts)* Something romantic.

TRILETSKI: It's quite a different matter when she's winning. 'I'm bored' means 'I'm losing.' If we don't continue, I shall assume you concede.

ANNA: Assume what you will.

TRILETSKI: *(Totting up.)* Very well, that's ... ten roubles you owe me ...

ANNA: (*A whip crack*) Yasha!

Yasha's at full stretch, corset all but accomplished; the call rips him off balance, the pole swirls dangerously around.

YASHA: (*Icy*) Could it wait, madame?

ANNA: Is there any sign of Zakhar and that other one? And what about the gypsies? Finish that at once and come and speak to me ...

She looks across at Triletski, who's emptied a biscuit bag and is now quietly inflating it; follows his eyes to Sergei, who's down on all fours some paces from the impassive mutt, mid-lecture. Triletski holds the bag out very deliberately, bursts it with a bang of the hand. Sergei yelps, rears.

SERGEI: Maman, tell him. I do despise that sort of thing ...

Anna chuckles, Sergei moves off for the hammock.

TRILETSKI: What about your debt? How will you pay me?

A moment. She gives him another smoulder. He braves it out. She blows smoke in his face.

ANNA: (*Rising*) Sergei, pay this clown ten roubles.

SERGEI: *(Sulking:)* ... No, Maman, no ... When father was alive ... I don't know ... *(He slumps into the hammock)* Even Voltaire doesn't love me ...

Yasha approaches, the pole held like a lance, the corset on the tip. He walks deliberately, headed for the house.

YASHA: *(On the move, eyes front)* A telegram has been dispatched to the gypsies. Zakhar and the other one left for the station first thing and are expected imminently ...

ANNA: Where did you find that?

YASHA: *(On and gone.)* In a tree, madame.

Triletski chuckles. Petrin stares at the corset from behind his paper. Porfiry, on the edge of things, looks away, embarrassed.

TRILETSKI: *(On his feet; posing a little:)* I think. I shall drink. A little wine.

He saunters off for the house. Passes the sitting dog, clicks his fingers without looking back. The mutt wags after him on cue.

SERGEI: Look at him. Look at him.

Anna stands for a moment, fixes eventually on Porfiry; smiles. Porfiry gives her his rictal bow.

ANNA: So, Porfiry Semyonovich. *(He waits, expectant.)* Won't you join me? *(He approaches the table, she indicates Triletski's chair, he sits, she joins him across the table, carefully removes the buffering chessboard.)* Woman *is* the better human being, did you say?

PORFIRY: *(A touch breathless)* Better. Most certainly. Oh yes.

ANNA: *(Low, intimate)* And you're a great lover … of women, is that right?

PORFIRY: I most certainly do … love them. Adore them. Yes.

ANNA: *(The tease on)* Them? How many have you known?

PORFIRY: Women?

ANNA: Mm.

PORFIRY: Believe me, Anna Petrovna, if I had known only one … and that one were you … it would suffice.

Long pause as she holds him in her gaze. He trembles.

ANNA: *(Soft, wicked)* Booboobooboooboo

Porfiry blinks. Giggles. Anna laughs. A loud flatulent blast draws attention to the house, where Triletski has reappeared on a first-floor balcony with wine, telescope and a hunting horn.

TRILETSKI: God be praised. Here come the Platonovs. At last!

SERGEI: Hurrah. Hurrah. Hurrah.

ANNA: Good. *(She looks at the three men about her.)* And what do we think of Platonov?

Silence.

PORFIRY: I lost a cufflink when I was mowing … Mikhail? He's a clever enough fellow … I'd better see if I can find it …

He wanders away. Petrin stands, folds his paper carefully, pockets his glasses. He's in his forties, neat, strong, meticulous.

SERGEI: Misha's a man among men. A delight to converse with.

Anna cues Petrin to give voice.

PETRIN: Talks well. Lacks sense.

TRILETSKI: *(Telescope up)* Ha ha. He's blown up like a bull, my little sister's risen like a bun loaf. They must have spent the whole winter at the trough.

Anna rises to greet the newcomers. **Platonov** *arrives, mopping his face and drying the band of his panama, his wife* **Sashenka** *some steps behind. She wears a pretty new flower-braided hat, a slender but worrying fraction too large for her head.*

ANNA: Welcome. At last. Would you care for tea?

PLATONOV: Tea? No. (*He sits heavily. Sergei greets Sashenka with a deep bow and a hand kiss.*) Well, I see there are still people in the world. We haven't encountered a soul for six months. Winters are God's greatest mistake. How are you then, madame? Still making your stepson miserable?

ANNA: Not at all. He's even started calling me Mama.

PLATONOV: Eat, sleep, talk to the walls ... Dreary.

SASHENKA: *(Joining them at table)* Dreary? Why so, Misha? A little dull, perhaps, but pleasant enough, surely?

She adjusts the brim of her hat, smiling, lovely and nervous. Platonov stares at her in a minatory silence for a moment, looks away. Nods greeting to Petrin. Glimpses Porfiry on the fringe, stooped in search of his cufflink.

ANNA: Well, you're both looking remarkably ... sleek. It must be a measure of how happy you are together.

Platonov glares at her a moment; leaves his seat.

PLATONOV: That you, Porfiry Semyonovich? You can't hide from me, I see everything.

Porfiry stands briefly, bows. Shows his shirt sleeve.

PORFIRY: Cuff. Lost it. Link.

He disappears again.

PLATONOV: *(Peering myopically.)* Sergei? Is it you? Where's the long hair and choirboy voice?

SERGEI: All gone, Misha. I'm a bass now.

PLATONOV: A bass, eh? Mm. (*Anna and Sashenka laugh. Platonov grins.*) Well, what does your stepmother have in store for us, mm?

ANNA: There are gypsies coming, God willing. And there's a small musical surprise on its way.

Thunder, remote, rolling in.

PLATONOV: Good. I like a surprise.

Silence.

ANNA: I believe it might rain.

Petrin moves to another chair closer to the house, resumes his tour of the paper. Platonov stands immobile, as if weighed down. Sashenka approaches him, giggles something in his ear.

PLATONOV: Sergei, Sergei, Sergei my dear fellow, got yourself wed and never said a word.

Sergei approaches shyly, pleased, takes the congratulating hand.

SERGEI: A whirlwind, dear friend. Blew me head over heels. Whoo.

SASHENKA: *(Kissing his cheek:)* Bless you, bless you. Now you will discover life's deepest joys …

PLATONOV: … You'll excuse my wife. Weddings make her heady.

Some laughter. Sashenka rebalances her hat.

SASHENKA: It's not weddings, Misha. It's order. You've made me very happy, Sergei Pavlovich.

SERGEI: *(Hugging and lifting her.)* Me too, Sashenka. I've never ever been so happy, never ever …

Platonov leaves them to their celebration. Stares at Anna darkly. She begins to chuckle.

PLATONOV: What's funny?

Anna turns away, hand to mouth. The separate moments die away. People stand on, smiling or not. Silence grows.

PETRIN: *(From nowhere.)* It says here a crow was caught by a girl last week in Syzran with blue eyes.

Pause.

PLATONOV: *(Quiet, deadly.)* Good old Syzran. Home of the blue-eyed crow.

ANNA: Porfiry, be so kind as to go and fetch Sophia. I believe she's on the pond.

Porfiry stands, bows, leaves. Thunder again, a touch closer.

SERGEI: Ah yes, thoughtless of me, I er … I hope nobody imagines I'm like some Arab sheik who keeps his wives under lock and key … *(He laughs nervously; Sashenka giggles; Platonov looks at his feet; it's clear no one does.)* … In any case, my beautiful wife is not at all the sort of woman …

A shot bangs out, loud, sudden, very close. The group leaps to life.

TRILETSKI: *(On balcony, hunting rifle in one hand, red wine in the other; calling.)* Long live my relatives! All hail the General's delicious widow!

Laughter, calls of reproach. Yasha comes out on to the veranda terrace to check on the latest madness; throws himself face down on the ground as Triletski looses off anther round directly above. Platonov has brightened; for the first time he smiles.

PLATONOV: *(Calling.)* All hail to the General's delicious widow's impoverished personal physician!

*The **Colonel** wobbles out, a gaunt ancient with a knitted shawl round his shoulders and a birch broom at the port in his bony mitts.*

COLONEL: What? What?

YASHA: *(Recovering slowly.)* Your son, Colonel. Having his fun.

PLATONOV: *(Advancing to house, wiping head with kerchief)* ... God, I can smell it from here, man, you must have been at it all day ...

TRILETSKI: *(Bottle aloft.)* Hail Jupiter, God and Bull! I shall bring you a glass ...

COLONEL: *(To approaching Platonov)* Misha, is it? Who's he firing at?

PLATONOV: Me. Who else would he fire at?

COLONEL: Why?

PLATONOV: You never taught him to shake hands, Colonel.

COLONEL: Did he hit you? *(Platonov ponders the question. The others have followed up the garden; the old man sees his daughter. Excited.)* Aha, the most beautiful planet in the Triletski firmament. *(Warm embraces: Sashenka, Platonov.)* Come and sit down. *(To Platonov.)* Sit, that's an order. Are you well, my lovely? I'm always well, heart's been a problem now and again, but that's the fair sex and quite incurable ... Where'd this broom come from? How's my grandson ...?

SASHENKA: Blooming. He sends his love.

COLONEL: Sends his love, eh? Bright baby ...

SERGEI: Metaphorically speaking, she means.

Anna arrives last, lighting another cigarette.

COLONEL: ... Anna Petrovna, my dear lady, I've bought myself ... *(Yasha walks past him, removes broom from his hands en route.)* ... What are *you* doing? ... I've bought a new shotgun, we'll hunt quail together ... Oh, look at her, I love 'em like that, there's female liberation for you, kiss her shoulder, she smells of gunpowder ... Goddess Diana, Alexandra the Great, your Excellency.

PLATONOV: You've been at the bottle too, Colonel, when did you start?

COLONEL: *(Cackling:)* Crack o' dawn. Sans doute. House was asleep when I got here, stamped my feet and lo! out she comes, Diana herself, with a laugh and a bottle of Madeira, she had a couple of glasses and I had the rest. Ha!

ANNA: *(Mock angry)* Tell the world, Colonel, won't you.

COLONEL: Aiee. I'm worn out.

Sashenka helps him to a chair. Triletski appears from the house, glasses, bottle, telescope in hands.

TRILETSKI: Eh bien. Me voici. *(Laughter, greetings. Sashenka claps her hands. He lays down his load.)* There you are, my little sister. *(They embrace.)* What's this? A new hat! Looks good enough to eat. *(He plays kid's teasing games with her, affectionate and patronizing, as he prepares his approach to Platonov.)*

Oh, and who's this? Not his Excellency! (*Platonov grins, stands. They approach each other in silence, look as if they might fight, segue into customary and personal greeting rituals. Eventually.*) Comment ça va, Michel?

PLATONOV: *(Slow:)* That's a long and very dreary story, Kolya.

The group has settled around them. Petrin is back to his paper; the Colonel heads back to sleep; Sashenka watches her brother and husband, a nervous smile on her face; Anna sits in a kind of quiet disinterested vacancy; Sergei stares down the garden, on the lookout for his wife. Triletski takes a false nose/moustache mask from his pocket, looks across at the preoccupied Sergei. Platonov follows the look, a smile's shared, Triletski dons the mask, the two men join hands and waltz gently around the terrace, humming their music for tempo. Arrive eventually behind Sergei.

TRILETSKI: *(Sudden; weird voice:)* ... Excuse me, my man, I wonder if you could ...

Sergei turns sharply, yelps at the mad face. Laughter.

SERGEI: *(Moving to other side of terrace.)* Nikolai Ivanovich, I do not care for your japes. Tell him, Maman ...

He whitters on. The laughter seeps away. People settle in the space. The Colonel snores thinly. Sashenka giggles, embarrassed. Silence.

TRILETSKI: How's the boy, is he well?

PLATONOV: He's well.

TRILETSKI: Haven't seen him for ... months and months. He must have grown.

PLATONOV: He's grown

TRILETSKI: Tall, eh?

PLATONOV: Ahunh.

TRILETSKI: What, really tall? Tall-tall?

PLATONOV: Perhaps. We'll know better when he can stand.

Sashenka chuckles along with the exchange from her chair by the house wall; watches others closely, to be sure things are well. The Colonel farts in his sleep: a slow tearing crack.

TRILETSKI: Oh dear!

SASHENKA: *(Crossing:)* Papa, please, Papa.

COLONEL: I'm awake, I'm awake.

SASHENKA: Don't sleep here, I beg you, Papa.

She fusses over him, can't shift him.

COLONEL: It's your brother's fault, he makes them put beans in the cabbage soup, last week he put salt in my tobacco and sewed up all my pockets.

Platonov laughs, Triletski chuckles, Sashenka shushes the old man quiet. Sergei has collected the telescope; gazes down the garden through it.

SERGEI: And here she comes! My beloved wife, Sophia Yegorovna. (*Platonov cuts mid-laugh at the name. Sergei lifts his voice.*) ... I thought you had stolen her from me, Porfiry Semyonovich

People drift to the front of the terrace to greet her. Platonov takes the telescope; refocuses; gazes at the approaching figures.

SASHENKA: Oh, doesn't she look lovely!

Platonov lays down the telescope, hovers uneasily, leaves for the house. Only Anna notes the departure.

SOPHIA: *(On the approach, flowers in her hand:)* It's wonderful here. The good Porfiry showed me everything.

PORFIRY: *(Toiling after her)* Wait till you see my place. She's promised you'll come over on Thursday, Sergei.

Platonov appears by a window, pours a drink swigs it down, takes another, disappears.

SERGEI: ... Thursday's fine. Perhaps we could all go, Maman.

ANNA: So long as we don't have to call on Yuspov on the way.

PLATONOV: *(Reappeared; quietly)* ... We could go via Platonov's little plot ...

PORFIRY: ...That's miles out of the way ...

SOPHIA: ... Platonov's? You know, I believe I knew him once, Misha Platonov, I don't suppose he's Misha any longer ... Mikhail ... what was it ...?

PLATONOV: ... Vasilyevich

SOPHIA: Vasilyevich. *(She nods her thanks to the stranger, returns to her flowers.)* Exactly.

Silence. Looks exchanged, glances at the still, amiable Platonov: something's on.

SERGEI: Cher Michel! Never stirs himself but nothing escapes him ... *(To Sophia.)* It's the man in question, my love ... See.

She turns, stares at Platonov.

SOPHIA: No. It can't be.

Laughter, a touch nervy.

PLATONOV: *(Sweet still)* Well, what is it, seven years? Eight? A long time, Sophia Yegorovna. If we were dogs, we'd already be geriatric. Horses too.

PETRIN: *(Over paper)* Horses live to eighteen. That's an average, you understand.

Laughter, some relief.

SOPHIA: Mikhail Vasilyevich is quite right, it was a long time ago … another age. He was a student then, I was going to be an actress, remember? Great things were expected of him, people said he'd be a future Minister of State. Or a second Lord Byron, mm? A long time ago. A long way away. How are you? What are you doing?

PLATONOV: I'm a teacher. Local school.

SOPHIA: No. You?

PLATONOV: Yes. Me.

SOPHIA: I just can't … Why?

PLATONOV: Why? Because.

SOPHIA: I'm sorry, what I mean is, with the whole world out there … and a degree.

PLATONOV: No degree. I gave up.

Silence. She frowns, mire ahead of her.

SOPHIA: Yes, but that hasn't prevented you becoming a fully realized … person, being, human being, has it?

PLATONOV: Excuse me? I'm not sure I've understood your question … What?

SOPHIA: Forgive me, I put it badly … (*She looks to Sergei for help, he smiles supportively: he's having a bad time.*) I mean: none of this stops you from wanting to create a better world, reform, progress, the rights of women, that kind of thing, does it? You can still serve ideals, can't you … ?

PLATONOV: … But of course, Sophia Yegorovna. Do not for a moment imagine we have let ourselves go here. I can assure you we are as abreast and as busy as any in the land, appearances notwithstanding … Triletski here, a simple district doctor you might think, but no, a *Darwinist,* mm, an evolutionist even, a man moreover who has dedicated much of his time – some might even say a disproportionate amount of it – to the Woman Question … Porfiry Semyono- vich, landowner, yes, but so much more – an authority on grass-mowing techniques. And popular hygiene. Shaves his peasant's skulls every week, a whole village, you'll see for yourself, they look like actors. We take all the major newspapers and journals, Petrin there kindly collates them and reads them out to us … (*He picks up Sashenka's straw hat, puts it on his head.*) So you see, dear lady, we certainly do our share of toiling here … Ah yes, I quite forgot, my wife … (*He gathers her by the arm, draws her forward.*) … my wife Alexandra, Sashenka, Sashenka, my wife, civic responsibility, reproduc- tion of the species, we've been busy multiplying, I have a son on whom to bequeath my ideas. No actual wealth, of course, but what's that compared with intellectual inheritance …

He sits, still wearing Sashenka's hat, as if drained by the passage from irony to mania. Sophia finds it difficult to look anywhere. Anna sits detached, ironically watchful; whistles a snatch of 'Una Furtiva Lacrima.' Silence. Yasha enters

suddenly with a tray of drinks, Triletski turns him around and heads him back off.
A train whistle in the distance. Sophia looks around her, trying to speak; can't.
Removing hat.

What is the matter with you people? Eh? You look like guests at a funeral ...
Sophia Yegorovna and I have just put on a perfect little comedy for you and
you can't raise a single titter. *(Sophia laughs, delighted at the relief)* Look at
'em, Sophia, I swear they've been embalmed ...

Laughter, lifting and swelling, as they take the bridge he's offered to safer ground.

SASHENKA: *(Proud, apologetic:)* My Misha can't bear it when things are calm.

SERGEI: Bravo, Misha, he's right, it's exactly what we deserve, he's the only one
of us who dares to live to the hilt, bless him. Without Platonov we'd all just ...
wither away completely ...

TRILETSKI: Brilliantly put, Sergei Pavlovich. And on the subject of withering away,
perhaps we could prevail upon our good hostess to furnish a little sustenance
before too long ... I could eat a pig whole. Your Excellency, I beg of you ...

He smiles down the terrace at Anna. She sits unsmiling a moment. Rises.

ANNA: How impudent and tiresome you have become, Nikolai Ivanovich.
Everyone else waits, why shouldn't you? How can you be hungry? When are
you ever not hungry? You spend your whole life gorging yourself. This morning
what did you have, hunh? Two glasses of tea, a mound of beef, five eggs ...

TRILETSKI: ... Four. ...

ANNA: Five, I watched you, amazed. Then you stole into the larder and
demolished half a pie. I've had no peace since daybreak with your guzzling
and your shouting ... *(Sounds off, people on the approach. Anna's wholly
convincing display of patrician temper finds a new gear.)* ... What in God's
name is all that noise? Stop it, damn you, stop that din ... *(She walks forward
to the edge of the veranda; stares down the garden fiercely; softens slowly, as
the voices advance.)* Aha. Eh voilà. My hero. Mon chevalier!

Shcherbuk *appears, toils up the garden, mid-tirade. He's fifty or so, burly, sweating
in the sun, voice habitually and cracklingly over the top. His nephew,* **Petya**, *ten, in
white uniform and shiny-peaked hat, straggles disconsolately behind him.*

SHCHERBUK: *(From off)* ... I shall be watching you, my boy, be in no doubt about
that. Put but a word or muscle out of place and by God you will pay for it, yes
indeed ... And I want that suit as spotless when we leave as when you put it on
this morning.

ANNA: *(From the terrace steps:)* Pavel Petrovich!

SHCHERBUK: *(Puffing up:)* I've had to bring my nephew, no one to look after him,
my daughters have gone off somewhere in their ludicrous green gowns, they
look like toads, lizards ...

He bows, kisses her hand, waves at the others assembling behind her.

ANNA: Now here is a real character, realer than any of you.

SHCHERBUK: Petya, he's called. *(To boy)* Pay your respects to her Excellency.

PETYA: Bonjour, madame.

ANNA: Bonjour, petit.

PETYA: Congratulations on your marriage.

Anna laughs. Shcherbuk clatters the back of the lad's head, spilling the cap.

SHCHERBUK: It's her son who's married, not her Excellency, you don't listen …
Pick it up boy. *(Petya collects his hat, raw-eyed, as Shcherbuk exchanges greetings with the company.)* And where, my friends, might she be, the one my soul burns to see …?

Sergei and Sophia stand by the house door. Anna beckons them forward.

ANNA: Pavel Petrovich Shcherbuk, friend, neighbour, admirer and creditor …

SHCHERBUK: … Not to mention close companion of his Excellency, the late General. May I?

He bows to kiss Sophia's hand. She pulls it away.

SOPHIA: Thank you, that really isn't necessary.

Shcherbuk stares, frowns. Sergei puts his arm round Sophia's shoulder.

SERGEI: I trust you're not offended, honoured sir. It's just that in our view hand kissing demeans women. We don't kiss men's hands now, do we? And we're opposed to all forms of inequality, inequality being, of course, the first step towards humiliation …

Shcherbuk sniffs, looks briefly around, sees the boy on the garden steps.

SHCHERBUK: What are you then, Sergei, her lawyer? *(To Petya)* Go and play. There's a lake over there. Stay out of it. *(Petya shuffles off. Shcherbuk returns to the fray with relish.)* Aha, what have we here? Liberals, is it? Humanists, progressives, your heads full of shallow nonsense, hunh? Liberty, Equality, Fraternity, Hogwash. Me? I'm a Darwinist, pure and simple. I have science behind me when I say that blood and breeding will decide the fate of the species. Noble blood equals pure breeding. Q.E.D. Not empty words, I assure you …

People have relaxed back into the veranda terrace. Petrin has resumed his silent reading. Sashenka has recovered her straw hat, is trying to get it to sit straight on her brow. Triletski watches Anna, who has her arm inside Shcherbuk's. Platonov appears at the house window, discreetly knocking back another chaser. Shcherbuk barristerially releases the pinned pair, wanders a little, addressing the jury.

Equality. I ask you. Was it some scummy peasant who gave us art, music, literature, science …? You think a bunch of wet-arsed slugs created Petersburg, do you? Ha!

Sergei tries to think of the answer. Goes to speak; Sophia tugs him to heel.

PETRIN: *(As if surfacing)* 'Hailstones the sizes of duck eggs fell on Kostowata last week during a storm …'

SHCHERBUK: Gerasim Kusmich, we are talking here, and you read aloud, hunh? *(Petrin stares at him calmly, gives him a thin smile.)* So, my friends, by not associating with scum, by not shaking their paws or inviting their snouts to my table, I further the laws of natural selection … In other words, I do my duty … *(He darts forward suddenly, kisses Sophia's hand. Laughs delightedly.)* Tell me honestly, does that demean you? I think not. After all: Quod licet Jovi non licet bovi. What befits Jupiter does not necessarily befit a bull, eh?

Platonov has returned from within. Sophia sees him watching her.

SOPHIA: Perhaps you'll pay us a visit one day, Pavel Petrovich, and we can argue the matter out …

SERGEI: Excellent idea. Together we will find the truth.

COLONEL: *(In his sleep)* Kalitin's bird dog farts when it points … Gives the game away.

Laughter.

SASHENKA: Papa, please, sleep inside if you must, it's so embarrassing.

COLONEL: *(Awakening)* … Wide awake, my love, wide awake. What's the matter, mm?

Silence. Anna surveys the company coolly, as vacancy settles across them. Yasha has appeared at the upper balcony, the telescope to his eye.

YASHA: *(Calling:)* Zakhar and the other one have just crested the ridge, madame. By my calculation, they should be here within the next half hour …

ANNA: *(Staring up)* Who said you could handle the General's telescope?

YASHA: How else am I to keep you posted?

ANNA: Put it back. At once. *(Yasha glares a moment, stifflegs into the house. A crash. Silence.)* A little lunch, I think.

She leads off indoors; Shcherbuk gives her his arm. Triletski follows Sergei and Sophia. Sashenka trundles her father in, waves anxiously at Platonov as she passes him in the doorway. Platonov stands for some moments; moves slowly forward to the veranda terrace steps; stares out at nothing for a long time. Is drawn eventually by sounds from the garden.

PLATONOV: Who is it? Who is there? *(Young Petya sits up in the hammock, face greasy with tears. Silence.)* Are you hungry? *(Petya stands, shakes his head.)* How about a swim? No? *(Thinks.)* Can you ride a bicycle? *(Petya nods, interested.)* There's one in the big barn … Over there. *(Petya sniffs, straightens his peaked cap, salutes, marches off for the barn. As if to Petya.)* Better still, bring the horse and carriage, we'll run away together … *(A **Servant**, just entered the garden to clear away, overhears him, looks around for whom he might be addressing. Quiet, as if cheery.)* It's all right. I'm just going mad.

The Servant nods, satisfied. Platonov very slowly slides to a sit on the top step. Silence. Sophia steps silently out on to the veranda, approaches the rail to one side of the steps, turns her back to the garden, careful they should not appear to be together.

SOPHIA: Mikhail Vasilyevich. May I speak with you? *(He nods, not looking.)* I need to apologize for my idiotic behaviour just now, that … stupid interrogation. I'll perfectly understand if you feel too angry with me to discuss it. *(He says nothing.)* Do you?

PLATONOV: Not at all. *(Looks at her.)* There was a time. Not now.

She looks at him, looks away at once. A river boat sounds a deep horn a mile away. Another answers.

SOPHIA: Where do they go? The boats?

PLATONOV: To paradise. Forgive me, that was puerile, I don't know where they go.

Voices lift suddenly in laughter, upstairs in the dining room beyond the balcony. She hears her name spoken.

SOPHIA: I wish there was somewhere we could talk …

PLATONOV: *(Wholly different track)* The landing pier. Remember?

SOPHIA: What? No, I meant here, now.

PLATONOV: The boat. The evening boat, what was it called?

SOPHIA: The boat? I …

PLATONOV: The old man with the banjo, the evening steamer, what was it called …?

SOPHIA: Mikhail, please.

PLATONOV: *Aurora.* Of course. *(Looks at her again.)* Why have you come looking for me? What do you want? Of me? Have you forgotten the lake too? The dog …? Under the bench? The boy crouched by the bridge with his fishing rod …?

SOPHIA: Stop, Mikhail … Your voice … You have quite misunderstood me … Sh.

She freezes. Platonov turns to look. Anna has appeared in the downstairs window, helps herself to a large glass of Madeira. She's inward functional; sees nothing. Tidies her hair, squeezes lemon on her neck. Leaves the frame. Eventually, her back still to him.

My God. She might have seen us. My God.

PLATONOV: And the fog. Rolling in from the sea. Remember? People disappearing.

SOPHIA: I beg you, no, no, it's not this I want, I've misled you … *(Voices, laughter again above. She rubs her face, searches for words.)* Mikhail Vasilyevich, the past was beautiful, extraordinary, I recall everything and regret none of it … I can see him now, the old you, Misha with the panama hat and the armful of books and the pockets bulging with tobacco … but you're a schoolmaster now, with a wife and a child, and I'm Sophia Yegorovna Voynitseva, wife to Sergei, the two of us dedicating our lives to useful work …

She talks softly, her back still to him. Platonov has sat motionless, eyes on the garden. Petya has returned, stands staring at Platonov, his hands supporting the bicycle. Platonov stands slowly, glides into the garden, makes a weird shuffling beeline for boy and bike. Unaware.

We must let the past remain just that. A young student loved a girl, the girl loved him, it's too trite a story to disturb us now … (*Platonov has reached the bike and straddled it. Lifts Petya into the front basket. Wobbles unsteadily off.*) Say I'm right, Misha.

Silence. She turns for his answer. Finds nothing. Works on her hurt and anger. Jumps at the voice behind her.

SERGEI: *(Arriving from house)* Sophia, my love, I just had this amazing thought and wanted to share it with you … (*Platonov wobbles back into the garden. Petya shrieks his pleasure. Calling:*) Watch out Misha, Mama's looking for you … (*Platonov waves, the bike veers wildly, he rights it and disappears again. Sophia watches, a touch bitterly.*) The thing is, Germany or Belgium are little places, mm? And the closer people are, the faster new ideas can be spread from one to another. Holland and England are the same, but here the country is so vast, in bad weather we can hardly reach our neighbours, let alone the people in Kamchatka or Siberia …

SOPHIA: … Sergei.

SERGEI: Yes, my love.

SOPHIA: Let's have some wine.

SERGEI: What?

SOPHIA: Some wine.

SERGEI: Of course, of course … (*He puts his arm around her shoulder, leads her in. Anna appears on the balcony, scans the garden.*) You know, I am so happy, Sophia. Voltaire, you, Mama … My cup runneth over … Really.

They enter the house. Anna calls 'Mikhail Vasilyevich' twice, re-enters the dining room. Platonov reappears, wiping dirt from his trouser leg; settles into the hammock; uses a stick to keep it swaying. Anna leaves the house. Yasha follows her out. The afternoon light has begun to dribble away.

ANNA: Mikhail Vasilyevich.

Platonov waves the stick above the hammock.

YASHA: I shall need your instructions for dinner, madame.

ANNA: Have we heard from the gypsies?

YASHA: Er. No, madame.

ANNA: Send Mitka to the station with another telegram. And go out yourself and hurry Zakhar in, they're holding things up … (*He goes to protest, she's down*

*the steps and headed for Platonov. Petya has returned, stands on the edge,
peering at Platonov in the hammock. Arriving; seeing him:)* Go and play. *(The
boy vanishes.)* So. Are you by any chance avoiding me?

PLATONOV: Does the earth avoid the sun?

Silence. She thinks about that.

ANNA: Is that yes or no?

PLATONOV: Never mind. What is it?

ANNA: Porfiry Semyonovich has asked me to marry him.

Silence. Platonov rocks on.

PLATONOV: All winter long we yearn for the sun, when it comes we can't bear it
and want it gone.

ANNA: Did you hear me? He wants me to marry him. (*Yasha walks past them,
fuming, buttoning a coat. Disappears.*) ... It's tempting, I'll tell you. I could be
rich overnight, pay off all my creditors, Petrin, Shcherbuk, Kalitin ... aiiee! I
could even put something into your schoolhouse ... All I'd have to do is learn
to mow. Seems a small price to pay. Oh and enter a loveless marriage. *(She
looks at him)* I'd like to know your feelings. Can I stoop so low?

PLATONOV: *(Casual)* Oh, I should think so.

ANNA: If this is a joke, Misha, shouldn't one of us be laughing by now? Are you
trying to be rid of me, is that it? Move over. (*She pushes his legs, he swings
them to the ground, she sits next to him.*) I know we haven't seen each other all
winter ... but if you have problems, let me know them, mm? Just don't play
the fool with me, Misha. Not me.

PLATONOV: I don't know. You're bright and good and lovely, Anna, and worthy of
... better than this ... *(He waves a hand at the hopeless terrain.)* Let's put the
past behind us. Let's just be friends. Your future's yours to decide, no one
else's ... Besides, I'm just a touch married myself ...

ANNA: Your wife is irrelevant, Misha, why raise her now? You think I'm blind?
It's that bloody Sophia, isn't it? You want to tell me what's going on, mm? You
don't have to be ashamed, my dear, no one knows better than I what a sewer
rat you are, au fond ... Without me, you'll drown, Platonov.

PLATONOV: Oh God. Ten years from now we'll sit in our deck-chairs and chuckle
till we weep at all this. And a thick fog will cover everything ...

YASHA: (*Arriving unheard behind them, a garden chair in his hand.*) ... Not quite
everything, there will always be Yasha, Excellency ...

He's setting his chair before them and is halfway to the sit.

ANNA: *(Fierce.)* Who gave you leave to speak, you oaf!

YASHA: *(Rising, retreating with chair:)* You told me to tell you when the surprise arrived, it's here, forgive me for breathing ... *(Radish and Zakhar have struggled on by a side path with the wrapped load.)* As for oafs, that doctor friend of yours is a bigger one, he set fire to Mr. Petrin's newspaper. *(Cackles maniacally.)* While he was reading it!

ANNA: Out of my sight!

The Peasants lay the load down in the garden, slump to earth, drained. Shcherbuk leads the Colonel and Triletski out on to the balcony, their wine glasses in their hands.

SHCHERBUK: ... There's no case for mixed breeding, none whatsoever. Richard the Lionheart had the heart of a lion, yes? But where did it come from, if not his noble and valiant parents ... Breed with scum and you'll get scum for your litter ... Aha, there it is, the surprise. Intriguing ...

COLONEL: *(Peering.)* What is it, a cannon? If it's a cannon, I'll drink to it.

SHCHERBUK: *(Clinking glasses.)* You'll drink to it anyway, Colonel.

ANNA: *(Sotto; still by Platonov in the hammock)* You must be losing your mind, Platonov. You have me. Isn't that enough? *(She leaves the hammock abruptly, clapping her hands and calling as she heads up the garden.)* Everyone out of doors, if you please, it's time for the surprise I promised.

Behind her, the hammock has swung violently, pitching Platonov to the ground. He scrambles up quickly, trying to cover the embarrassment. The three men on the balcony disappear indoors. Anna stops midway to instruct the load-bearers. They struggle to their feet, caps in hand, to listen. People begin to drift out on to the terrace, some still busy on the cold collation. Platonov tidies himself as he moves up the garden to join them. He glances in Anna's direction as he passes her; she ignores him, goes on instructing the two peasants in idiot-English.

SOPHIA: *(Linking arms with Sashenka)* ... I really do love children, you know. And hearing you talk so warmly about yours has given me a splendid idea ... Listen, everyone, if you'd be so kind, I'd like you all to hear my plan. *(Shcherbuk leads the Triletskis out on to the terrace; they form, with Sashenka, Sergei and Porfiry, a sort of arena for the announcement.)* Tomorrow, my friends, I shall go to the village, and arrange the bottle-feeding of all those babies whose mothers are at work in the fields. I would like to ask now for volunteers to assist me. Sashenka, say you will come ... *(Sashenka looks to Platonov for guidance: he frowns.)* Anna, what about you?

ANNA: *(Arriving; curt)* Sorry, I shan't be up until noon at the earliest ... Yasha!

Sophia scans the watching group for support. Sergei's eyes brim with love and admiration. Platonov looks on darkly.

SOPHIA: Well, perhaps we could go to bed early ...?

ANNA: Out of the question, the gypsies are coming. Yasha ... *(He arrives, stone-faced, a tray in his hand.)* There you are. The chairs, man, the chairs ...

She begins showing him the arrangement she requires. The others direct their attention to the object down the garden, where Radish and Zakhar have begun loosening the cowhide wrapping. Petya has reappeared; tries to help.

SHCHERBUK: *(Calling)* Hands off, brat. Never touch what isn't yours.

ANNA: *(Sotto, to Yasha)* You've been at my drink again, haven't you?

YASHA: *(Above it)* I haven't touched madame's spirits, stealing is beneath me ...

ANNA: Liar.

SOPHIA: I hope to meet your son one day. Your wife has told me miraculous things about him.

PLATONOV: She makes them up. All kids are the same, it's only the parents who differ.

SHCHERBUK: Not at all. Different parents breed different offspring ...

ANNA: *(To the company)* Enough! Take your seats, if you will ... Yasha, go.

People sit or stand, form a loose line along the veranda. Yasha leaves haughtily, drops the tray just inside the door, his hand grabs it as it rolls back on to the terrace. A handclap.

Zakhar!

The two men strip the hide from the object. The company stares at a brightly burnished mahogany upright piano. A handclap.

Chair!

Radish carries a garden chair, sets it down before the keyboard.

SHCHERBUK: A piano? Where's the surprise in a ...

ANNA: Sh. *(A handclap.)* Zakhar!

Zakhar looks at Radish, smiles palely, wipes his hands and feet, sits, lifts the lid, stares at the brilliant keys. Raises his hands above them.

Play!

Zakhar's hands go down, Rachmaninov swells and twirls around the garden. The terrace people watch as if tranced.

COLONEL: *(Peering:)* It's not a cannon at all.

SHCHERBUK: This is not possible. Not possible.

ANNA: Zakhar!

Zakhar stands, bows, edges nervously away from the still playing pianola. The terrace people stand paralyzed, deep in the event, nervous uncertainty edging towards fear. Anna takes them in one by one, enjoying herself. Thunder; closer. Sashenka sways, grows unsteady; slumps finally in a faint across the balustrade. Sophia moves to help her, Platonov is balked by the Colonel, curses as he rounds him.

SOPHIA: Take her indoors, please, I have some drops ...

SHCHERBUK: Leave her, she needs air.

Platonov moves her to a chair, crouches to look at her, rubs her hand in his.

SASHENKA: *(Reviving:)* Forgive me, Misha.

PLATONOV: What's the matter with you? You're behaving like Anna Karenina ...

SASHENKA: The heat, I grew frightened, and my head ...

PLATONOV: Why come out with a headache in this heat? You could have stayed at home. (*He tries to straighten her cock-eyed hat, she flinches away from him, tries to straighten it herself.*) And take that hat off, will you, I can't bear the sight of it.

Sophia hurries forward with drops and water. Sashenka removes the hat.

SOPHIA: Here, I have the drops, they're a little bitter but they're what you need ...

PLATONOV: *(Exploding)* Are you just going to stand there, she's your sister, attend her!

TRILETSKI: *(Pouring more wine:)* Yes, yes, yes, yes ... *(Moves forward to Sashenka and Sophia)* Now, what's the matter with you, tubby. *(To Sophia)* What's that?

SOPHIA: Drops. I had them from my ...

TRILETSKI: Drops? Ba. In the best circles one prescribes sherry. (*He holds his glass to Sashenka's lips, she chokes a little.*) See. Better already.

Platonov grimaces, moves to the steps. Anna has re-entered the garden, closed down the music, gathers the piano roll and holds it above her head.

ANNA: See.

Some ragged laughter at the trick she's played. Shcherbuk scowls, trying to smile.

SHCHERBUK: Trickery! I said a peasant couldn't do it, didn't I? It's beyond them. It's a machine, nothing more.

PETRIN: (*Approaching balustrade*) How much?

ANNA: Two thousand. Don't be so bourgeois.

PETRIN: Two thousand for a fainting fit? What do you say, Platonov?

Platonov says nothing, walks into the house. People begin to settle again on the terrace. Sophia stays with Sashenka, eager to nurse. Triletski picks up a guitar, begins posing and strumming between the tables. Platonov reappears in the downstairs window, pouring a long drink of vodka. Sergei moves forward suddenly to the edge of the terrace.

SERGEI: Your attention, friends, if you please. As you know, Sophia, my wife, plans to visit the village tomorrow to help the peasant women. Well ... I find that very inspiring. Very. I believe she has shown us the way forward. And I believe that we ... the men ... are honour bound to respond. So. I have decided to give the peasants all my old suits, every last one of them. And all my old shoes.

He gazes along the terrace at Sophia, who smiles a touch unhappily, aware of the bored silence the announcement has evinced. Thunder again, closing in still. Platonov begins laughing in the window. Rolls out on to the terrace, the mirth rising in desperate waves.

PLATONOV: ... I just had this picture ... of how extraordinary they're all going to look ... mowing in their frock coats ...

He doubles up, close to explosion. Laughter ripples across the space, taking everyone in its path. Down the terrace, Sashenka turns in her chair to join in, happy he's happy.

SERGEI: *(Through laughter)* You know, that never occurred to me... That's very funny.

Sophia stands slowly, levels a bitter stare at Platonov, who hangs helpless over the balustrade, face greasy with tears; walks slowly into the house. Light very slowly fades. In the garden, Petya has crept back to the pianola; he sits now, lid open, playing on air.

Black

ACT TWO

Black. Thunder, rolling, dying. Sounds of voices, slow hammering.

Fade up: garden, evening, light almost gone. Servants trail out from the rear of the house to a long table being laid for dinner. Above, on a crude ladder footed by Zakhar, Radish hammers up a waterproof awning over the dining area. Yasha troops importantly in and out to supervise, holding the ring between kitchen and table. Laughter, excited shrieks, off from the house.

ANNA: *(Off calling)* Come along, come along, am I to wait all night ...?

The casual, concrete images of invisible labour underpinning the life of the house slowly crossfade to veranda terrace, now beaded by small variously coloured overhead lamps that give it a festive feel. The pianola stands against the house wall, ready for use.

Anna sits at a green baize table; shuffles a deck of cards.

Petrin sits some distance away, reading a paper by lamplight.

More laughter from the house.

Petya appears on the balcony, lays his lamp on the balustrade, stands immobile, telescope to eye, staring into the far darkness. A train weeps its way across country, miles away.

Anna walks casually along the terrace, stopping at tables to memorize the little stacks of playing cards already consigned to the game. Petrin watches her; she ignores him.

PETRIN: *(Reading)* 'A strike of all two thousand workers brought production to a standstill at the giant Pulilov plant in Moscow yesterday ...'

Laughter again.

ANNA: Bring the wretches out! I'm growing bored here ...

The door opens, people spill out on the terrace in a bubble of laughter, dragging the Colonel and Porfiry, the forfeit players, with them. Sophia and Sashenka, in men's panamas and droopy Fu Manchu moustaches, parade the two men before Anna's table. Versions of applause from Platonov, in Sashenka's hat; Sergei, in brilliant silk peasant costume; and Triletski, in false nose, spectacles and moustache. Anna reviews the parade: Porfiry's dressed and made up as a harem girl, the Colonel, giggle-drunk, as a Moscow tart.

PORFIRY: *(Holding out his playing card.)* Mercy, madame, have mercy, release me from this servitude, I beg you.

ANNA: Booboobooboo. You may return your card when you have danced with la jeune fille de Moscou. Allez, allez!

She claps her hands, Petrin leans laconically forward beyond his paper to engage the pianola, which lurches clumsily into a polka. Porfiry and the Colonel fumble each other around the space, helplessly adrift from the music. Servants, laden, move by in the garden dark, glance blankly at the revel as they go. The dance ends; the Colonel's spread across a table, his rouged and mascara-ed face garish in the beady light. Applause, help; cards are returned, the forfeits paid. Petrin leans forward to disengage the pianola. Platonov and Sashenka move to their table. He mops his face with the band of Sashenka's hat, puffed.

SASHENKA: *(Full of him.)* Mishenka, I'm so glad we're us. You're so ... funny and clever and ... oh everything. With you I'm so happy, so sure of things ... You fill my days.

She kisses him, a sudden awkward lunge.

PLATONOV: *(Trying to disengage her arms.)* Sasha, please ... I'm hot enough as it is, there are people. You can do that at home.

ANNA: *(Piercing; missing nothing.)* On, please. Sophia, your call.

SOPHIA: *(Taking the proffered card.)* Let me see, let me see. Whoever holds this card must ... must.

SHCHERBUK: *(A bellow:)* ... ride a pig around the house!

SOPHIA: Precisely! The Knave of Spades!

The men ruffle through their cards. Sashenka vets Platonov's, who stares darkly at Sophia.

TRILETSKI: *(Moving forward.)* Je l'ai. C'est moi. *(A formal bow to Anna)* Let the pig be summoned.

ANNA: Sergei, tell Yasha to bring a pig! A quiet one, mind, one with a little grace, if you please. *(Sergei exits dutifully, blows a kiss back to Sophia. Laughter at something down the terrace.)* Colonel! Enough. *(The Colonel's on all fours, grunting and squealing.)* A pig has been sent for, you are de trop, sir.

COLONEL: Look no further, dear lady, ye'll find no finer pig in all Russia …

SASHENKA: *(Approaching to tend him)* Father, please, you'll tire yourself …

TRILETSKI: … God willing.

PLATONOV: *(Joining Sashenka)* Come along, Colonel, we'll find you a nice sty upstairs.

COLONEL: Haven't had my supper …

PLATONOV: … We'll put some swill in a bucket for you.

The Colonel waves them away, clambers mazily to upright, wades unaided to his chair with odd hauteur. Thunder.

COLONEL: See. Nothing.

He sits heavily. Giggles. Yasha's arriving from the house, Sergei in his wake.

SERGEI: The idiot claims not to understand your instruction, Mother …

YASHA: … If you please your Excellency, the General's son here tells me I'm to embark on some polar expedition for a pig.

ANNA: *(Curt; ignoring him)* Yes? *(To guests)* Who's next?

YASHA: If you could put yourself in my place, madame, you would see at once how unthinkable your orders are. *(She looks at him curtly.)* Who will serve your guests their dinner, do you imagine? The pig-ignorant Zakhar? The other one …? Deaf Polya with the skin complaint …?

ANNA: Send one of them then. See to it. *(To terrace)* Come along, who's left?

Yasha bows, edges off. Eventually speaks with Zakhar, who peels off into the night.

SERGEI: I haven't had a turn yet, Mother. And there's Shcherbuk …

SOPHIA: I do believe Mikhail Vasilyevich has not yet been called …

SASHENKA: *(Moving forward:)* … I haven't named a forfeit yet, may I?

ANNA: *(Card in hand)* The card is drawn, my dear, I'm sorry, you take the next one. Whoever has this card must come and kiss me. *(She looks at it carefully.)* The Ace of Hearts.

Cards are checked; blanks drawn.

PORFIRY: Whoever has it, name your price, I'll buy it from you …

SASHENKA: *(Checking Platonov's)* It's here, you have it, my love. *(Holds it up.)* See, Anna. Now you must kiss my Misha.

She giggles, nervous.

PORFIRY: Mikhail, I beg of you, name your price …

ANNA: … You think my lips can be bought, sir? Enough. Come, Monsieur Platonov. Pay your forfeit.

*Anna rounds the table, lays the card face down on the baize, calmly awaits his
approach. Platonov dwells a moment; moves slowly forward. People watch
intently. Mutters, whispers, chuckles. Petrin angles his paper a little to take it in.
The two face each other for some uneasy moments, Anna amusedly impassive,
Platonov uncertain. Anna carefully lays her arms on his shoulders and draws his
mouth to hers in a long and increasingly intense embrace. Lifetimes elapse, stars
die in the silence. Porfiry's crest, shaky at the best of times, slowly falls: he
collects a lamp and heads off unseen into the dark. Sashenka falters softly around
the edge of things, an uncertain smile on her lips, checking others' faces for
reassurance it's just a game. The smash of glass cuts the kiss, pulls all eyes down
the terrace. Petya's telescope swings with them. Sophia stares at the debris by her
feet, looks up at the others.*

SOPHIA: Forgive me. It slipped from my hand …

SERGEI: … It's a sign of good fortune to come, my love …

ANNA: Oh, I'm sure it *is*. *(Moving towards her.)* Take care, you'll hurt yourself …
   (Shouts.) Yasha! *(Stoops to help her.)* Yasha will look after it.

*Yasha ghosts in, pulls a face. Petya arrives on the terrace, sees the excitement's
died, heads for the gramophone.*

YASHA: Leave it to Yasha, dear ladies. Yasha does everything …

SOPHIA: I can't think how it happened.

*Platonov has moved to the garden steps, stares out at the night. Sashenka edges
towards him, stops some paces away. He sees her, looks at her sombrely for a
moment; suddenly makes a face at her. She grins, winks at him, hugely relieved.
Anna has returned to the card table. Petrin's there before her, the forfeit card in
his hand. He shows her the card: she gives him a blank cool look.*

PETRIN: (Soft:) The Ace of Hearts, hunh?

ANNA: *(As soft; a smile:)* Tais-toi, mon vieux. *(To the gathering:)* On, on. Who's
   next? Monsieur Shcherbuk … Entertain me. Something elevated, if you please.

*Shcherbuk moves reluctantly forward, pleased to be asked. A spatter of applause.
Platonov pads off into the garden. Sophia watches him from the terrace rail.*

SHCHERBUK: Well, I suppose I could give you something, a little impression I
   picked up from Prince Sergei Konyaev … His excellency performs it far better
   than I do, of course … it's the mating call of the Siberian moose, King of the
   Forest, Monarch of the Glen. I shall need assistance and a few moments of
   preparation … Petya, you'll do for one … Now then, who else …?

ANNA: *(A handclap at the passing Radish.)* You there, what's your name, come
   and help monsieur.

Radish lays down his ladder, approaches the terrace, cap in hand.

SHCHERBUK: Know how to whistle, d'ye?

RADISH: Whistle?

SHCHERBUK: Whistle, dummy, *whistle*. Like a bird, birdsong … (*Radish puts fingers to teeth, produces a perfect blackbird.*) Enough, fine, follow me, it's not your show, you know … Beggar thinks he's a genius. *(Over shoulder)* Amuse yourselves, dear friends, we shall return …

He leads Radish and Petya away into house.

ANNA: *(Handclap.)* Music. Let there be music.

Petrin pushes the lever, the pianola sets up on a wobbly pavane, the group pair off into dance: Sergei and Sophia; Sashenka and her father. Anna looks for Platonov; summons Triletski. Platonov stands mid-garden watching. The great table is all but ready. Yasha surveys it, delicately threading his fingers into white serving gloves. Thunder. A **Stranger** *appears at the bottom of the garden, glasses, thick moustache, begins the approach to the house.*

YASHA: *(Seeing him:)* You there, what's your business …?

PLATONOV: *(To Yasha)* It's all right, I'll see to him. *(To Stranger)* Can I help?

STRANGER: *(Mud-spattered, tired from his trip:)* My name's Gorokhov, clerk at the timber mill, I need the doctor, I'm told he's here.

PLATONOV: … Happy to meet you, Mr. Gorokhov.

GOROKHOV: I doubt that. You're about as happy to meet Mr. Gorokhov as I am to be him. If you'll just …

PLATONOV: He's up there, the tall one.

GOROKHOV: Thank you.

The Stranger heads for the steps. Platonov ambles after him, amused; watches him remove his boots before taking the steps, as the revellers whirl crazily past him. The Clerk gazes at the extraordinary scene a moment, crosses himself as if to ward off the danger he senses.

COLONEL: *(Still the tart, en passant)* What is it? What d'ye want?

GOROKHOV: *(After him)* Name's Gorokhov. I'm looking for the doctor …

People spin on past him. Triletski hands Anna to Petrin, approaches the steps. He still wears false nose, moustache, glasses.

TRILETSKI: What is it?

GOROKHOV: It's my wife. It's all here. *(He hands him a letter, watches the whirl as Triletski reads it)* What is it, spiritualism?

TRILETSKI: … Look, if this woman's your wife, what's the point of a letter, why not just tell me?

GOROKHOV: I wasn't sure I'd be let in. I could've left the letter …

TRILETSKI: Mm. Well, I'm afraid tonight's out of the question. Tomorrow maybe. In the evening.

GOROKHOV: My boss has lent me transport, I could take you there and back, couple of hours at the most ... I can pay, I have the money.

TRILETSKI: That's as maybe, tonight is not possible. Possibly tomorrow. Day after at the very latest.

He tucks the letter into Gorokhov's top pocket, his attention already back on the dance. Thunder.

GOROKHOV: Your Excellency, please come with me, I beg of you, sir, she's not well, she's ... *(Triletski has removed the half-mask. The Clerk reads the cold eyes.)* Forgive me, sir, I do understand. Please excuse me ... *(Triletski returns to the revel. Gorokhov sits on the bottom step to draw on his boots. Sees Platonov approaching.)* You might've told me the doctor was otherwise engaged, now I've made him angry he may never come.

He stamps his boots on the grass, stumps off into the dark. Platonov watches him a moment, as the music ends up above; climbs up to the terrace. Triletski's pouring himself a drink.

PLATONOV: The man's wife is sick, why didn't you go?

TRILETSKI: Oh Lord, here we go ... spare me the bloody sermon, will you? I am what I am and do what I do, just leave me alone ...

SASHENKA: ... But if the woman's ill, Kolya, and you are here, that's wicked ...

TRILETSKI: *(Rounding on her.)* ... Who asked your opinion, you're scarcely out of nappies?

PLATONOV: *(Huge; smashing table with fist)* Don't you dare speak to my wife like that, you idle bastard! You're the only doctor in the area, you swore an oath to tend the sick and the needy, it's your moral duty to show compassion ...

TRILETSKI: ... All right, all right, you want me to go, I'll go. Jesus. I'll have my dinner and then I'll go. *(Silence. Platonov rubs a bruised fist, still seething; catches Sophia's gaze, the new admiration there in the eyes; looks away, finds Anna's mocking face.)* But while we are on the subject, dear friend, you're not exactly the world's most dedicated schoolmaster either ...

PLATONOV: *(A new fury.)* Aha, so it's all my fault, I'm a lousy teacher so you don't have to tend the dying, you're free to let 'em pop off while you souse yourself in booze, eh? Listen, friend, I left university before graduation, I gave my place to someone else, but you bloody well didn't, so buckle to and do your duty.

An extraordinary mooing sound sets up down the terrace. Shcherbuk's arrived, flanked by the twittering Radish and Petya, giving them his celebrated Monarch of the Glen. Platonov sighs his exasperation. Glares across at Triletski. Shcherbuk dins relentlessly on. Triletski grins nervously at Platonov, who softens to a chuckle. The company moves to laughter, another crisis negotiated. Porfiry reappears at the garden steps; stares up at the weirdness above.

Fade to black.

Trail, from darkness, sounds of people at table.

ANNA: *(Unseen)* Well, friends, this might be the appropriate moment for everyone to drink to my health ...

Fade up: garden. Table. Night. Servants carry on more lamps as the dinner progresses. Yasha serves more cutlets with finicky precision. Anna heads the table, Porfiry sits by her, Platonov's flanked by Sashenka and Shcherbuk, Sergei's seat at the foot is empty, Sophia beside it; Petrin sits with Petya facing Platonov. The low hum and chomp of people deep in a meal.

ANNA: *(On; calling.)* Sergei, for heaven's sake where are you?

SERGEI: *(Emerging from house, book in hand)* Coming, Mother.

COLONEL: *(Waking)* ... This policeman claimed earthquakes are caused by evacuation.

TRILETSKI: ... Evaporation ...

COLONEL: ... Exactly. Some German discovered it. Said we must put our faith in haemorrhoids.

TRILETSKI: ... Metalloids ...

SASHENKA: Papa!

TRILETSKI: Go back to sleep, eh?

COLONEL: Don't make fun of me, boy. Maybe I'm alive today because I sleep so well.

SERGEI: *(In his chair, search over:)* Found it! I knew it was in here. Listen everyone ... 'Russia is a vast unending plain on which only men of courage and character may stand.' There.

SHCHERBUK: *(Spraying food from stuffed cheeks as he speaks)* Yes, and who are these men of character, pray? *(He stands awkwardly, wine-sodden. No one pays him much heed, used to him.)* Bluebloods, that's who! Whatever's good, whatever's *best* on this earth is the work of the aristocrat. Absolutely. But today what do we do, mm? We smile on every kind of riff-raff. Kulaks, bottle washers, clerks and postmasters, no ideas, no ideals ... Civilization itself is under threat. Like germs, the scum will gobble everything they touch. Peasants, shopkeepers, scum everywhere, as far as the eye can see. Where are the bluebloods now, eh? Where are your Pushkins, your Lermontovs, your Gogols and Goncharovs, mm?

PLATONOV: *(Factual)* Goncharov was a merchant, wasn't he?

SHCHERBUK: *(Unstoppable)* The exception proves the rule, my friend. Always. Not that Goncharov's genius is unassailable either ... *(Resuming)* Plague and pestilence stalk the land, friends, and our duty to the race is clear. Unite, while we may, and deal the common enemy a mighty blow. Let me appear before this rising scum not as Pavel Petrovich Shcherbuk but as Richard Lionheart. *(Petya slides slowly under the table, as his uncle screeches on)* All our kindness and sensitivity, where has it got us with these degenerates, eh? It's time to speak out clearly, straight to their ugly faces: 'Know your place, you rabble.' Pah. *(A spitting sound.)* Straight in their ugly mugs.

He sits heavily, drunkenly pleased with his oration. Sophia gives Sergei the hard eye, pressing him to rebut. Sergei clears his throat unhappily, not up to the task. The Colonel chunners, head on the table. Triletski gently strokes the old man's head.

PETRIN: *(Casual; from nowhere.)* Fine. But count me out of it, all right?

Silence. Shcherbuk blinks at him across the table.

SHCHERBUK: Really? And why is that, pray?

PETRIN: *(Calm, objective.)* Because my father was a worker and his a serf. And if anyone here finds that unpalatable, I'm perfectly happy to leave. But just bear in mind, will you, that what you've eaten and supped here tonight was bought from my pocket. And the fireworks, mm? And the gun, the piano? I'm the reason you people survive. It's scum like me keeps you afloat. All you're fit for is preaching to others, how they should live, what they should believe. But what about your own lives, your own beliefs, what are they? Pavel Petrovich Shcherbuk, the mighty Lionheart, son of aristocrats, proud to be a blueblood … but what use are you to anyone? You think the world's prepared to go on feeding you forever because you've blue blood in your veins? What do you actually *do*, mm? The mating call of the Siberian moose? (*He moos, softly, horns his fingers around his head, chuckles, rises from the table, takes out a good cigar, heads for a lamp on a side table to light it.*) Believe me, friend, the world has no need of you. These days, the world needs scum. I'm scum … nice word, eh? … and I can turn my hand to anything. My dad was terrified of this place, wouldn't come near it. And I've sat in every room in the house exchanging pleasantries with her Excellency. Not bad.

He lights his cigar carefully at the lamp. The table bears the weight of his meaning.

PORFIRY: *(Eventually.)* Gerasim, Gerasim, what's got into you, my friend, talking like that in another's home, it's not right.

Petrin smiles, unapologetic. Platonov slices a cutlet, forks a piece into his mouth. Anna sips her wine, impassive. The Colonel snores and snuffles a little.

SOPHIA: *(Nervy; keen to normalize)* Dear Gerasim, would you do me a great kindness and deal with that lamp, it's smoking, do you see? If there are two things in the world I cannot bear, it's draughts and smoking lamps …

Silence. Petrin produces a penknife, begins trimming the wick.

PETRIN: *(Soft)* I bought the oil too.

ANNA: *(Sharp)* Eat. Everybody eat.

SHCHERBUK: *(Lurching upright again)* Thank you, I ate before I came, I haven't touched a morsel …

He begins to walk away, struggling for dignity he can't quite achieve.

PLATONOV: *(Laying fork down)* Excellent. Really good.

The swoosh of a needle groping for a groove, Caruso full belt from the terrace gramophone: 'Una Furtiva Lacrima.' Hearts stop, small shrieks bubble to lips, heads swivel up the garden. Petya stares at them from the terrace, a defiant smile on his face.

SHCHERBUK: *(Released into fury:)* You little monster! Let me get my hands on you, I'll give you the braying of a lifetime.

He rips a switch from the garden, lumbers after the already fleeing boy, cuts the record en route for the house. The din of the chase persists for a while, dies. Silence.

PORFIRY: *(Gently, his hand on Anna's.)* My dear lady, pay him no heed, what Petrin says is of no importance.

ANNA: *(Removing her hand; pitiless.)* Porfiry Semyonovich, you're old enough to know better, make-believe will get us nowhere … The General's wife was one thing, the General's widow is quite another. Let me look askance at any creditor, I'll be out of this house before I can say booboo … I've known it for years: the estate or my honour. I choose the estate. Gerasim Kusmich Petrin is a man of courage. And character. And great wealth. He could sink me without a trace. Instead, he keeps me afloat. *(Raises her glass to Petrin.)* Your health, sir.

Petrin smiles, makes an ironic formal bow.

PORFIRY: Dear Jesus, how painful it is.

SERGEI: You see, Sophia? Poor, sad, unending Russia.

PLATONOV: *(A sudden spit:)* Jesus God, leave Russia out of it, will you?

SERGEI: I only meant to say.

PLATONOV: … You've only been meaning to say for fifteen bloody years, man. Give your mouth a rest. Talk, talk, talk … The Russian soul, the common weal, our hopes and fears … it's a wonder our tongues haven't shrivelled with it all. You yap on about Russia, Shcherbuk about scum, Porfiry about love and chivalry … and flies wither on the wing from our wise pronouncements. Talk, eat, sleep, talk, talk some more, talk and more talk, all with a clear conscience. The only thing we take from the modern world is our sense of self-importance, everything else about us is back with the Neanderthals …

SOPHIA: … How can you say such things? It's disgraceful, it's immoral …

PLATONOV: *(Fierce:)* What is? Recognizing one's own mediocrity? Well, what about bottle-feeding village infants and handing out frock coats to their fathers? You don't find *that* just a touch immoral …?

SERGEI: Ding dong ding dong, there's no stopping you, is there? You're like a church bell.

PLATONOV: ... We're all like church bells, friend. The difference is, I toll only what I myself feel; for you, any cause at all can start your clapper banging ... You've been down from university what, three years? And what do you do? Nothing. And what d'you plan to do? Nothing.

SERGEI: ... I'm not starving, I've a long life ahead of me, what's the hurry ...?

SASHENKA: Stop, Mish, stop. You're wearing everyone down, my love ...

PLATONOV: *(Standing, suddenly unsteady)* ... Then don't listen, my darling. Sleep, like your papa there. He hears nothing. That way he can go on loving us all ...

TRILETSKI: What has the old man ever done to you, eh? Have a go at me if you like, but leave him alone.

PORFIRY: *(Standing:)* He's not interested in the argument, he's just looking to show us how clever he is. They can't afford servants any longer, he has to find someone else to vent his spite on.

A weird yowling noise from the darkness. Heads turn. Eyes peer.

ANNA: Now what.

YASHA: *(Looming:)* The beast has arrived, your Excellency.

ANNA: What?

Zakhar looms behind him, a black and white sow in his arms.

YASHA: The pig, madame. For Mr. Triletski, I believe.

Relieved laughter, applause, another crisis bridged.

ANNA: Perfect! Enough philosophising, Kolya's forfeit is to hand. Come, sir!

PLATONOV: *(Ambling away.)* Fine. The pig's here. Go to it, learned doctor.

TRILETSKI: *(Rage and pain growing:)* You go to hell, Platonov. What do you take me for, a clown, is it? It's what you all take me for, isn't it? The perfect clown, the court jester. What do any of you know about me, mm? What do you know of me? *(He's close to tears; the rage turns inward)* Do any of you have any idea how bored I am in this wasteland, mm? I have no life here. Waking at night if a dog so much as mewls, for fear it's someone coming to drag me off to some sickbed. Clattering over dreadful roads with hopeless horses, knowing I'll find diarrhoea at the end of it, terrified it'll be cholera ... Oh, the books I've read on cholera ... and feeling nothing, not a thing, for those who have it. Choking on shame and fear and self-disgust, sickened by living and drinking the way I do ... *(People watch him, horrified; Sergei can't bear it, moves from the table to stand in the darkness.)* I turn my head and see the whole of my future behind me. It's so unbearable to know how little is possible, to know that nothing can ever really be changed.

SASHENKA: *(In pain:)* Kolya, please, I beg of you, do stop. All of you, please stop.

Platonov has collected a guitar, now sits on the swing, begins a soft strumming. Lamps flick and splutter in the dark space. Triletski wipes his eyes with a napkin.

YASHA: What shall we do with the beast, madame?

SERGEI: *(Erupting:)* Take it away, just go, go!

YASHA: *(Standing his ground as he retreats)* I wasn't actually speaking to you, sir. It was her Excellency who ordered the pig.

He mutters on as he and Zakhar move off. Platonov's guitar takes hold again. Anna stands; scans the company; raises her glass.

ANNA: Well, I'll drink my own health.

She drains the wine, lays down the glass, leaves in silence for the house. Passes Shcherbuk, switch still in hand, returning. Petrin has moved softly forward from dark to light and taken Anna's chair at the head of the table. Shcherbuk sees him, heads for Sergei's vacant seat by Sophia.

PETRIN: Imagine the irony. At precisely this moment, in some warm tropical place, a man sits by his canoe on a perfect white beach debating whether to go and get himself a banana. Mm.

Silence. Platonov strums on in the near darkness of the swing.

PLATONOV: *(Eventually)* I came across a story recently, I don't remember where. Quite a short one, but rather good. About a girl who fell in love with a student, he with her. He'd read books to her, she loved to listen. Sometimes, at dusk, they'd go down to the river and watch the lights of the boats pass by. They sang together, dreamed, kissed, swore their love ....

The table listens in silence. Sophia takes more wine, Sashenka scans faces, uneasy again.

SASHENKA: Who is it by, Misha, the story?

PLATONOV: Don't recall. The girl wore her hair long then, below her ears, and always on her skin the smell of spring water, and life for them both seemed to unfold like some unending festival ... dedicated by a kind world to honour their love. And they were happy. One day, she told him she had to go to St. Petersburg for a couple of days. 'Do I have your leave?' she asked him. 'Of course,' he answered, 'but you will be missed ...' *(Sophia stands carefully, glass in hand, stares into the darkness at the storyteller.)* She took the midnight train, he saw her off at the station, she hugged him tenderly, he squeezed her hands and spoke not a word, scared he would weep. He watched the tail-lights dwindling, mile after mile, and whispered, 'my dear good girl. My wondrous woman.' *(Pause. His guitar chords fill the silence.)* A day passed. Two. Five. A month. She didn't come back. The student kept watch at the station, met trains, drank vodka in the station bar. Finally he stopped going. Came to his senses. Grew up. Became an ordinary person.

The chords end. Platonov sits, his face averted. Long silence. Sophia drains her wine, gazes around her, as if trapped.

SERGEI: Terribly good story. Sounds like Uspenski ... or Leskov maybe ...?

Platonov turns slowly in the swing to face the table. Sophia bangs her glass down, heads off for the house, in tears, a napkin to her mouth.

SASHENKA: *(In tears herself.)* Oh God, what have you done now, Mishenka. Must you hurt *everybody* ...?

A rocket blasts into the sky behind the house, bursts above them, washes them in a strange pink glow. The stare up at the night.

ANNA: *(Calling from the terrace.)* Enough, my friends. Everyone to the river. Magic time!

Black.

SASHENKA: *(Calling from the blackness.)* See, Misha, see. Look how beautiful they are ...

The first of a series of brilliant flare-like explosions convulsing their settled world order. Sophia moves quickly through empty space, a lamp in her hand, spectral in the weird off-white glow. Platonov appears in her wake: he wears a long off-white open Burberry, mid-calf like a Long Rider's coat.

PLATONOV: ... Wait. Listen. For Christ's sake, woman, hear me out. Please ... *(She stops, half turns. He gulps for air. They stare at each other across the ghostly space.)* Dear, wonderful woman ... My life's gone, I know it, but yours? What's become of you? Mm? Where's that ... simplicity and ... spirit, unh? Where has all that gone to ...?

SOPHIA: Stop. You're a wild man, you're out of control ...

PLATONOV: ... All right, but be honest with me, in the name of what we once had, why did you marry this man?

SOPHIA: I married him because he's a fine person.

PLATONOV: ... He's a *nothing,* and you know it, ...

SOPHIA: ... He's my husband.

PLATONOV: You could have married *anyone.* You could have married someone with drive and courage and imagination, instead you choose a pygmy, soused in debt and paralytically idle. Why, my love? Why?

SOPHIA: Oh God. Please, Mikhail Vasilyevich, I beg of you, don't destroy my life again, laugh at me if you want, deride me, think of me what you will, but this is the only life I have now ... There's nothing else. Nothing. *(The flare fades fast: she stands in the blackness, lit only by her lamp.)* Mikhail. *(Pause.)* Mikhail ...

She takes a pace or two forward: he's gone. She stands for several minutes as if dead, eyes closed, a slight postmortem tremor in the limbs.

PLATONOV: *(From behind her:)* How I loved you. My God, how I loved you …
(Another great explosion, another great flare of spectral light washing the
space. She turns, moves towards him; he wraps her tight in his arms. Low, tiny
voice.) Dear good girl. Wondrous woman. You know my problem? I believe in
an afterwards. And life doesn't deal in such things. We kid ourselves that
everything's still up ahead, waiting to be discovered, waiting to be lived, never
mind what we do *now,* there's always 'later,' there's always an 'afterwards' to
put it right … And there isn't. There isn't. Back then … I didn't know that. I
watched your train disappear … I let your train disappear. And.

SOPHIA: Oh God, my heart almost stopped when I saw you today.

PLATONOV: Remember the landing pier?

SOPHIA: Yes.

They move slowly into a kiss. At the point of closure, she pulls back with a tiny
yelp. Platonov follows her gaze: sees Sergei, cloak over arm, watching from a
distance. Silence.

SERGEI: *(In shock; voice wobbling)* You asked for your cloak, my love. I'm not
here … on purpose. Purposely … You said you were cold.

SOPHIA: Dear Lord. How banal.

She walks away; disappears. Platonov watches her go; turns to face Sergei.
Silence. Flare fading.

SERGEI: *(Eventually:)* I don't imagine you'll ever understand what I'm … *(He*
can't finish. Silence. It's almost black again.) Congratulations, Misha.

Another great explosion. Black. Slow soft flare across the empty space. Black.
Another.

Another flare washes the terrace. Anna sits in a chair, legs crossed, foot swinging
softly forward and back. Porfiry kneels on one knee before her, head slightly
bowed, eyes fixed on the swinging ankle boot, rabbit to snake.

PORFIRY: … At least give me some small hope, madame, some glimpse of possible
happiness, I don't say now … and I don't ever expect you to … love me … as
I love you but I need meaning in my life. I need hope, Anna.

He looks up from foot to face. Anna gazes blankly back at him.

ANNA: And I, Porfiry, need time. You must try not to be selfish in this matter.

SERGEI: *(Off yelling, hopeless)* Maman, Maman, where are you, I need you …

ANNA: *(Standing briskly.)* Oh my God, what now? *(Calling.)* Here, boy, here!

Sergei appears in the garden, dishevelled, distraught. Stops at the foot of the
steps. Porfiry levers himself embarrassedly to upright.

SERGEI: I need a horse, Maman.

ANNA: You need a horse.

SERGEI: I have to get away from this bloody place.

ANNA: Why, what has this bloody place been doing to you, then …? Is it me or is the whole world insane?

SERGEI: Maman, Anna, Maman, listen. I can't bear it. Tell me what I must do. I'm alone again. I'm on my own again. It's unbearable. Why me? Why me, Maman?

ANNA: *(Deliberately:)* What happened? Has someone done something?

He lurches away. Returns.

SERGEI: You're looking at a cuckold, Mother. Sergei Pavlovich Voynitsev; cuckold.

ANNA: *(Judging it)* Sophia? *(He nods dumbly.)* You caught her? (*He nods again*) Platonov?

SERGEI: Sophia, Sophia, Sophia, Sophia, Sophia. Put me in an asylum, Mother, I'm the one who's insane, I still believe in love and truth and loyalty … Or just put me down, like a dog gone mad, no one needs me, I'm in the way …

Anna opens her arms for him, he lumbers up the steps to her, she hugs him to her quite tenderly.

ANNA: … Booboooo. Calm yourself. Everything will be as it was. Platonov doesn't need that silly little thing. He's far too sharp to fall for all that 'progressive' nonsense. Everything will be as it was, you'll see. Sophia will stay with you, Platonov with me, Sashenka with him … (*Porfiry recoils, handkerchief at mouth to stifle the horror. She doesn't notice.*) Who needs this silly little flirt of a wife of yours, eh? Calmes-toi, enfant.

Sergei has begun to pull away from her, horrified too. Flare fading.

SERGEI: How can you say such things, Maman? How can you?

He runs past her into the house. Anna looks for Porfiry: he's gone. Black a moment; another brief flare blossoms. Triletski stands watching her broodingly from the garden steps.

ANNA: My physician. Boobooboooo. Why so glum?

TRILETSKI: *(On the edge of something.)* Excellency, I … Anna.

Silence. She laughs.

ANNA: *(Replicating his tone exactly)* Anna? Anna? It's a game, dear man. All of it. Who ever wants the one he may have? Sine qua non.

Silence. He laughs; in pain. She begins to massage her shoulder by the neck. Light fading.

TRILETSKI: If I did not love you quite so much, madame, I believe I might find you rather hateful …

ANNA: *(A small laugh)* No, you wouldn't.

TRILETSKI: *(Indicating her stiff neck)* Sometimes you hold yourself too tightly …

ANNA: I know.

Black.

Another explosion, lighting the dining room balcony. Sashenka and Petya stand hand in hand, marvelling at the brilliant sky. Black.

Explosion; flare over empty space. Platonov appears at the trot, knees bent, hands in the pockets of the long Burberry, floating in weird weaves across the terrain like a great bird, intoning a yadeda version of 'Una Furtiva Lacrima.' Stops. Stares. Porfiry stands at the edge of the space, a lamp in one hand, an uprooted sapling cudgelled in the other, watching him. Platonov lights a cigarette. Coughs a little.

PLATONOV: Is it me you want, old man?

PORFIRY: It is. I want to tell you, Mikhail Vasilyevich, how much I hate you. You are a knave, sir. You have destroyed my life, as you have destroyed others'. You hold the world in contempt and ridicule everyone in it save yourself. You scatter lust and faithlessness wherever you go and you do it with impunity. You go unscathed, yet you deserve to be broken, beaten to a pulp.

He raises the sapling. Silence. Platonov draws on the cigarette; coughs again.

PLATONOV: You think life hasn't broken me too, old man? Nothing goes unpunished. But I'll tell you what: I don't give a weasel's tosser what you think of me. I know you decent honest folk. You're honest and decent because you haven't got the guts or the imagination to be otherwise. Sinning's beyond you, you grow old and you can't get it up any more, hunh? So you turn your bile on those who still can …

They stare at each other for some moments, as if frozen. Flare slowly fading. Platonov glides suddenly forward, completes mazy surreal circles around the old man, yadeda-ing as he goes. Disappears. Light fades to black. Porfiry raises his lamp, hurls the sapling after him with a dry scream, spits impotently several times in Platonov's general direction, finds most of the spittle lodged on his lapel, wipes it tearfully off with his free hand.

Black.

SERGEI: *(Off yelling:)* Yasha, Zakhar, Mitka, where in God's name are you …? Asleep, are you? Who gave you leave to sleep when you're needed, you lazy swine …?

A whoosh; a flare floats briefly across the space. Sergei's bent double, lugging a heavy travel trunk across the ground. Flare fading fast.

… When the General was alive you came all right, oh yes, at my beck and call you were then, the master's son, now you only answer to her …

*Black again. Grunts, moans, sounds of a heavy fall. Servants run on in
nightclothes: Yasha, Zakhar, Radish. Their lamps reveal Sergei on his face, the
trunk upended, its contents spilled out on the ground. Screaming.*

Where the hell's the horse I ordered? Where's my bloody horse?

YASHA: You don't have a horse, sir.

SERGEI: *(Hysterical)* Fetch me a horse. I want a horse. Here. Now.

*Yasha looks at the other two; gives them a nod. They leave. Yasha takes a pace
forward, shines his lamp on Sergei's prone form.*

YASHA: Might I suggest the young gentleman retires to his bed …?

SERGEI: *(Full force still)* And where's my hat? Where the hell is my hat? I've
    looked everywhere.

*Yasha stoops, pokes among the spillage from the trunk, locates the hat in question.
Sergei sits up, stares at the hat. Yasha leans forward, gently places it on Sergei's
head. Turns. Leaves. Sergei weeps pathetically in the silent blackness. A flare
briefly re-lights the space: he's trying to remove his wedding ring; can't budge it.*

Fade to black.

Wail of a slow train, a long way away.

PLATONOV: *(From the darkness)* Dearest Lord, how little one needs to be happy.
    To sit in a warm train, take tea by lamplight, idly chat with the chance fellow
    traveller opposite, headed somewhere, anywhere, but away from this
    miserable, meaningless life. One thing I now know: only once betray, only
    once deny what you love and believe in, and the web of pretending and lying
    you spin will hold you fast forever. Dearest Lord, save me, give me strength,
    show me a way.

*The small bead lamps on the terrace fade slowly up. Platonov kneels in the
garden, mud-streaked, worn. Stands slowly. Slowly approaches the sleeping
house. Climbs up to the terrace. Surveys the building. Approaches the door: finds
it locked. Shivers in the predawn cold.*

SOPHIA: *(Soft, unseen)* I waited for you. (*He turns. She's been crouched by the
    terrace rail; stands now; lays a tied bundle of clothes and belongings on a
    terrace table. Platonov stares at her wanly.*) Come, Misha. We can go. You've
    brought me back from the dead. I'm happy again. And every day I will thank
    you for it. We'll start a new life, fresh as spring water, bright as the sun. We'll
    work till we drop and eat only the bread we earn, we'll find our joy in work and
    each other. Our lives will be a festival of truth and justice and honesty. You'll
    teach, I'll help you. We'll live simply, simple clothes, plain food. Come, Misha.
    Take me. (*She closes her eyes, extends her arm.*) Here's my hand on it. Feel it,
    it's frozen, I've waited so long … (*She waits a little longer: nothing. Platonov
    tries the front door again. She opens her eyes.*) Mikhail Vasilyevich.

PLATONOV: *(Slowly)* No, Sophia. No. It's no use. Won't work.

He returns to the locked door, rattles the handle stubbornly. She stares on at him. He turns round again to look at her; shakes his head; resumes the pointless rattling. Sophia picks up her bundle, takes the steps, falters a few paces into the near-dark garden. A thin snoring sound meets her. She approaches quietly; makes out the indistinct form of Sergei, asleep on his trunk. She turns to look at the house; Platonov's begun banging on the door; lays down her bundle, sits on it. Lamps begin to blossom within the house, voices rearing from sleep. Platonov's begun shouting, a new incoherent fury building within him. Night-clad figures appear in lamplight, above, below: Triletski leans over the upper balustrade, his father and Shcherbuk in nightshirts behind him.

TRILETSKI: What is it, Misha, are you hurt?

PLATONOV: *(Huge, hopeless voice)* I'm thirty-five years old, that's what it is, I'm thirty-five years old and yes I'm hurt, I'm hurt, I'm hurt … All gone. Thirty-five years, all gone, I'm nothing, do you hear me? *(He begins turning chairs and tables over, wrecking the terrace. Screams from the house.)* Thirty-five years of age and a complete nonentity! Lermontov died at twenty-seven, Napoleon was already a general, I've achieved nothing! Nothing! Sasha, where are you? You've ruined my life, ruined it. *(Sashenka arrives on the balcony above, screams as she sees the havoc. Platonov sees her.)* I'm nothing because of you, d'you hear me? A useless, worthless, hopeless nothing! *(Sashenka hurries indoors, calling his name. Platonov smashes the pianola with his fists: a sort of crazy music leaps from it, he throws himself blindly against it, kicking and yelling.)* Stop it, stop it, you … machine, you …

Sashenka arrives on the terrace. Others crowd after her. Predawn moves very slowly to dawn as they gather.

SASHENKA: Misha, I beg you, stop, please stop all this …

PLATONOV: *(Still blind)* Where's my mind gone? My strength? My talent? *(She moves forward to restrain him. He sees her. Looks at his barked knuckles.)* You're here too, are you? My keeper of the cold hearth. D'you know how much I despise you, eh? With your cabbage soup and your canaries. I know, you've nowhere else to go either. To see you day on day on day, to hear your silly voice and despise you almost as much as myself, and know nothing's possible …

She takes his hands, tries to draw him to her. For a moment he seems spent, then pushes her violently away. Triletski catches her spinning tumble. Calls of 'Shame,' 'Brute!', 'Shame on you'.

TRILETSKI: How dare you treat my sister that way? Who do you think you are, you louche uncouth bastard, you?

PLATONOV: *(Blinking; scanning the group)* I'm looking in a mirror. I'm just like the rest of you. A nothing. *(A small movement by the door draws his eye.)* It's all right, no need to leave, I'll do that for you … Wake you all up, did I? Ruined your beauty sleep, have I? Fine. You'll be better off when I'm gone …

He glares round the terrace, looking for a place to leave. Sophia and Sergei stand by the garden steps. Platonov shakes his head crazily. Lunges for the terrace rail. Sashenka runs forward again, grabs him round the waist, he swings round viciously, his elbow sends her flying to the floor, he vaults the rail into the garden, charges off into the dark. People crowd round the floored Sashenka, who struggles to her feet screaming his name and takes off after him. A still moment, as people gather sombrely at the front rail of the terrace to chart their shouted progress. The voices slowly die.

ANNA: *(Finally:)* Yasha!

Black.

Sashenka's voice, distant, slowly closing: Misha, Misha, Mishenka …

Fade up: ghostly dawn light, moments before sunrise. Platonov stands motionless, eyes closed, on the plank bridge on which the day began. His wife's voice grows closer.

PLATONOV: Forgive me. Forgive me. *(He opens his eyes. The faintest tinge of pink touches his skin from the rising sun.)* Not another day. Not another day.

SASHENKA: *(Closer)* Misha. Mishenka.

He climbs out, ready to leap. Black. Light up. Sashenka appears on the bridge almost at once. A deep thudding splash below. She stares down in almost comical horror, fingers stuffed in her mouth. Rushes from the bridge. A slow, salmony blush begins to colour the space. Silence. A figure slowly rises down below: Platonov, drenched to the skin, fetlock-deep in shallow water. He stares hopelessly at the heavens.

PLATONOV: You make it hard, Lord. Really.

Sashenka rushes on, wades out to grab him to her. He stands in her arms like a rag doll as she speaks, water dripping from his panama hat.

SASHENKA: *(Part litany; all love)* Misha, my dearest man, my love, my husband. You live, then I live too. I love you so much. Misha, you're my world, air, food, roof, everything. I fear nothing now, nothing I cannot endure, no one will ever love you as I do. Sleep, Misha, you must sleep, rest and we'll be happy again, so many fine days ahead of us, luck will smile on us, we'll see a bright new life, new friends to understand and forgive us. But you must learn to love, Misha. Love. So long as there's love, there's life too, long and happy.

Sounds of the others arriving at the lakeside. She holds him out to look at him.

PLATONOV: Dear Sasha. Save me. Why is it always like this?

SASHENKA: Sh. Come.

She leads him off. He stops. Stoops to rub his leg.

PLATONOV: Forgive me. I hurt my leg. I thought it was deep. It isn't …

She leads him off he goes on whimpering, her child again. The rest of the household, in various stages of undress, stand in rough line to greet them. Yasha fusses up and down, with coats and capes and wraps. Greetings, hugs, kisses: another crisis over.

ANNA: Nothing will change, my friends.

The sun suddenly strengthens. They turn, like spectres, to watch it lift over the hill across the lake.

COLONEL: The sun.

TRILETSKI: The sun.

SOPHIA: *(Hand in Sergei's)* Another day.

PLATONOV: Another day.

SERGEI: God bless us all.

PORFIRY: He will, he will.

TRILETSKI: Of course, I was a younger man then, and just a touch shy.

PETRIN: *(As if reading:)* 'On the fifteenth of July, at the Black Forest spa of Badenweiler, his wife by his side, the playwright Anton Chekhov died smilingly. His last reported words were "It's a long time since I drank champagne".'

SHCHERBUK: Aristocrat of wines.

ANNA: Nothing changes. Everything will be as it was.

RADISH: *(From above; unseen)* Grass dies. Iron rusts. Lies eat the soul …

The radiance spreads upwards; reveals Radish and Zakhar, Petya between them, holding their hands, on the plank bridge. Looking down on the spectres below)

… Everything's possible.

Fade to black.

END

THE GULF BETWEEN US

or

THE TRUTH AND OTHER FICTIONS

An interview for the West Yorkshire Playhouse

How did you come to write The Gulf between Us?

I'd started working on an idea with Paul Slack and Dave Hill some time before Christmas 1990 and the idea involved building a wall in real time, on stage, every night. Originally I wasn't involved as a writer, I was just there as a sort of ideas man and a possible director for this project – it interested me, and the idea of creating a company to do new work interested me.

While we were discussing this, talking through these ideas, the deadline was set for the Gulf War. So out of the corner of my eye I was always watching the geopolitical scene and sensing with increasing horror that this was a deadline that would not be met and that was intended not to be met. The Western Alliance had decided that it needed this war of retribution.

When the war actually began, on the night of 16-17 January 1991, I was in America discussing a screenplay I'd just written about Eastern Europe with the director Bob Rafelson, and I watched the bombs dropping on Baghdad from the relative safety of a Beverly Hills hotel. I remember the sense of rage and horror and pity in me, feelings that were going to grow and grow over those forty-four horrific days of slaughter. When I got back home, about a week after the outbreak of war, I called Dave Hill and said, 'I think these guys should be building a wall in the Middle East,' and that's really where *The Gulf between Us* started.

I followed the war drowning in rage and pity and an awful sense of impotence, and I began to try and think of how this play might be set in an Iraqi city. As I talk I'm still working on the play – there are sections of it I haven't managed to write yet – and I guess the work will go on up to and beyond the opening night, because that's the ways plays are; I mean you try to get them right on the page before rehearsal, and then in rehearsal you have more writing to do – some that you've done anyway and some that you thought you'd done, but now as you stand it up and work it you see that it needs to be taken further.

How did the theme of the Arabian Nights *occur to you?*

I set myself a kind of literary research task. I wanted to read the Koran, I wanted to read the *Tales of a Thousand and One Nights*, I wanted to read the *Epic of Gilgamesh*, I wanted to read anything and everything that I hadn't read or had forgotten that I'd read, that might help me into the minds of these people at the crossroads of the East and the West. When I began this play all I could think was blood and pain, but the further I got away from the War, the more – I think – balance I got. When I started writing it I discovered that it was going to be a rather strange comedy – and you make these discoveries on the page, you don't make them by agreement with yourself in advance. I also realized that it was not going to be a naturalistic play – that there were going to be elements of it that were shimmering and trembling away from *Tales of a Thousand and One Nights*. What's interesting about the *Thousand and One Nights* is that it's the first literature in Arabic that challenges the rule of the priests and the law-makers and the kings, basing itself in the lives and the language of the people. Then I realized that there was something there that I needed for this play – because this is not a play about presidents and secretary-generals and prime ministers, it's a play about people much closer to the earth – building workers, British building workers and the Arab workers of one kind or another. Also, because the *Thousand and One Nights* was popular it was irreverent, it was satirical, it was comic, and it dealt with the details of everyday life in ways that the Koran or the great epics didn't.

Did you find that when you were writing it, it became a very personal piece, or were you writing it for other people – for all the people who were victims of the Gulf War in one way or another?

I think that writing – all my writing anyway – is probably first of all self-addressed; I mean you write because you can't address the problem without writing: that's the joy and the trap of writing. And there is, I think, in this play a great deal of the pain and the pity and the impotence that I've talked about and that I experienced and continue to experience about these events. But I also know that I want it to be seen in the region, in the Middle East. There was no way that this could be written only for a Western audience. It has to be seen there as well and part of the ambition of The Building Company is to take the play, possibly in this production, out to Palestine and Syria and Iraq if possible.

When I finished the first draft of the play some important things emerged. There is a sense in which the Brits in the play are quite definitely the foreigners – so it's an odd experience reading it and watching it, I suspect, to feel that you're on the outside looking in. Even though the Brits are at the heart of this play, they're not at the moral centre of it. At the moral centre are Arabs who are experiencing this crushing, horrific, punitive, exemplary war which is being handed down to them by the Western Alliance for reasons and values that really don't stand up to even the most cursory scrutiny. To murder a quarter of a million people, at the most conservative estimate, to consign another one or two million people to death in the aftermath and to bomb the country back five thousand years, very nearly, seems to me a pretty unpromising and unpropitious way of trying to create a new world order. Especially when that country was indeed the cradle of civilization and was the origin of so much that we in the West have inherited in the way of art, science, mathematics, medicine, literature, language – even our alphabet.

The country in which the play is set is not named as Iraq. The war is not necessarily that war. It's an un-named country and an un-named city in an un-named war. The references suggest Iraq and the West, but I hope the play generates thoughts and feelings about more than just the most recent conflict. As I said, the moral centre of the play is occupied by Arabs, and because I hadn't known when I began to write that that would be the case, it became very important that this production should honour that event, that discovery. So we decided to cast Arab actors in the four Arab roles, people who had the lived experience of being Arabs and who were, indeed, in the region, living their lives and suffering these traumas, during the Gulf War.

I chose Palestinians partly because the play demands politicized people, people who would, by dint of their own experience, understand the issues that this play deals with. It's not a play about Palestine or Israel, but Palestinians are much more political than almost anybody else in the region by virtue of their own history; and that hunch, about the essential contribution they would make to the production, has proved right.

I don't know that *The Gulf between Us* is the whole of my reaction to the Gulf War: it's not a documentary, it's not a journalistic piece. It's a kind of dreamplay. My personal reaction will probably come out as poems or song lyrics – I've written some songs already. But the play is certainly emotionally and morally very much about responding to the events of the Gulf War.

Leeds, 1992

The Gulf between Us was first performed at The West Yorkshire Playhouse, Leeds, on 16th January 1992. The cast was as follows:

O'Toole   Dave Hill

Ryder   Paul Slack

Chatterjee   Kulvinder Ghir

Dr Aziz   Salwa Nakkarah

Ismael   Akram Telawe

Ancients
Yacoub Abu Arafeh
Ahmad Abo Sal'oum

Director   Trevor Griffiths

Designer   Hayden Griffin

Lighting   Rory Dempster

Associate Director   John Tams

Consultant & Translator   Fateh Azzam

Sound   Mic Pool

Assistant Director   Vicky Featherstone

The play was produced in association with The Building Company.

The Gulf Between Us

ACT ONE

Black.

Slow fade up to chill moonlight over glimpsed desert. Mid-ground, the black outline of a large Bedouin tent.

O'Toole *appears foreground in tight golden spot: 'The Gilder's Lamp'. He's large, pushing fifty, with long black hair and a full beard, dressed in the grubby garb of an Arab worker. He carries a large battered grip, an instrument case slung from a shoulder.*

He turns to face the auditorium.

O'TOOLE: 'In the name of Allah
The Compassionate
The Merciful
Blessings and peace eternal
Upon the Prince of Apostles,
The Master Muhammad.
'The annals of former generations
Are lessons to the living; men and women
May look back upon the fortunes
Of predecessors and be warned;
And by contemplating
The history of past ages
Be purged of folly.
'Glory to the One who has made
The heritage of antiquity
A guide for our own time …'
'… For it is from
This heritage are drawn
The Tales of the Arabian Nights
And all that is in them
Of fable and adventure.'

He turns to look behind him again.

Allahu Akbar.

God is good.

The spot fades, O'Toole with it.

Bleed in –

A coil of Arab voices in quotidian discourse: souk, bazaar, schoolroom, state radio, tea-shop, mosque. Threads of English start up, within the coil: an endless lexicon of words invisibly ingested from the Arabic; a discontinuous mesh of readings detailing the Near East origins of our alphabet; commercial jingles; a

*moral litany from First World leaders justifying the punitive use of force against
Third World intransigents.*

*The light has gradually thickened to pre-dawn. The voice-coil eventually gives
way to a muezzin calling the faithful to first prayer. The call holds, grave and
pure, for some moments; becomes, almost seamlessly, a city siren wailing the raid
to come. The siren builds, grows harsh, violent; cuts abruptly as the raid begins.*

*In the deep silence, mute cockpit-videos of famous strikes on bridges,
buildings, installations replace the pre-dawn light on the sky-cyc.*

A final Western voice defending the action, then sound and image fade.

An abrupt plunge into daylight, harsh, strange.

*Mid-ground, left, an Arab Ancient spades a slow ant-like path across a
wilderness of rubbled buildings, searching for personal effects and valuables, a
large black bin-liner tied to his waist. Mid-ground, right, a tent-like structure,
green, solitary, unfathomable, rears above the wasteland.*

*Foreground, a second Ancient laboriously strings red tape across an arc of
metal stakes driven into the earth.*

Ismael, *late teens, in shirt, slacks and good shoes, stands motionless between
mid- and foreground, a kid's football balanced on his raised right foot.*

Silence.

*The youth calls out to the two Ancients, holds up his arms, like a footballer
demanding acclaim from the terraces. The Ancients stop their work to gaze at
him; exchange a look; return impassively to their work.*

*A phone rings. Ismael crosses to an old oil-drum where he's laid his gear,
fishes out a phone. The ball goes with him, wobbling at his ankle, the elastic band
holding it now clearly visible.*

ISMAEL: (*In Arabic; phone*) Ismael. Yes, sir, it's done, Major, completely screened,
the area cordoned off, I'm still waiting for labour …

*He listens for some time. Turns upstage to stare at the tent, shakes his head,
gradually oppressed by the growing gravity of what he's hearing. Turns
downstage again, face grim, concentrated. Frowns. Asks for something to be
clarified. Dumbly nods assent.*

*The call ends. He stows the phone. Stands a moment, as if in shock. Calls the
Ancients to leave the site. Stoops to detach the ball. Straps on shoulder holster,
slips on his warm-up jacket, pitcher's hat and shades.*

*Two armed People's Militia arrive, pushing a middle-aged man in bus-driver's
uniform ahead of them. The man weeps, distressed, terrified. One of the militiamen
hands Ismael a document, Ismael orders them to take the driver to the tent.*

*The man's pushed roughly to his knees, wails, hopeless. Ismael reads out the
document aloud over the weeping driver, folds it, pockets it, walks behind the
man, draws his pistol, lays it to the man's head, fires.*

*The driver flops forward in a spray of blood. The militiamen move impassively
in to drag him off face down across the rubble. Silence.*

*Ismael stands, blank, white-faced, swaying and kecking a little. Gathers at the
sound of women's voices, raised, anxious, some way down the block. Holsters the
pistol. Picks up the phone. Pads out a number. Sees blood on his shoe.*

Aiee!

O'TOOLE: (*Tape relay*) Wherein it came to pass, on the twenty-first night was told the Tale of the Builder, the Gilder, the Minder and the Gulf between them …

Lights up, less bright.

Billy Ryder *stands amid the rubble, just arrived, two large grips and a suit-bag in his hands, taking in the Ancients slowly laying a duckboard roadway across the wasteland.*

He stacks his gear carefully, rubs his eyes, whacked; sniffs, sniffs again.

RYDER: (*Calling the Ancients*) This it? (*They look at him.*) This the er …? (*Nothing.*) OK, forget it …

He wanders over to the tent, deliberates a moment, moves towards the flap-entrance, freezes as a volley of shots, off, scatters the shrieking women.

Ismael in fast, bawling back a question at a perimeter guard. The guard responds: the women have retreated. Ismael checks watch and sun, chivvies the Ancients, who work on as before, mute, lava-like; flicks the kid's ball up into the air, punts it in the direction of the tent; sees Ryder.

ISMAEL: Hey. You.

RYDER: Talkin' to me?

ISMAEL: Over here. (*Ismael sits on his oil-drum, studies a clipboard of papers. Ryder collects his gear, approaches, some tension evident inside the self-assurance.*) Name?

RYDER: Ryder. Billy.

ISMAEL: I.D. (*Takes it.*) Ryder William. What's Billy?

RYDER: It's short for William.

ISMAEL: Mm. You here alone?

RYDER: Ahunh. Listen, son …

ISMAEL: I'm promised two persons …

RYDER: (*Looking round*) Aye, well, you're one short. (*Takes I.D. back.*) Do me a favour, will you, call the head honcho, I've got a letter from Colonel Faqir down at the Water Filtration Plant …

ISMAEL: What is it concerning? This letter?

RYDER: Well, it's actually addressed to the senior man here …

ISMAEL: Nevertheless …

RYDER: OK. Number one, I've been slavin' down at the water plant since the dawn raid, OK?, an' I'm knackered. Number two, I'm meant to be getting an exit visa an' a ticket out today, I mean the Ministry gave me their word, anyway they're not at the hotel, so I need a couple of hours to call in at the office and erm … collect 'em. You understand any o' this?

Ismael stands, checks his watch, looks at the sky.

ISMAEL: OK, Ryder Billy, I show you the job ...

RYDER: Excuse me, you don't seem to be hearing me, hey ...

ISMAEL: (*Hard*) Hey!

RYDER: (*Fast*) What?

ISMAEL: Don't hey to me. I do heying.

RYDER: That's fine.

ISMAEL: You bet.

RYDER: (*Letter in hands; reasonable*) I just wanted to draw your attention to the fact that this is an official correspondence, I mean someone in authority ought to read it ...

Silence.

ISMAEL: OK. I see to it.

He puts his hand out. Ryder looks at it.

RYDER: How do you mean?

ISMAEL: (*Telephone*) I read it to my Major.

RYDER: Oh. Right. Excellent. (*Hands it over. Looks around him.*) You got labour? (*Ismael indicates the two Ancients.*) Terrific. I meant craftsmen, you know, brickies ... Splat clunk.

ISMAEL: A person's coming ...

RYDER: I hope so, cos my job's not hands-on, I'm more management ...

ISMAEL: (*Sharp*) Hey.

RYDER: What?

ISMAEL: I'm the boss.

RYDER: Sure.

ISMAEL: And.

RYDER: Yes?

ISMAEL: I have a boss.

RYDER: I understand.

ISMAEL: So. This building here inside ... a missile came through a window and out the back wall. My boss instructs Ismael mend the wall before sundown, no if no but, before dark (*Looks at sky*) you see the picture ...? I show you the job.

RYDER: Ah, I see, it's a complete misunderstanding, time's of the essence, we're saying the same thing ... I was just about to suggest I size the job up, work out what you need, how long it'll tek, while you can be reading the Colonel's letter to your Major … Division of labour. (*Silence. The men eye each other; a slightly scary stand-off. Tacking into sincerity*) Look, er … Ismael, that's your name, right? D'you mind …? Ismael, you have every right to be angry at what the white … at what the West is doing to your people and your country … It is, it's horrible, horrible, but … I could've left with everyone else, spent Christmas with the wife and kiddie, I chose to stay, I chose to help, right up to the deadline and beyond, right up to this day, I put my life on the line, told the Ministry my services were at their disposal, you know … Then three weeks ago I got news my wife had been very seriously injured in a car crash, a bus … they say the driver was drunk, I don't know … (*Sniffing, reeling him in*) I am not trying to be obstructive, friend, I'm just fairly desperate to get home, you know …? (*Looks at his watch.*) What can I say …?

Silence again. Ismael checks the sky.

ISMAEL: You got tough shit, Ryder Billy. (*A new commotion erupts down at the tent-side perimeter line, men's voices lifting in fervid anger.*) You size the job. I call the Major.

RYDER: (*Hand out*) God bless you. (*Ismael takes it.*) It's a deal.

ISMAEL: You have my hand, you have my word.

RYDER: You're a brick, sir.

A call from a militiaman labouring up from tent-side perimeter. Ismael takes him in. Watches Ryder readying for work.

ISMAEL: Hey.

RYDER: Yessir …

ISMAEL: In here is. Ancient holy place. You stay out of. Such a place is not for your eyes. (*In Arabic*) Yes, I'm coming. (*The approaching militiaman stops on the crest of the mounded rubble. A second man lumbers up behind him.*) You understand?

RYDER: Absolutely.

Ismael crosses to speak with the guards. He gives one of them Ryder's letter and murmured instructions, sends him on his way. Ryder, out of sight now in the lee of the tent, peels seamlessly from his studied zeal, chuckling as he lights a fag and begins changing into working gear.

Dear dear dear. Like takin' sweets off a child. Bloody wife in a car crash, Jesus, there's one born every day … Perfect. Just what I've bin lookin' for …

ISMAEL: (*Calling*) Hey.

RYDER: (*Fast*) Yessir.

ISMAEL: (*Phone up*) I see where second man is, OK?

RYDER: Fine. No time to waste.

More din from the tent-side perimeter. Ismael completes the call, instructs the remaining militiaman to guard the site, yells at the Ancients to help Ryder, hurries off to deal with the disturbance. The Ancients plod across to the tent, begin peeling away the entrance flaps. Ryder weighs up what's on site, lays out tools and a metre-stick, closes in to assess the damage.

Little by little, the rear wall of a pre-Muslim shrine is uncovered, a huge chunk of masonry bitten out by the hit, the surviving stonework charred by flash-marks. Beyond the hole, a second hanging thick-mesh screen blocking further access; through which, suggested rather than seen, a solitary stained-glass window tinily lights the blackness.

Ryder feeds readings and measurements into his Psion II. The Ancients gaze at him incuriously.

RYDER: (*Uncomfortable*) OK. Piss off. Scram. (*They stand; mute, immovable.*) Go on, get outa here … Imshi, Imshi. (*He claps his hands behind them, like a man shooing geese. The Ancients seep back to their duckboards. Ryder busies himself measuring and feeding in, launched on a tuneless version of 'Let Me Go'; turns for a moment to check the sky, as a distant siren starts up to the west; sniffs, keys his Psion for print-out, reads it.*) This'll be no pushover either … (*O'Toole emerges from the shrine. He's in frayed denim shorts, an old Man United shirt and sandals, carries his Arab work gear on one arm. Stretches. Yawns. Seriously startled*) Jesus Christ, who the fuck're you …?

O'Toole checks watch, sky; listens a moment, as the aerial attack begins some miles away.

O'TOOLE: (*Strong East Lancs voice*) You woke me up with your yammering. I was taking a nap.

RYDER: Unbelievable. Ha. I thought I were t'last on board, put it there, old son, Billy Ry-

O'TOOLE: (*Uninterested*) Ryder, yeah. Heard you hustling the kid.

He re-enters the tent, reaches out his gear from beyond the thick mesh, carries it out on to the site. Checks his feet; the shoes are caked in a black, shiny goo.

RYDER: (*Tracking him*) In there? 'S off limits, din't anyone tell you, you'll get me shot …

O'TOOLE: (*Thinks; frowns*) Why would they shoot *you*?

RYDER: (*Back foot*) Because I'm bloody meant to be in charge …

O'TOOLE: Are you? (*Shakes head.*) You could be in for a really trying day, sunshine.

RYDER: What, that? (*The hole*) Coupla hours, piecea cake, two brickies on the job …

O'TOOLE: You're a brickie, are you?

RYDER: 'S matter of fact, I run my own firm, but yes, that's my trade …

O'TOOLE: (*Looking around*) Where's the other one?

RYDER: What?

O'TOOLE: You said two.

RYDER: Well, what're you?

O'TOOLE: Not a brickie, son, that much I can tell you …

He sits. Fiddles in his instrument case, brings out a can of Stone's. Looks at feet again.

RYDER: Oh, Christ. (*Studies him.*) Have I missed something …? I mean, who are you? How come you're here in the first place?

O'TOOLE: No comment.

RYDER: 'S that mean?

O'TOOLE: Whatever you want it to.

RYDER: You're trouble. I can smell it.

O'TOOLE: (*Studying sandals*) 'S probably these. Trod in something back there. Cat-shit mebbe. (*He begins trying to clean them, smells the stuff, stares back at the hole, looks again at Ryder.*) I can get you a brickie.

RYDER: Oh aye? What you gonna do, ring the job shop?

O'TOOLE: Please yourself.

RYDER: I can lay the buggers meself if I have to, there's time …

O'TOOLE: (*Checking sky; listening*) Don't count on it.

He wets a finger, holds it up for the wind.

RYDER: How d'you mean?

O'TOOLE: That's the refineries being blitzed again. Wind picks up, you're gonna be needing braille.

Ryder listens. Bites his lip. Looks at O'Toole.

RYDER: Who are you?

O'TOOLE: Name's O'Toole.

RYDER: What are you doin' here?

O'TOOLE: 'S a long story. Yours too, eh?

He grins, hands Ryder the can. Begins slipping into his Arab work trousers. Calls something in Arabic to the guard above; the guy tells him to wait.

RYDER: You're a weird fucker, I'll tell you. (*O'Toole gives a scaly chuckle.*) How come you can get a brickie?

O'TOOLE: I know the turf, friend. 'S my patch.

A woman calls, another answers, another; regrouping. The guard picks up his rifle, dumps his fag. Ismael's voice calling, still distant, on the approach.

RYDER: Fuck me. Teks all sorts …

O'TOOLE: (*Quiet*) Put it this way. I'm all you've got.

RYDER: Oh aye? I've got a deal with the kid. He does his stuff, I'm out of here.

O'TOOLE: Sure. 'You got tough shit, Ryder Billy.' Do me a favour.

RYDER: I'm telling you, that letter's for real, two hundred quidsworth of it.

O'Toole chuckles again. Picks up the ball, twirls it on his finger. The guard calls something down to the approaching Ismael.

O'TOOLE: You haven't the first idea, have you? You've got Shias ready to riot over there, you've got women going crazy the other side, I haven't worked out what the hell's going on here, but I'd lay a small wager it's gonna be something truly awful, I mean a lot worse than Blackpool, a lot worse, and you think you've got something going with the kid? (*His eyes burn black across the space between them.*) Trust me. Not a request. You muck around with Ismael, you'll get us all shot … (*Ismael crests the rubble ridge, exchanges words with the guard, begins the descent to join them. To be heard, a seamless segue*) … The guy says, 'This doesn't seem so bad, knee-deep in dog-shit, sure, but I always imagined Hell'd be a lot worse than this,' then the door opens, this bugger with horns and a tail blows his whistle and shouts, 'Tea break over, back on your heads …'

ISMAEL: (*Beckoning*) Hey, you. You're late. Where you been?

A moment, as O'Toole studies the youth.

O'TOOLE: Graveyard. Burying the dead.

ISMAEL: I.D. (*Takes it. Checks clipboard.*) How you say this?

O'TOOLE: O'Toole.

Ismael hands it back, studies him carefully.

ISMAEL: O'Toole. (*The distant explosions tail off. The two stand in silence, locked. A siren sounds all-clear. Silence.*) OK. (*To Ryder*) You size what we need, mister?

RYDER: (*Print-out in hand*) 'S all here.

ISMAEL: No problem, hunh?

Ryder glances at O'Toole, who's studying the sky.

RYDER: Be a push. It can be done.

ISMAEL: You say the boys what you need, they fetch and carry, truck's on the corner here … (*Yells instructions in Arabic at the Ancients*) Let's go, let's go. (*To O'Toole; sharp*) You stay here.

RYDER: I was wondering if there was any word on the visa thing …

Silence.

ISMAEL: My Major speak with the Ministry, they check. They give him a strong maybe.

RYDER: Strong maybe, hunh? (*Another glance at O'Toole.*) Fine. Fine.

He leaves with the Ancients. Ismael watches a moment, slips off his jacket, casually repositions his pistol, sits down for a smoke, his hands trembling a touch. O'Toole collects a long-handled shovel, begins clearing a work area around the shrine wall. Ismael watches, broods. Takes out phone, keys a number, rattles something in Arabic, we hear 'O'Toole' twice. Pockets phone.

ISMAEL: Your team, yes?

O'TOOLE: What?

ISMAEL: Your team. Man United.

O'TOOLE: Right.

ISMAEL: Good team, eh?

O'TOOLE: The best.

ISMAEL: Red devils.

O'TOOLE: Right.

ISMAEL: Sir Matt Bussaby.

O'TOOLE: Yeah.

ISMAEL: You skinhead, hunh? (*O'Toole smiles.*) You know Gazza?

O'TOOLE: Gaza? Never bin, no.

ISMAEL: Gazza. Gazza?

O'TOOLE: Gazza, right. Sure.

ISMAEL: Great, hunh?

O'TOOLE: Pretty good. Bit of a prick.

ISMAEL: Bit of a prick, sure. You wanna sell?

O'TOOLE: What?

ISMAEL: Ten dinar I give you.

O'TOOLE: Uhunh.

ISMAEL: Fifteen.

O'TOOLE: You like it?

ISMAEL: 's OK.

O'TOOLE: Cost me two hundred.

Ismael thinks.

ISMAEL: OK, twenty. (*O'Toole laughs.*) What?

O'TOOLE: Tell you what. Maybe I'll give it you. How's that sound?

ISMAEL: Why?

O'TOOLE: Because.

ISMAEL: Because.

O'TOOLE: We'll see.

Phone again. Ismael answers: gets the result of the check on O'Toole; is told to expect Dr Aziz, from the Ministry, on site to help with the women. O'Toole works on, always within earshot.

The Ancients have reappeared, struggling an antique diesel-powered cement-mixer on to the site. Billy Ryder follows, carrying tools and gear.

RYDER: I'm gonna need help, chief, these boys don't understand a word I say …

ISMAEL: I fix. (*He hurls instructions to the guard above, who bawls down to the perimeter for assistance; snarls abuse at the Ancients; generally puts himself about.*) Let's go, let's go …

RYDER: Get these sorted, will you? I'll start getting the blocks in … (*O'Toole pitches in. Two militiamen arrive; Ismael directs them to the truck. Sotto*) 'S happenin'?

O'TOOLE: This guy's in trouble.

RYDER: How? Shit. What d'you mean?

ISMAEL: (*Loud*) 'S go! (*Ryder and the helpers move back off to the truck. O'Toole begins stripping off the shirt.*) Where I saw you?

O'TOOLE: Spent a lot of time here. I was in this place before you were born, son.

ISMAEL: O'Toole.

O'TOOLE: O'Toole. Here. (*He wraps the shirt into a ball, underarms it across the site into Ismael's waiting arms.*) All yours. You're on the team.

ISMAEL: (*Slowly*) Why you do this?

O'TOOLE: I'm fifty next month. It's starting to look foolish. (*The youth deliberates the binding gift; eventually stoops to stow it in his case; lifts his head to listen as a fierce high-pitch ululation sets up around the women's perimeter. O'Toole pads across to look and listen. Fear and grief wash the site.*) What is that?

Ismael gives a fierce look, returns to packing the shirt.

ISMAEL: Just women. It's nothing.

O'TOOLE: Friend, if you have a problem …

ISMAEL: (*Standing*) Problem? I have no problem.

O'TOOLE: A man without problems has a problem.

ISMAEL: (*Staring off; the howling thickening*) I follow orders, no problem.

He looks up suddenly, stares at the sky.

The light begins to bleed away, strengthens for a moment, darkens again, as a pall of smoke blocks the sun – continues to end of the act.

The returning helpers stop, heads lifted, to look.

Ismael barks at them to move. A guard hurries up from the women's perimeter, reports the situation. Ismael sends him back, prepares to follow, stops on the rubble ridge, turns to scan the labouring traffic. Ryder's back, bossing the boys, organizing materials in the rough work area.

ISMAEL: No if no but, Ryder Billy. Tick tick, eh? You play the game, Ismael will do you OK. (*Looks at O'Toole.*) You fuck him around, he blows your legs off. Tick tick.

He calls an instruction to the remaining guard, moves off.

RYDER: (*For Ismael; keen to please*) Come on, let's get crackin', lads, we haven't got all bloody day … Watch that, for Christ's sake, no no no, like this, see, carry it like this …

Breezeblocks, tools, lime, sand, cement, water and a rough do-it-yourself scaffolding gradually find their way from truck to work area. Ryder nips and harries throughout, nervily checking the minder's whereabouts.

O'Toole gathers his Arab work tunic, slips it on, carries his bag and instrument case to safer ground downstage. Opens another can of Stone's. Stares out at the city below.

Ryder sees him, checks Ismael's gone, joins him.

RYDER: You're not getting ready t'do a bunk, are you? (*O'Toole looks at him calmly, looks back at the city.*) Why you wearing that stuff?

O'TOOLE: Why are they?

RYDER: Cos they're fucking Arabs, I don't know.

O'TOOLE: Deep. You've really given that some thought.

RYDER: Listen, don't piss around, we've gotta pull together on this one. You said the kid was in trouble, what's he told you?

O'TOOLE: The kid's scared. He's on the line with this thing, you can smell it …

RYDER: Who gives a shit? Trouble for these buggers is leverage for me, man, that's all I care about. I've shelled out a small fortune down at that bleedin' office 'n' I'm getting nowhere, they're just milking me dry … I've had three weeks o' this nightmare, I've gotta get out, I can't take this, I made a deal, they're fucking me over. You put your back into this one for me and I'll see you right and that's a promise. Now just tell me what you can do and I'll work round you, OK … I mean you do have a trade, right, just … I mean what are you?

The howling breaks down. Ismael's voice, megaphoned, addressing the women. O'Toole listens.

O'TOOLE: (*Eventually*) All right. I'm not sure if you're ready for this, Ryder Billy ...

RYDER: (*Nervy*) What?

O'TOOLE: I'm a reporter. For the *Sun*. Undercover.

Silence.

RYDER: Oh Jesus.

O'TOOLE: (*Deliberate*) No no. You're supposed to say, 'Don't be daft, the *Sun* doesn't have reporters ...

He chuckles, oddly pleased.

RYDER: Funny. Ha bloody ha. I think the sun's shrivelled your brain-pan or someat. Personally, I don't get the joke ...

O'TOOLE: Look at it (*the site, the world*). Look at it, will you. The new world order. We're the joke.

Ryder surveys the scene. The Ancients have squatted in the sand to rest.

RYDER: (*Calling*) Hey, come on, let's be having you, there's plenty more where that came from ...

He gives O'Toole a final wither, returns to his tasks, eventually leads the Ancients to the cement-mixer. His efforts to start it up and make mortar cover most of the next sequence.

O'Toole opens his instrument case, takes out a dulcimer, squats cross-legged, lays it on his lap.

A golden spot grows around him, as the lowering light behind dims the work action to a sort of lurid shadowplay.

O'Toole tunes briefly, plays. The sounds are picked up, enlarged, redistributed, remade; voices in Arabic thread in and out; male, female, anger, grief; fade eventually back to O'Toole's unaccompanied dulcimer.

O'TOOLE: Outside the besieged city, the massed ranks of the Christian host from the north pitilessly prepare the next assault, cold in their resolve to render life impossible for the unfortunate citizenry huddled within and so bring the Caliph to his knees. Already, between one moon and another, their great engines of war, their mangonels and petraries, have turned the days into nightmare, poisoning wells, destroying riverbanks, killing crops and livestock, leaving infants to suckle in vain on shrivelled breasts. Smoke covers the noonday sun like a death-shroud; deadly vapours, cries of the bereft and the dying, choke the narrow streets; sweet order collapses into murky chaos. And down in the Caliph's courtyard, so recently despoiled by enemy fire, our heroes scheme and plot their survival in a tiny war-play of their own. The Builder smells advantage on the poisoned air; the youthful Minder searches for manhood on the sticky paths of duty; and Finbar, our Wandering Gilder, his plans deep laid and all but ready to spring, struggles to recall the details of his tale from the wearying darkness that engulfs him. A phrase bubbles in his brain-pan: 'One clean heart, one clean heart.' What? Who? Ha. Of course. He had quite forgotten. The Good Doctor.

He looks up suddenly. A woman appears, front of stage, on the other side of the red-tape picket: Arab dress and headgear, strong leather briefcase. She takes in the scene for a moment, steps over the tape, triggering a return to the previous lighting state.

O'Toole begins returning hammers and instrument to the case. She calls the militiaman: gives name, position, business, asks for the man in charge. The guard points to the women's perimeter, indicates she should await his return.

She takes some paces towards the shrine, the guard calls, shakes his head; she nods, wanders back to front-of-stage, stops to light a cigarette, gives O'Toole a perfunctory look, gravely scans the sorry site again, turns to gaze out at the city.

DR AZIZ: (*A murmur; remembering*) 'My name is Ozymandias, king of kings:
Look on my works, ye Mighty, and despair!
Nothing beside remains. Round the decay
Of that colossal wreck, boundless and bare,
The lone and level sands stretch far away.'

She sniffs.

O'TOOLE: Shelley.

She turns sharply, as if seeing him for the first time. He smiles, stands, salutes her with his can of Stone's.

DR AZIZ: Are you …? What are you?

O'TOOLE: Just part of the circus.

DR AZIZ: But British, yes?

O'TOOLE: (*Afterthought*) Yes.

DR AZIZ: Strange.

O'TOOLE: Yes. (*Beat.*) I wish there were something to offer you, I have only this (*shows her the can*) … I realize it's not quite the thing …

DR AZIZ: Well, as it happens I'm a Christian, but alcohol doesn't agree with me, thank you …

O'TOOLE: Me too. That's why I stick to this.

She smiles. A silence. She turns away, gazes again at the city. O'Toole checks the site. Ryder gets the diesel mixer to start. The helpers applaud. It putters on for a few moments, then dies, the applause with it. Ryder curses.

I love this city. Do you see the Monument? Bottom of July 26ᵗʰ Boulevard, just before the Southern Highway. Sixty-five metres high, is that. We finished that the day before the first bombs fell. See the gold on the President's shoulders? Mine. If you were closer, much closer, you'd see he has a gold tooth. I did that too.

DR AZIZ: Does he have a gold tooth?

O'TOOLE: He does now.

He smiles, sucks on the can.

DR AZIZ: You're a building worker?

O'TOOLE: Ahunh.

DR AZIZ: Who reads poetry.

O'TOOLE: Why not?

They exchange a look, return to the city.

DR AZIZ: Aren't you afraid?

O'TOOLE: Oh yes.

DR AZIZ: But you stayed on.

O'TOOLE: Yes.

DR AZIZ: Because you love the city?

O'TOOLE: I like to leave places when I'm ready. As it happens, I've been waiting for someone, a friend. He's been detained.

The women begin wailing, drowning out Ismael's mollification. Dr Aziz turns to listen. Guards bawl for quiet; the women subside; Ismael's voice reasserts, a touch desperate.

DR AZIZ: (*Calling the Guard; in Arabic*) Tell him I'm here, will you, I need to speak with them … (*The guy wavers.*) Go! (*He leaves for the women's perimeter. Dr Aziz lights another cigarette.*) God help us all.

O'TOOLE: Amen.

Ryder shepherds carriers towards the work area, transferring bags of lime, cement, etc.

RYDER: (*Calling*) Come on, O'Toole, let's go, let's go …

O'Toole waves, fastens his instrument case, drains his can.

O'TOOLE: Nice to meet you, ma'am.

DR AZIZ: Indeed.

O'TOOLE: What will you tell them? The women?

DR AZIZ: I'll tell them the truth. The children are perfectly safe, a bus took them to the Al-Mansur shelter across the river last evening, we'll keep them there until it's safe to return them …

O'TOOLE: God's wounds. I see. One of these was a school …

DR AZIZ: A crèche. I'm crèche supervisor for the Sector …

O'TOOLE: The kids didn't come home after the raid ...

DR AZIZ: It's our policy to bus them to safety, this the mothers know, but their fears are understandable ... I heard the crèche was hit before I heard they were in the shelter. It was not easy ...

Silence. Ismael's voice, on the approach, hoarse from his efforts.

RYDER: (*Calling*) For Christ's sake, will you get over here, man ...

O'Toole ignores him, focus utterly on the woman.

DR AZIZ: As to how your countrymen can justify a district crèche and a dozen dwellings in a workers' suburb as legitimate targets ...

She turns to look at him.

RYDER: (*Calling*) You're gonna get me shot, O'Toole, you know that, don't you ...

O'TOOLE: (*Still*) Try to think of it as 'collateral damage', ma'am. Seems to do the trick on my side of the water.

She looks at him fiercely, the irony having trouble registering.

Ismael arrives, the militiaman in tow, scrambles down the slope towards Dr Aziz, draws her to one side to fill her in and set her to work on the women.

O'Toole joins Ryder in the work area. Light slowly builds again, as smoke clears the sun. The Ancients stand by as if elsewhere. The helpers have returned to perimeter duties.

RYDER: (*Looking up from his mortar-mixing*) Wind's changin'. We'll have two hours at least, I lay, you labour, a doddle ...

O'TOOLE: (*Checking sky*) You're gonna need another brickie, boy. Tek my word.

RYDER: Give it a rest, will you. I've got this licked. (*Checking the talking couple*) What's the bird here for?

O'TOOLE: One o' these was a nursery.

RYDER: Oh shit.

O'TOOLE: Save the tears, the babs were elsewhere. (*Ululations set up again. Ismael grows aggressive, Dr Aziz reluctantly accepts his argument.*) They're scared the women'll overrun the site 'n' stop the work. She's sent to calm 'em.

Ismael calls the guard to show Dr Aziz down to the women's perimeter. Phones his Major. Reports.

RYDER: (*Back to his mixing*) A nursery. What a carry-on.

O'TOOLE: 'S wrong with the mixer?

RYDER: They're out of oil, aren't they. Couldn't organize a shag in a brothel ...

O'TOOLE: So. Are you gonna back me up or what?

RYDER: What you talkin' about?

O'TOOLE: I'm gonna tell the kid we need another trowel …

RYDER: (*Blowing, fierce*) No fuckin' way, José, forget it, this is my job, my deal, I'm fast, man, never mind the quality, check the speed, you start buggerin' around there's no tellin' what'll happen … (*He gathers himself*) I'm gonna show you what to do, OK?

O'TOOLE: (*Calm*) You won't be told, will you.

RYDER: Just. Let it lie. (*A glance at Ismael, ending phone call.*) You put your back into this, I'll get you out of here, that's a promise.

ISMAEL: (*Call over; calling*) Hey! Ryder Billy!

Ryder turns abruptly. Ismael holds an envelope aloft in his hand. Beckons him over with it.

RYDER: Yessir. (*To O'Toole*) This is gonna work. I know it is.

O'Toole collects a sledgehammer, steps inside the hole, begins flattening out irregularities in the fringing masonry. Ryder clambers across to join Ismael. The women quieten; Dr Aziz's megaphone voice lifts, strong and clear, in the silence, inviting them to take tea with her in a neighbourhood school canteen. Murmurs of assent. Voices fade.

ISMAEL: Passport.

RYDER: Passport? 'S in my bag.

ISMAEL: Fetch.

Ryder twitches back to fetch his passport. O'Toole chuckles softly as he nears him.

RYDER: (*Returning*) Look, I'm not sure what this is about, friend, where I come from this here is a pretty sacred document … (*Ismael checks it, tucks it in his pocket.*) Hey, come on …

ISMAEL: Hey. I hey. OK? (*Hands him the envelope.*) Visa, ticket. You build the wall. I give you passport. You bugger off.

RYDER: (*Thumbing contents*) Jesus. You came through, Ismael.

ISMAEL: My word, my hand.

RYDER: You scratch my back, eh?

Silence.

ISMAEL: (*Frowning*) We ready?

RYDER: Sure thing.

ISMAEL: (*A question there*) This O'Toole.

RYDER: Comedian.

ISMAEL: Funny man. Jokha.

RYDER: I can handle him.

ISMAEL: He help, hunh? He can do splat clunk fast?

RYDER: He'll do what he's told.

Ismael's head flicks away towards the men's perimeter. Distant approaching sounds of men's voices on the march. Guards call nervously to each other.

ISMAEL: You build the wall, you perform great service, Ryder Billy. That's a message from my Major. In daylight we can keep away these madmen, these looters and criminals. Come the night, come the bombs, set your clock by it, how we do it then, eh? Many holy things, hunh?

RYDER: Got it.

ISMAEL: Here. (*He holds out the passport. Ryder takes it. Soft*) Let's go.

He clambers off to speak with the guard. Ryder returns to the shrine, gets busy gathering tools, looks around for O'Toole.

RYDER: (*Sotto*) Hey. You there? For Christ's sake, O'Toole, give me a break, will you. . (*Approaches hole; nervous*) You in there? (*Peers in.*) Listen, I've got mine, I can get yours, trust me ... (*O'Toole's head and shoulders slowly emerge at roof height from beneath the covering canvas. His face is still, expressionless, fixed on nothing. Edging nervously across the wall*) He's fucked off, I know it ... Bastard. Selfish old get. Shit! Serve him right if they bloody shoot him ... (*O'Toole directs his gaze down on the twitching Ryder, who chunners on, panic rising. Out again; hoarse, urgent*) Are you there? Where are you?

O'TOOLE: (*Soft*) Up here.

RYDER: (*Too loud*) Aagh!

O'TOOLE: Sh. You'll wake the dead.

RYDER: What's that? (*He indicates the length of scorched coaxial cable in O'Toole's hand. O'Toole looks at it; shrugs.*) What're you doi–?

O'TOOLE: Just checkin'. No point buildin' a wall if the roof's gone ...

RYDER: Is it?

O'TOOLE: Roof's fine. Burnt to buggery but it'll do. (*He swings down in a sort of forward roll, using the lintel as a bar. Lands with a grin at Ryder's feet.*) So. Are you winnin', Ryder Billy?

Ryder takes out the envelope, holds it up.

RYDER: I'm doin' OK.

O'TOOLE: (*Eyeing it*) Tell me.

RYDER: Visa. Ticket to ride.

O'TOOLE: Nice work. All you need now is your passport back ... (*The march has reached the perimeter. Cries, chants, slogans, a few shots loosed into the air, the sudden pop and whoosh of petrol bombs, frenzy building. Ismael crosses the ridge at speed, calls down to the other guard post, militiamen hurry across to reinforce the men's perimeter. Ismael calls his Major. O'Toole watches it all with care. Ryder produces his passport, draws O'Toole's focus back with it.)* I don't believe it.

RYDER: O ye of little faith.

O'TOOLE: You checked it? The visa?

RYDER: Course I checked it.

O'TOOLE: You read the language, d'ye?

RYDER: What?

O'Toole holds his hand out, Ryder bites his lip, hands him the envelope. O'Toole studies the contents.

Warfare erupts, down at the men's perimeter. Volleys ring out, screams and moans of men hit on the scatter, several petrol bombs reach in to the site, gutter out in sand and rubble. Ismael stands immobile on the ridge, staring off, hand on gun butt inside jacket: little Napoleon.

O'Toole looks up from the visa and ticket, stares in silence at Ryder. Shakes his head.

RYDER: What?

O'TOOLE: *(Slow)* Bad news, boy.

RYDER: What?

O'TOOLE: Looks like you pulled it off.

RYDER: *(Snatching it back)* Give it 'ere. Prick. How can it be bad news …?

O'TOOLE: We'll find out.

RYDER: You were wrong, just admit it. This may be your patch, O'Toole, I know the score, OK?

O'TOOLE: You may be right.

RYDER: I didn't get where I am today by being wrong, believe you me.

O'Toole scans the appalling wasteland: no comment. Offstage, the engagement stutters on. Men moan.

O'TOOLE: Billy. You're OK. I like you. I like your spirit. I like your optimism. It's rare. I was wrong. You're smart. You conned the shit outa the little sod. Comprehensively. Rafael O'Toole. Put it there. *(Ryder takes the large mitt.)* I think we can do business.

RYDER: First we can do some work, OK?

O'TOOLE: Putty in your hands, Mr Ryder.

They share a chuckle, move into work mode.

Music, patched-in words, on relay.

Elements of their talk lift and fall back, as they work. The engagement, off, has ended; its sounds abate. The Ancients struggle on another load of blocks, begin their precarious trek across the site.

Ismael leaves his watch, sits halfway down the rubble slope to monitor the Brits' progress. Smokes. Lies on his back to stare at the sky. Eventually takes out his phone, keys a number, asks for someone, waits, gets through. His talk, in Arabic, eventually readable as being with his girlfriend, patches into theirs.

RYDER: Keep these (*indicates blocks*) about this high, will you.

O'TOOLE: Right you are, chief.

RYDER: Here, take this. (*Hands him string.*) Keep us straight. Secrets of the craft. You'll get the hang of it.

Ismael's chat is light, bantering, shy, hesitant, vulnerable: for these minutes, the war has no presence for either of them. He has asked her to marry him; wants her answer.

Ryder lays the first blocks, establishing rhythm and work pattern. O'Toole becomes part of it, replacing each block taken from the block stack with a new one. Each time Ryder comes back up for one he calls out its number, a deep work habit, part of his process.

RYDER: What's the story anyway?

O'TOOLE: Been waiting for a guy, we've got a job in Java waiting on us, little devil's been held up ... (*Ryder chuckles, shakes his head.*) How 'bout you, Bill?

RYDER: Long story. Deals 'n' stuff. Bit above the Paddy's head I think, O'Toole.

O'TOOLE: Try me.

On the phone, Ismael's talk becomes serious, even painful.

RYDER: I'm standin' there, British Airways, queuin' a buy a ticket out, hundreds of us down there, scramblin' a get 'ome ... terrific din ... (*Long silence. He's back there, in the moment.*) An' like everything went quiet, like that ... An' I had this brilliant thought: what if there's no war? Four weeks on and this place'll be doin' business as usual. And he who dares, wins. Next day I'm down the Ministry doin' deals, talk about a field of clover, there's queues formin' round me, The Brit who refused to Quit. I've contracts for millions in that bag there ...

They work on in silence, rhythm, pattern, calls returning.

Ismael's tone is now angry, jealous, persistent; a boy.

Ryder begins laying the second course.

O'TOOLE: (*Eventually*) Pity about the war.

Ryder snaps a look at him. O'Toole's deep in work, as if unawares.

RYDER: (*Suspicions abating*) Deep. You really gave that some thought.

He chuckles, swells, pleased with himself. O'Toole smiles. Each dips again to his work. O'Toole's up at once.

O'TOOLE: So when d'you reckon I should be hittin' the kid with *my* list, William?

RYDER: I'm workin' on it, OK? What fuckin' *list*?

O'TOOLE: 'S not a list, just a coupla things …

Ryder swings up for a block, numbers it out loud, glares up at O'Toole. Ismael giggles at something she's told him.

RYDER: Visa. Ticket to ride. List ends. If I can. That's the deal. (*They work on.*) Don't get greedy, kid's on a tightrope, imagine what he's going to be like when we get up to here (*hand above head*), yeah? And the light's a bit murky? And the looters're back?

O'TOOLE: The what?

RYDER: He told me. These fuckers're after the goods, relics and shit … If we don't close this up for him before the next raid, the place'll be unguarded and his bollocks'll be in the mangle.

O'TOOLE: He told you this, Ryder Billy?

RYDER: I just told you. (*He comes up again, calls its number as he collects the block.*) Billy Ryder. Who knows the score. Makes it his business. Just don't go getting foolish on me, eh? (*Ryder winks, his friend. O'Toole nods compliance. Ryder dips to lay the block; O'Toole dips to keep the stack three high. Up again; number over block.*) Make sense?

O'TOOLE: Can't fault it.

They go down again, up; Ryder calls the number, takes the block; O'Toole replaces.

RYDER: Still with me?

O'TOOLE: All the way, Billy Ryder. We'll drink to it. (*He moves off to fetch drink from his case.*) Stand by, my friend, you could be in for a real experience.

RYDER: (*Moving out*) I need a leak … Fags, I'm out.

O'TOOLE: Fags. Not a problem.

He's reached the case, takes out a lemonade bottle half full of clear liquid, pouches it in his work robe, watches Ryder round the tent for his leak, pads silently across to the still-phoning Ismael. Inserts his shadow across the youth's face to announce his presence. Ismael blinks, swivels, sits up, stares; puts girlfriend on hold, coiled to act.

O'TOOLE: (*In Arabic*) I come in peace.

ISMAEL: Go work. Fuck off.

O'TOOLE: Mr Ryder wondered if you might spare him a cigarette, he is without them ...

ISMAEL: (*Handing pack*) Take. Skedaddle. (*He moves back to reconnect with his girl, sees O'Toole hasn't moved, fishing out one cigarette and returning the pack.*) What?

O'TOOLE: One's fine. Sufficient unto the day ... (*Ismael returns to his call, only slowly realizes he's no longer connected.*) I pray the day confer success upon your endeavours, Ismael, son of Akram, brother of Said. I give you a charm for the journey, from the prophet Jeremiah. Life may indeed be just a bowl of cherries, you've still got to look out for the stones ... (*Ismael curses in Arabic, waggles the phone around. Ryder's returning to the wall. O'Toole holds up the cigarette. Leaving*) I think you'll find that's the battery ... (*He's gone. Ismael smacks the phone with his fist, pissed off. Ryder's laying, calling numbers. Back*) Here we go, pal. (*Pours tot into bottle cap.*) May the good Lord smile on our efforts.

RYDER: What is it?

O'TOOLE: This? Elixir of Life. Crushed velvet in the mouth. Poteen. (*Bottle up*) Slanje.

RYDER: (*Smelling it*) Smells like meths.

O'TOOLE: Drink. It'll help you with the pain. Success. (*They drink. O'Toole recaps the bottle, pouches it.*) Save the rest for the topping out, eh?

He checks out Ismael, who's occupied despatching a guard for new batteries. Resumes work.

RYDER: Pain? What pain?

O'TOOLE: What?

RYDER: You said it helps wi' the pain. I'm not in pain.

O'TOOLE: 'S just an expression. You know, like 'Here's mud in your eye' ...

RYDER: You get the fags?

O'TOOLE: Oh aye. Fag actually. He's short. He's sendin' out for some ... (*He's fiddled the cigarette from his pocket, waits for Ryder to dip back from the stack to lay his next block. Laying it on the top of the block stack*) There when you want it, Bill ...

RYDER: (*A brief look, busy*) Right, I'll get it in a tick ...

O'Toole calmly moves the cigarette along and down on to the block left uncovered by the block Ryder's now laying, talking as he monitors Ryder's progress.

O'TOOLE: Serendipity. Happy circumstance. You 'n' me meetin' up like this. (*The brick's almost laid.*) 'Long indeed is the day that does not have surprises in it.' Ezekiel.

He ducks down to gather a block, carefully angling to keep Ryder in peripheral vision.

Ryder stands, cleans his hands on his shorts, looks for the fag: no number. Checks Ismael out. Looks up at the sky.

O'TOOLE: (*Firming grip for the swing up*) You're goin' along, nothin' really happenin' for ye, then suddenly, outa the blue …

RYDER: (*Somewhere else*) Right, I'll have that fag …

O'TOOLE: (*Up and across, slams the block on to the reaching hand*) Bang!

RYDER: (*Huge*) JESUS … CHRIST.

O'TOOLE: (*Perfectly incredulous; horrified*) What happened?

A chaos of blocks and screams, oaths and recriminations spills across the site. Ismael legs over, yelling in Arabic. Militiamen run on, guns in hand. Ryder squirms and contorts his way around the place, somewhere between apeshit and agony. O'Toole follows him around, trying to tend him.

(*Over and over*) Billy, how was I to know, you didn't call your number, I'm truly sorry, what can I say …?

RYDER: (*More than once*) Just leave me alone, will ya, you're not safe …

ISMAEL: Hey. What's happening? Why you do this …?

O'TOOLE: Accident, friend. A brick trapped his fingers.

ISMAEL: Show. (*He squats over Ryder.*) Show. (*Ryder's hand emerges from his belly. Ismael takes it gently in his own; they study the mess together.*) Move.

RYDER: Shit.

ISMAEL: Move. (*Studies movement.*) No bones. It's good. You be OK?

RYDER: Yeah yeah …

ISMAEL: You finish wall in time?

RYDER: Yeah yeah, 's not the trowel hand … give us a minute or two.

ISMAEL: (*Reaching for it*) I take this … (*He gathers one of the cotton gloves Ryder wears in his waistband.*) What is it …?

O'TOOLE: Glove.

Ismael tums to look at him.

ISMAEL: Glove, yes. (*To Ryder*) Make you better.

He carries the glove away, searches for something in the rubble, eventually rounds the tent. Ryder lies back a bit, eyes closed, still in pain.

RYDER: I think I'm gonna be sick …

O'TOOLE: (*Eyes on sky to west*) Get it all up, son. (*Looks about him briefly.*) You're not likely to spoil aught.

Ryder looks across at him.

RYDER: (*Hard, mean; quite brutal*) I knew as soon as I clapped eyes on you, I'll tell, you thick Irish twat ye, Paddy, clumsy bogtrotting pig-ignorant get ye, we're fucked, thanks to you we are totally and comprehensively fucked, out of the goodness of my heart, did I need to? No way, I cut you in, you crush my fuckin' hand with a fuckin' breezeblock, is that life or is that, Jesus God, no wonder you dress like 'em, Seamus, you're exactly their fuckin' level. (*O'Toole turns to look at him. Silence. Takes out a wallet, fiddles out a pad and pencil, rummages the wad. Suddenly*) That's my wallet!

O'TOOLE: It is.

RYDER: What're you doing?

O'TOOLE: (*Preoccupied with wallet*) Just now I'm doing what I have to. And praying rather fiercely my eye doesn't wander from the ball.

He pockets two hundred dinar, takes out an extraordinary contraption, multiple lenses set in a worked metal half-medieval headpiece, slips it on, lenses up, begins writing something in the pad.

RYDER: (*Slow*) You're mad. He is. O my God. O'Toole. O'Toole. Thinks he's Lawrence of whatsit. You're. Mad. (*He barks*) Sun shrivelled the brain-pan.

O'TOOLE: Or. (*He writes on.*) What?

RYDER: You tell me.

O'TOOLE: When you need to know, if, then I'll tell you.

RYDER: Out of his tree.

O'Toole folds the bills inside the note, pouches them. Stands to watch Ismael returning with the glove.

O'TOOLE: You listen but you don't hear, Ryder Billy. You look but you don't see. You've no smell so you can't taste. You speak but you don't mean. You touch but you can't feel. How shall we define this 'mad', Ryder Billy? Indeed, how shall we define major peckerhead? Sorry I had to whack you. I'm not fond of violence. You left me no option. A man who believes he knows the score is a desperate encumbrance. Particularly when he hasn't an inkling of the game he's in.

RYDER: (*Slow, low*) You. Cunt.

O'TOOLE: Warm, Ryder Billy. Friend Ismael …

ISMAEL: (*Kneeling*) Hand. (*He takes it gently, eases the cotton glove, wet and oozy now, on to the hand.*) How it feels, that?

RYDER: Aye. Not bad. Sorta warm. Mm. What is it?

ISMAEL: Old Bedouin doing.

RYDER: Ahunh.

ISMAEL: It's er pitch. And er … (*Looks for word again.*)

O'TOOLE: Piss.

Ismael turns again to stare at him.

ISMAEL: (*Smiles, shy*) Piss. Thank you.

RYDER: Yes, indeed.

Ismael stands. Scans the western sky. Isn't keen on what he's seeing.

ISMAEL: Half-hour, ten minutes, it's good, OK, tip-top, take easy, your man will do clunk splat …

RYDER: Yeah yeah. Absolutely.

ISMAEL: (*Stands; looks at O'Toole*) So. We build the wall.

O'TOOLE: That's the plan.

ISMAEL: Tick tick.

He's seen the militiaman returning with batteries and bars of chocolate. Heads for him. Sits to eat his chocs and reactivate phone. O'Toole gathers a new can of Stone's, takes out the note and bills.

RYDER: (*Bleak, dark; some fear there*) I don't get you. I don't get you at all. What sort of a man, eh, cold-bloodedly and by design, eh? Tell me. In words of one syllable: what game on? What're you playin' for? I want out, I've been honest with you. What do you want? I've a right, in common decency, in the same shitheap, to some fuckin' answers.

O'Toole stoops, picks something up from the sand by Ryder's feet. Stands with it. It's the cigarette, crushed and bent.

O'TOOLE: Done for. I must cadge you another.

He pads off, headed for Ismael, who's getting someone to call him, checking the bell.

RYDER: (*After him*) O'Toole. You are definitely on my shitlist.

O'TOOLE: Mine too.

Ismael sees him coming, cuts call, stands, arms folded, to watch him in, forces him to talk from below him.

ISMAEL: What? Get lost. You walk around, build the goddamn wall, you say nothing I wish to hear, you know the time …?

O'TOOLE: I do. It's time to cut the crap, Ismael, son of Akram, brother of Said. The schoolboy who played wag to come to the Winter Palace with a football under his arm to strut his stuff before the infidel workers and the talks he'd hang on for with O'Toole the Gilder … Mm? The man who taught you how to bring a ball down on your instep?

ISMAEL: O'Toole. Cut the crap. I know this story. Once I was a child. Today, this day, you deal with a man … The rest is bullshits …

O'TOOLE: Just so. OK. Simply stated, you're fucked. The facts. You'll be lucky if Ryder can reach 25 per cent of laying speed. He's not good with pain. Plus your confidence in my building prowess is wholly misplaced. I am a master gilder, the builder on my I.D. is a typographical error, a master gilder does not build walls. I'm hoping you're right about being a man, Ismael, there's choices to be made, it'll take a man …

ISMAEL: A man serves his country and his people. When a man treads into choices, he calls his Major …

O'TOOLE: Even when he knows he'd be safer slashing his own throat? Here. (*Hands him note and bills.*) You can phone the Major or build the wall, not both. This man is a layer, I know him a little, he's available, that's where he's staying. Call this guy, right, Case Officer, the dinars are a present for his son's wedding, he'll see he's bussed over, you get your wall, the Major saves his skin, buries whatever it is, Christ knows what, you can smell it, it's everywhere, and no Ministry in sight, keeping it local. You've about (*Looks at sky, at watch*) no time at all. Make the right call, eh?

He leaves. Ismael sniffs. Spits.

ISMAEL: Why? What's for you in this, O'Toole?

O'TOOLE: (*Going on*) The pleasure of helping friends. The satisfaction of thwarting an enemy or two. All the old bullshit.

ISMAEL: Bullshit, sure. Hey, this I handle, you think I don't have the bottles? Fuck you.

O'Toole heads back for the prone Ryder, who whimpers, sleeping.

Ismael paces and frets about the ridge, dealing with crisis. Looks up suddenly; the pall thickens again, the air dims. He hurls an instruction down to the truck, a voice answers.

He sits. Takes out the phone. Studies the note, face vacant, digging deep.

O'Toole sits by the sleeping Ryder. Gathers a pair of pebbles, bangs them rhythmically together, swaying a little. Ryder wakes, turns, stares at O'Toole.

RYDER: 'S happenin'?

O'TOOLE: He's sendin' for the brickie.

Ryder turns on his other side to look. Ismael sits immobile, the phone pouched.

RYDER: How do you know?

Ismael stands, takes out the phone, keys out a number, disappears over the rubble ridge as the call connects.

O'TOOLE: He's got no choice.

Militiamen move up, lit paraffin lamps in their hands, begin rigging them about the work area.

Music; low.

Very slow creep up, houselights.

Ryder gets to his feet, peels off the glove, moves gingerly over to the work site area, working the damaged mitt.

RYDER: I'm gonna see what I can do, if that's all right.

O'TOOLE: Need a hand?

RYDER: Thanks. I have one.

A muezzin sets up. His voice washes the site. The Ancients lay down their long shovels, wash in the burst-main pool, approach the forestage, turn towards Mecca to worship.

Houselights on.

Ryder builds painfully, drives himself a bit, in a sort of dull rage. He brings the wall to perhaps five courses before pain and fatigue lay him out.

O'Toole half helps, half wanders, checking out. Mixes more mortar.

The Ancients finish their worship, squat in the sand to eat their snap, make music with tabla and oud, leading to dance.

The wall crawls upward. Ryder rests the hand a lot. Ismael reappears, goes again, phone at ear. Later, a call from perimeter fence; he answers, leaves.

Houselights eventually to slow fade. The site's weirdly dark, the lamps bright.

ACT TWO

The Ancients have returned to their recovery work among the rubble. One of them has left the site; returns with a wheelbarrow; snails his way with it across the wasteland to rejoin his comrade.

Ryder has rounded the tented shrine to take a piss. He's not in good shape.

O'Toole climbs a fragment of nibbled building, stoops to gather the bus-driver's cap, stares at it a moment as his gilder's spot glows in on him.

O'TOOLE: (*Narrative voice*) The dance was real. It happened. Yet it was not written; rather the dance wrote itself. Rose up from the sand, already inside these unrecorded peasants, and brought the foreigners gently to their senses, stilled time itself, wrought place anew, shared out joy and ease in common purpose, stopped the sun in its tracks, to cancel the coming slaughter. But the music died; and the day and the war – the Grand and the Petty – resumed their customary clamour. Voices, questions, ifs and buts, echoed round his brain-pan: had he the story aright, would the young Minder risk all for all and have the Apprentice brought, to give his plans for rescue the chance to prosper? Would the battered Builder fall in line or splinter underfoot like brushwood, most of all, would the Gilder's own failing memory and crumbling eyesight last the journey? The waiting minutes slid away as he reviewed the possible outcomes and his joy was very far from unconfined. But honour held him fast, he told himself, he had given the Apprentice's family his solemn word he would be cared for, no master leaves his pupil in the lurch, etc. Besides, one should in truth add, the Gilder well knew how bleak his own future as a craftsman would be without him. Madness Rafael might have by the bucketful, but there was method in there too …

The spot dies, the remains of the day struggle to reassert against the gloom.

Guards push on a young Indian, T-shirt and shorts, chained hand and foot, a hood tied on his head.

O'Toole turns, sees Ryder, returned from his pee, staring at the chained and hooded prisoner.

RYDER: I don't believe this …

O'TOOLE: What?

RYDER: You've had him send for a *gaol*bird …?

O'TOOLE: You will rush to judgement, Billy …

RYDER: He's in chains, for God's sake …

O'TOOLE: He's being held on suspicion, a minor infraction, no evidence, a trumped-up charge, rozzers're the same the world over, the boy's blameless …

RYDER: (*Distinct*) He's a prisoner, O'Toole. That means I'm gonna have a gun trained on me the whole time he's here … (*Looks at sky.*) I'm going to die. It's certain. (*Ryder shivers, begins to wander downstage, face bleak, feet aimless, headed for the perimeter tape. O'Toole watches.*) I'm cold. (*Rubs himself.*) Is it cold?

O'TOOLE: Don't ask me. I'm always cold. (*O'Toole collects a garment from Ryder's bags, eyes fixed on the wandering Ryder.*) Billy …

RYDER: Can't hear you.

O'TOOLE: No exit, Billy.

RYDER: Can't hear you.

O'TOOLE: You won't die.

RYDER: Can't hear you.

O'TOOLE: It isn't written.

Ryder stops abruptly, drops into a kneeling slouch in the sand. Stares out, fingers joined at lap.

RYDER: Fuck off.

O'Toole carries a jacket over. Lays it gently over Ryder's shoulders. Ryder scarcely notices, his lips moving on a prayer that won't form.

O'TOOLE: (*Squatting; mouth to ear*) It's in hand. This time tomorrow you're poolside at the Cairo Hilton, this time next week you'll be on *Wogan*, an overnight hero, millions of small businessmen the length and breadth of Britain hanging on your every whopper. Trust me. (*Ismael yells at the guards, on the return. O'Toole stands, lays a hand on Ryder's shoulder.*) My hand, my word.

ISMAEL: (*Pumped up*) Give me your name. I want your name. O'Toole!

O'Toole moves off up the rubble slope towards the group around the prisoner.

Ryder's hand moves slowly up to cover the touched shoulder, his desperate loneliness for a moment palpable. Somewhere inside the pain of things, his fingers recognize the Armani.

RYDER: Oh Christ. Not my best suit.

He looks down. The hem trails in oil-soaked sand.

On the ridge, the guards are removing the wrist irons; Ismael questions the still-hooded prisoner, his details on a card in his hand.

ISMAEL: (*To O'Toole*) This guy don't hear me, he deaf, mister …?

O'TOOLE: (*Stopping halfway*) Try losing the hood. (*Ismael sniffs. Begins unfastening the tie-cord. To prisoner*) Welcome to the nursery, Chatty. Today we're building a wall. (*A mangled phrase from beneath the hood: possibly 'Fuck off, O'Toole.'*) Remember Habbakuk: 'Silence is golden.' All will be revealed.

The hood comes off. The young Asian, twenty-five or so, blinks a scan of the place, ends with a heavy glare at O'Toole down the slope.

ISMAEL: (*From card*) Chatterjee Anand, yes?

O'TOOLE: Correct.

ISMAEL: Builder, yes?

The Asian glares again at O'Toole.

O'TOOLE: Definitely.

ISMAEL: Why he don't answer? He deaf, yes?

O'TOOLE: He's dumb.

ISMAEL: What 'dumb'?

O'TOOLE: Mute. (*Gives the word in Arabic.*) Someone accidentally ran a laser through his larynx, back in wherever it is he comes from. He thought of reporting it to the authorities, but since the accident took place in a police cell, he decided not to pursue the matter … (*Ismael stares hard at O'Toole, sniffing for treacheries. A sudden braying chuckle from Ryder down below, on his feet again, taking it all in.*) What's the problem, he's here to lay bricks for your sweating Major, not seduce us with his oratory ...

ISMAEL: Shut up your trap, gilder! (*To Chatterjee*) OK, you do clunk splat, you do it fast, we get the fucker done ... (*He growls instructions, the guards push Chatterjee towards the shrine. O'Toole stays put. Calling*) We work, Ryder Billy, you too, you see this one do good, OK?

RYDER: (*Oddly buckshee*) Putty in your hands, *mein Führer*.

ISMAEL: (*To O'Toole*) Hey. You too.

O'TOOLE: What about his legs, Ismael, how's he gonna ...?

ISMAEL: I tell you once, I tell you twice, your boy fuck around I blow them off. (*O'Toole sniffs, turns to leave.*) Major's orders.

Silence.

O'TOOLE: I thought we'd put the Major behind us, Ismael.

ISMAEL: My Major knows everything. You think I'm crazy? He fix this, no problem.

A guard calls from the women's perimeter. Ismael swings round to look, sees Dr Aziz headed slowly up towards the site.

O'TOOLE: (*Dealing with the news*) Your Major's in deeper shit than I thought.

ISMAEL: Hey. Maybe you don't notice, British, we fight a war here ...

He barks instructions down to the two guards at the shrine, wheels off along the ridge to confront the approaching woman. The guards unsling their Stens, retreat to vantage points – the ridge, the forestage perimeter – to cover the workers.

O'Toole watches Ismael and Dr Aziz begin low-pitched exchange for a moment, then pads back to the shrine. Ryder's slipped into his jacket, arrives ahead of him.

RYDER: Hi, welcome to the nuthouse. Name's Ryder. Billy.

CHATTERJEE: (*Hand out*) Yow yu.

Ryder gingerly offers his own, wipes it on his shorts, a largely unconscious gesture.

RYDER: Sorry about the er ... (*He indicates throat. Chatterjee nods. Ryder hands him his trowel.*) We've less than an hour, I hope you're fast ...

O'TOOLE: (*Returning, businesslike*) Forget it, Bill, he's no more a brickie than I am, just another typo ... Now, for God's sake, look handy, will you ... More mortar, Billy ... Chatty, give 'and wi' this ...

He begins assembling the crude scaffolding ready for the higher courses. Chatterjee clanks over to help, seriously angry yowls escaping from his clenched teeth.

RYDER: (*Distinct*) What did you say? (*O'Toole waves him quiet, eyes fixed on the meeting on the ridge as he works on. The talk is low-toned, rational, but Ismael has kept Dr Aziz at the bottom of the far slope, still not on the site proper.*) O'Toole?

O'TOOLE: (*Working, watching*) This may come as a bit of a blow, Ryder Billy, but I've not been entirely honest with you up to now.

CHATTERJEE: Yyin yun,

O'TOOLE: Dummy up, kid. It's in hand. (*He looks at Ryder, who's going crazy with the mortar.*) This is not the moment to freak out, Billy …

RYDER: I can't hear you, you're gone, ppp, you're a loony, whatever you've got in that horrible … diseased … bent brain of yours, sorry, can't hear you … WHO'S GONNA BUILD THE FUCKING WALL?

Ismael turns to look briefly at the builders, returns to the troublesome Dr Aziz.

O'TOOLE: (*Toneless; deeply calm*) I'm coming to that, Bill. OK?

RYDER: Can't hear you, sorry.

Dr Aziz crests the ridge. Ismael's hand moves inside his coat, falls clear. O'Toole watches and listens.

ISMAEL: (*In Arabic*) I have my orders …

DR AZIZ: (*In Arabic*) What is the problem? It will take a couple of minutes, and I can also send the women home happy before the bombs start falling …

ISMAEL: (*In Arabic*) The Major's orders are explicit …

DR AZIZ: (*In Arabic; tough*) Then call the Major. Report the problem. He will understand, I promise you.

A small stand-off. Ismael yanks the phone out, keys a number. Dr Aziz waits for connection, picks her way down the rubble. Stands below in silence, trying not to stare at the shrine, a fret of concern worrying her lips.

O'TOOLE: (*Watching*) Building the wall's not a problem, Chat can do a bit, I can do a bit, you can do a bit, I mean we're not after a RIBA award or aught, are we … The problem now is timing …

RYDER: Lost you again, sorry … I think I'd better have a word with friend Ismael. (*He stands. O'Toole nods to Chatterjee. Ryder takes a pace, the Indian's big hand noiselessly arrests his forward motion by the scruff of the neck.*) All right, all right, all right. What's the plan then? (*Chatterjee's hand relaxes.*) Gonna call a chopper in, fly us all out, that'd be good, that'd get my vote, definitely.

O'Toole scans the ridge. Ismael stamps along it and back, phone to ear, on hold, waiting for the Major's meeting to finish. He looks across at Dr Aziz. She's staring at him, half reproach, half entreaty, the tugs powerful for both of them. He pulls away, an act of will, fixes on Ryder.

O'TOOLE: Timing, Billy. Between the siren and the raid. We finish the wall. That's the only chance this poor afflicted bastard has of flying the coop ... (*Ismael's voice, low, urgent; he's through. O'Toole checks Dr Aziz. She's turned to watch Ismael; turns again to return his gaze. Soft; inward*) God's wounds. This was also written. I remember me ...

RYDER: What about *this* poor afflicted bastard (*himself*), O'Toole?

O'TOOLE: She says ...

DR AZIZ: (*Seamlessly; low across the space*) Might I have a word, please?

RYDER: (*Clenched teeth*) I have my papers, I wanna be in a shelter when that fuckin' siren goes, not arsin' about helpin' your Paki friend skip ...

CHATTERJEE: (*O'Toole's voice*) He says ...

O'TOOLE: (*Across the space*) With you directly, doctor.

RYDER: Who said that?

O'TOOLE: I did.

RYDER: (*Looking from one to the other*) Oh God, I know what you are, you're special, oh my God, you're special ops, aren't you, you're ...

O'TOOLE: Ryder. I'm just me. Rafael Finbar O'Toole, the Wandering Gilder. Trying to survive in rather difficult times. Praying the Good Doctor does not blow us off course ... Trust me. Build.

He slaps the scaffolding section he's just finished. Sees Ismael finish the call and house the phone. Heads for the woman, collects the bus-driver's cap as he goes. A slow rhythmic handclap sets up from the women's perimeter. A cry from a guard: the women are back. Ismael yells at the onsite guards, the man on the ridge heads off for the women's perimeter, the other takes his place on the ridge. Ismael calls reinforcements up from the men's perimeter.

O'TOOLE: (*Stopped, some way from her*) Can I help?

DR AZIZ: I need to make a brief inspection. I have to file a report for the Department. An inventory ...

O'Toole nods, scans the rubble. An Ancient empties his full bin-liner into the wheelbarrow.

O'TOOLE: You should speak with the men here, they're gathering ...

DR AZIZ: In there, I mean.

He looks at her, turns, stares at the shrine. Ryder and Chatterjee have laboriously begun the next course.

RYDER: (*Reasserting*) No no, for Christ's sake, *this* way, right ...?

O'TOOLE: The shrine?

DR AZIZ: The crèche.

Silence. Guards pour across to the women's perimeter. A rhythmic chanting builds around the handclaps.

O'TOOLE: (*Lost*) The crèche.

DR AZIZ: The shrine became a mosque, the mosque a crèche, in this part of the world we learn to nurse our resources ... Perhaps you would ask your men to stop, I shouldn't be long ...

O'TOOLE: What about him?

DR AZIZ: (*Looking across at Ismael*) He's checking with his superior. He's a boy. He should be playing football, learning a skill ...

O'Toole nods, turns towards the shrine, looks back at Dr Aziz.

O'TOOLE: Talking to the mothers didn't help, hunh?

DR AZIZ: What do you mean?

O'Toole stares on at her.

O'TOOLE: I'm not certain I can afford to care about this. I am, as they say, powerless to help. But if you're going to make an inspection and file a report, you're going to have to do it unauthorized, you're not stupid or naïve enough to believe the Major and his handlers will say, 'Stop building, let her proceed.' The Major will say ...

ISMAEL: (*In Arabic; calling, headed down slope, jacket in hand*) You will report to your superior, they're sending a car, the work has priority ...

He slides, loses balance, pitches forward, his jacket arm plunging into standing water. He curses, scrabbles in pockets, fishes out the dripping phone, moves doggedly on, shaking as he goes.

O'TOOLE: Your boss wants to see you, they're sending a car, build the wall ... Take a look. (*He nods at her to look at the sprawled minder.*) This good soldier is not a well human being. Half of him's a pistol on legs, half's all at sea. How important can it *be* to make an inventory of a burnt-out shell? A thousand gallons of fuel burning at fifteen hundred degrees, what d'you think's gonna be left? In the meantime ...

ISMAEL: (*Limping up; in Arabic*) In the meantime, you will go down to the perimeter and reassure the unruly women you have seen with your own eyes, their fears are groundless ...

O'TOOLE: Your orders are to lie to the women. End of story. (*Ismael frowns a look across at O'Toole, who twiddles the found cap in his fingers.*) Builder says ...

RYDER: (*Calling*) Could we have a ruling over here, please? (*He's trying to help Chatterjee climb the scaffolding, the leg-irons the problem.*) I mean, either he keeps these buggers on or we can build the wall ... I mean it's up to you, boss, but I am a builder, I do know about these things.

ISMAEL: OK, I look at. (*To Dr Aziz; in Arabic*) You go, Dr Fadia, it's best for all ...

RYDER: Take your time, we've got minutes and minutes …

ISMAEL: (*Arabic*) The only thing these women have to fear is their own frenzy driving them to interfere with our work here, for then they will surely get hurt, I cannot disobey my orders … (*Dr Aziz blinks. Bites her lip. Searches for an answer. Pulls her headshawl tighter.*) Excuse me, ma'am …

He heads off for the wall. Sizes up the problem. Eventually begins unkeying the leg-irons.

O'TOOLE: (*Climbing to look at the women's perimeter*) Don't even think about it. He had the Shias mown down for trying to stop them violating their ancient shrine with unclean labour, the women'll go the same way … As it happens, you do not even have to lie, there really is nothing to see in there to cause them concern, I've seen it for myself, inspected it earlier, what you have basically is the inside of a large Tandoori oven … no desks, no tables, no soft toys, no hard toys, no chairs, no wall-paintings, no gilt. Ash. Bitumen. End of inventory.

DR AZIZ: (*Low; unable to complete*) No …?

O'TOOLE: A. B. No C.

DR AZIZ: Can I believe you?

O'TOOLE: Do I look like a liar?

DR AZIZ: If liars looked like liars, who would believe them?

ISMAEL: (*Fierce, sudden call*) O'Toole, over here, now …

O'TOOLE: Yessir!

He shrugs, peels away, rejoining the wall group.

Dr Aziz stands on; turns sharply; heads eventually for the women's perimeter.

Her subsequent address to the mothers persists for much of the sequence that follows and, even at distance, remains in tone and content audible and intelligible throughout. It culminates in shouted expressions of gratitude, deep relief and praise to Allah; and eventual dispersal.

Ismael has freed the Indian's legs; ordered Ryder and Chatterjee to resume building.

ISMAEL: OK, O'Toole, better we talk …

RYDER: Better we build this bloody thing, Ismael. O'Toole, thirty more blocks, mek it forty, let's go …

O'Toole calls the Ancients in Arabic. Looks at Ismael.

ISMAEL: Two minutes.

He points where, wanders up there, shaking the phone, needing it to work. Crosses to the ruined hulk, looks down towards the women's perimeter, listens, stone-faced, blank-eyed, to Dr Aziz's address.

O'Toole gets the old guys cracking. Looks up at Ryder who's painfully pulled himself up on to the scaffolding to join Chatterjee laying.

O'TOOLE: Bill.

RYDER: (*Routine*) Fuck off.

O'TOOLE: The story. We're still workin', nearly there, the secret's all but buried, right? The siren goes. Thirty seconds later … at the most … I've *seen* these boys shift for that shelter … it's just Ismael and us.

RYDER: I'd say we were still heavily outnumbered.

O'TOOLE: Thirty seconds after that, it's just Ismael and me, you're off to the shelter, next the world … You hearing me yet?

RYDER: (*Deliberate*) I have. My papers. O'Toole. Even if you manage to stop me leaving tonight, I can leave. Tomorrow.

O'TOOLE: Oh dear. If you believe that, Billy, you'll believe …

He shakes his head, peels away.

RYDER: (*After him*) Hey, pull the other one, I showed 'em to you, you seem t'forget that …

O'Toole pads away towards Ismael up at the watch-post. Dr Aziz is winding up, the women begin to respond.

Ryder watches O'Toole for some moments, face puckering as he begins to suspect faulty reasoning somewhere. Turns to find Chatterjee staring at him and shaking his head in contemptuous disbelief, there well ahead of him.

RYDER: He's lying, right?

CHATTERJEE: Uhunh.

RYDER: He's lying. I'm telling you.

They return to laying. Ryder repeats 'He's lying' as he works. Chatterjee drops in a few 'Uhunhs' and a 'Yo-yay', to stir the pot.

O'TOOLE: Last orders, friend. (*Ismael swivels to face him, eyes dark. O'Toole holds out his passport.*) Save your breath.

ISMAEL: (*Taking it*) How you know this?

O'TOOLE: It was in your eyes. And I'd read the book. (*Hands him I.D.*) And I.D.? Of course. (*O'Toole sits to face the city. Ismael calls the remaining guard over, gives him the papers, mutters instructions, the guy heads off. Throughout*) I've been minded all my working life, Ismael, across Africa, Asia, South America, wherever I can find some appalling little shite in a crown, some beast in a beret, some ermined vermin with power to spare and the desire to indulge a passion for giltwork, minders and gold-leaf, it's all I've known. Was it not the holy Balalah, the Prophet's uncle, who said, 'The mind of the minder is as an open sewer ateem with the crimes of obedience, on which only the pure of heart may gaze, and then only if they can handle the stench' …?

The Ancients trundle in with their block-laden barrows. The wall-builders work on in muttery silence.

Sounds of the women dispersing, calls in the evening streets.

O'Toole turns, sees Ismael eyeing him, the papers despatched.

O'TOOLE: You wanted to talk.

ISMAEL: It's done. (*Hands O'Toole his own note from Act One.*) We fix the wall, we get the prisoner back to police cell, same man returns your documents ... I send them bye bye.

He chuckles, pleased at the neatness. O'Toole stands, chuckles with him.

O'TOOLE: Nice one, friend. You'll make major yet, you see.

He lays down the driver's cap very carefully on a slab of rubble. Pulls the mesh of scorched cable from the roof out of his tunic, lays it carefully beside the cap.

ISMAEL: What you have here?

O'TOOLE: One cap, peaked, bus drivers for the use of, City Transport Department (Schools). One length of coaxial cable, from a concreted gully let in to the roof of the holy place there ...

ISMAEL: You're crazy, man. You walk about, you talk, it's not good, why you bring this crap ...?

O'TOOLE: I was hoping you'd tell me, Ismael.

ISMAEL: Hey. What you know?

Silence. A guard calls something up from the women's perimeter.

RYDER: (*Slumping back on scaffold*) That's me. I'm fucked.

(A car arriving, women's perimeter, siren blaring. Ismael flicks a look.)

O'TOOLE: Exit the Good Doctor.

Dr Aziz enters as if on cue, at the side of the tented shrine. She stands, back against wall, drawing breath, shielded from the site by the building. She's drained; not sure what she's doing; slides to a squat, back to the wall.

Raised voices from the perimeter, shouts, a guard struggles up to speak with Ismael.

O'Toole waits until he knows enough, returns to the wall area, opens a can of beer, hands it up to the knackered Ryder. Serious hoo-haa develops around the site, calls in Arabic for Dr Aziz to make her way to the women's perimeter, the car is waiting ... A couple of dogs join the search. Pressure builds on Ismael; a second guard moves in, the minder sent to escort Dr Aziz wants him down at the car right away. He calls up two men to cover the builders, eventually heads off at speed.

Through this –

O'Toole goes to sit beneath the scaffolding, his back to the wall edge, all but visible to the now seated Dr Aziz.

O'TOOLE: (*Remote; inturned*) Ease down, Chatty.

RYDER: (*Gas gone*) Pay him no heed. He's all self, that one.

Chatterjee reaches for the can, dowses his head, drinks, stares, scans the city, the sky above it. Smiles, a seraph.

CHATTERJEE: (*O'Toole's voice*) There y'are, y'old bugger, off ter bed, is it …?

Pale intense light bursts slowly across the site, turning it spectral, on the edge of Magritte, the sky wholly black, the earth and brick vivid, unearthly, as the sinking sun shafts in from below the smoke pall.

The four watch it in their separate silences.

(*Vera Lynn's voice; a soft croon*)

> There'll be bluebirds over
> The white cliffs of Dover
> Tomorrow is another day.

(*Silence.*)

RYDER: How d'ye *do* that, O'Toole?

O'TOOLE: It's uncanny, innit, I know. I suppose it's a gift.

RYDER: 'S the story?

They listen: men, calls, dogs; the attention of the men covering the site already sucked to the search.

O'TOOLE: Time you got, Billy?

RYDER: Stopped. Thanks a bunch, Rolex.

O'TOOLE: (*Taking waterproof package from tunic*) The woman's done a runner, the heavies've arrived to drive her to a place of unsafety, she very sagely decided to hop it … Nice one, doc. (*Checks watch. Gathers pace.*) It'll be about a brick a minute, lads, rough guide, no more than six or eight left on the siren, I'll tek them, you'll wait for Chat, Ryder, he'll show you where, I'll join up with you at the river …

He's removed three passports from the waterproof, studies them, lens-crown on. Ryder angles from above to get a look at him.

RYDER: What's that?

O'TOOLE: Just sorting out a couple passports, just in case, Chatty's without, the little bugger just took mine … Right, give it a bit o' welly, Chat, look handy … (*A glance up at Ryder who's levering himself up for work.*) This time we'll slip out the back door, so we won't need 'em … Getting into the next place, who knows, maybe it'll be easier goin' through the front … Aught else?

He stands, restows the gear, stretches.

RYDER: One question, O'Toole …

DR AZIZ: (*Quiet; distinct*) May I speak, please?

Silence. No one moves.

RYDER: Who said that?

O'TOOLE: (*Scanning the guards*) She did.

DR AZIZ: Will you hear me?

Ryder, then Chatterjee, stare into the shrine, tracing the voice.

O'TOOLE: (*Soft*) This is not written.

DR AZIZ: I have no wish to be a bother to you. But you must understand it is my intention ...

O'TOOLE: Too late for new pages.

DR AZIZ: ... to carry out an inspection of my crèche before I leave this place.

RYDER: Crèche? 'S she talkin' ab –?

DR AZIZ: Not because I believe I sent the mothers off with a lie. But because I cannot know the truth unless I see for myself. These are not small things I speak of, gentlemen. Breach of trust. The responsibilities of care. Mothers and children ...

O'TOOLE: (*Shaking head*) Oh shit. (*He turns to the shrine.*) Let's get this over. Chatty, let that flap down, son, we'll be blinded else ...

RYDER: The sun's over 'ere, what're you ...? Hey, give your brain a rest, O'Toole, no one goes in here, we let this one, this place is gonna turn into a rifle range and we're right in fronta the butts. You're GONNA GET ME KILLED, O'TOOLE. Fuck you ... I say we call Ismael, right now ...

Chatterjee brings the flap down in a great sweep across the top of the scaffolding, blocking eyelines for the guards on the ridge.

Dr Aziz has levered herself upright. Neatens her dress into some kind of order. Ryder's voice has drawn a couple of them out of the search and back to the site.

O'TOOLE: (*Over shoulder, light, casual*) You're such a prick, Ryder. It's breathtaking. It's in the voice, man, this is a woman in the act of drawing a line, she won't be deflected this side of paradise. So. Time could suddenly grow very short if this ... spreads, right? She slips in, she slips out, two minutes, she's gone ... (*He carries the tunic back to the scaffolding, drapes it, another screen, to dry.*) Call Ismael, this could outlast the war. What do I know, I'm making this up ... (*He moves to look directly at Dr Aziz down the side of the shrine.*) My mistake. I remembered you as a doctor. I should've remembered you as a woman. See for yourself. If you must.

She walks past him with care, enters the shrouded passage, finds the steps to the scaffold, Chatterjee helping.

Ryder edges around the site, hand hurting, looking for ways of not dying if she's spotted.

O'Toole returns to the crater, squats before it, checks watch, sky. Stares into the water. A faint gold glow strikes up at his face from the pool, turning it ghastly. The glow comes and goes, like his fragmenting narrative. Shouts echo around the site. The sun's on a slow dip; reddening.

(*Blank*) Gilder Builder Minder Soldier Major

Caliph Wall War Play Lamp Crown

Prisoner Doctor …

(*Tries again.*)

        Doctor …
        He had not lied, he told himself.
        Lying.
        Between the alarm and the attack
        Between the heart and the brain-pan
        Between us the Gulf …
        The dark.
        Two minutes, in and out, the barn would be repaired, they would
            gain their release …
        Long ago, on an arch in the great Alhambra, he had written in
            letters of gold the words of Gilgamesh, king of the first city,
            builder of the first wall:
        Be what you are. Seek not what you may not find. Let your every
            day be full of joy. Love the child that holds your hand. Let
            your wife delight in your embrace. For these alone are the
            concerns of humanity.
        And now, the dark.
        Half blind. Half gone in the head. Half …

Ululations set up abruptly, single voices, tiny clusters, this time out front. The pool lamp flickers out. O'Toole stares at the city. Ismael barks instructions, on the approach. The sentries turn to see him in. He's telling them to help in the search; they slither away.

ISMAEL: You finished, Ryder Billy?

RYDER: (*Edging back towards shrine*) All but, chief.

O'TOOLE: (*Calling*) How we doin', Chat? Almost ready to unveil?

Chatterjee moves into vision, downstage end of scaffolding, waves his trowel, smiling benignly. The women's calls lift, grow more intense.

ISMAEL: Show. Uncover. (*Chatterjee doesn't move.*) Ryder Billy! Do it.

Ryder looks at O'Toole, begins to haul the canvas back and up from the scaffolded wall. Several blocks have been picked out from lower courses, to ease her entry . Ismael moves a pace or two forward. O'Toole stands.

ISMAEL: (*Slow*) What you do here? (*Scans the three.*) What the story? O'Toole?

O'TOOLE: The story. Let me think …

A strange unearthly sound begins to build from within the shrine: dog breath, shrieks of infants, the crack of burning bone. The calling women fall abruptly silent. The site reddens, sun dipping on. At the heart of the sound, Dr Aziz's voice, a growing wretched terrifying wail, outlasting the rest.

Silence.

Ismael edges forward. Stops at movement beyond the wall. Militiamen begin to appear on the ridge. Ismael sends them away. Dr Aziz returns through the gap in the wall, her headshawl bundled around something in her hands.

ISMAEL: (*In Arabic throughout*) Put it back. You put that back, that's an order.

He opens his jacket. Dr Aziz looks at him steadily.

DR AZIZ: (*In Arabic*) May God forgive you, Ismael. (*She scans the three workers; in English*) May God forgive you too. (*A glance out front.*) May God forgive us all …

She heads for the crater. Reaches Ismael. He stands for some moments, turns abruptly away, goes back to his perch on the hulk above the site, stares out towards the perimeter.

O'Toole sits on the rubble ridge, face blank, in the dark.

O'TOOLE'S VOICE: (*Relay*) The bits we never remember. The bits we edit … out.

Dr Aziz has sat by the pool. Rocks a bit, the bundle held close to her breast.

A single mother's voice, close, awful, calls her child's name: Ibrahim.

DR AZIZ: Al-Aker. Ibrahim. Three years four months. (*To the sky beyond the city*) Who do you think you are? Mm? Who do you think we are?

She lays the shawl down on earth. Unwraps it. Examines the contents.

Perhaps. How can we tell?

A second mother calls a name: Hanin.

On the shawl, an almost abstract shine-black sculpture of abbreviated limbs and torsos fused and reworked under intense heat, gleams on the cloth.

Al-Kurdi. Hanin. Four. Recently recovered from dysentery. (*To sky*) What have we done to you, mm? What awful wrong? That you would kill children …? (*To the charcoal*) Hanin, is it? What shall I write in my report …?

MOTHER'S VOICE: Mamdouh. Waseem. Fadia. Eman. Shamma'eh

DR AZIZ: (*To sky*) I have travelled in your countries, taken food in your homes, shared feelings and hopes, thought of you as brothers and sisters in the long struggle for human dignity. And I have seen you, Mr President, with your sensitive expression and sorrowing eyes on my television screen … And I had forgotten, what you will not acknowledge but the world knows, that yours is a country forged and shaped in brutal genocide, the destruction of whole peoples, lives, customs, beliefs, men, women and children who had learned respect for the place that nourished them, who had learned to tread gently on this good earth …

A WOMAN'S VOICE: (*A child's name*) Ghazi.

DR AZIZ: (*To sky still*) You destroy your past with these acts. Your future too. Wars only have beginnings. No endings.

ANOTHER VOICE: (*Another child*) Samzi.

DR AZIZ: What kind of world have you in mind, Mr President, Mr Prime Minister, Mr Secretary-General, what kind of world do you work to preserve, where a mere 20 per cent on your side of this tiny planet take and hold and consume a full 80 per cent of its bounty? Tell me, please. I would know this. I would know this ...

VOICE: (*Name*) Nidal.

She looks down again at the charcoal figure.

DR AZIZ: Qassem. Nidal. Four years one month. Hard of hearing. I will pray to my God for you, child. (*She looks up again.*) And what will you say to yours? No no no, please, this will not be justified by invoking the evil of my rulers or the unavoidability of your 'collateral damage', gentlemen. This world is full of evil rule, look at those you bought or bribed or bullied to give you houseroom here, look at those you would restore to their thrones, and tell me how we are worse. As for the unavoidable, how stupid, how very stupid you must think us, to imagine a decent human being believing you for one second, when you have told us and you have shown us your ability to tell the time on a child's wristwatch from one hundred miles, the side a woman parts her hair, the stubble on a man's face. We have a holy place, a place of worship, a place your cameras tell every day is filled with children. And you send a missile, not a wayward falling bomb, to burn it up ... In the name of God? In the name of humankind? In the name of ...

A FINAL VOICE: Suad.

She stands, gathers the charcoal sculpting in her hands, holds it to her face to kiss it.

DR AZIZ: Jubeh. Suad. Three. Arab. How can it matter? Yes. Not quite ... one of you. Arab. Yes. But when the mouth takes the nipple, the womb shivers just the same. (*Silence.*) Gentle. Men. (*She peers around the space. Ryder looks away. O'Toole sits on, retruded, scarcely there. Ismael stares out at the perimeter. In Arabic*) You knew? Are you mad?

ISMAEL: (*Not looking; in Arabic*) I had my orders.

DR AZIZ: (*Slow; in English*) So did they. They had their orders too ...

Ismael calls to the perimeter, harsh, certain. Dr Aziz looks around her, as if dazed. Chatterjee climbs down from the scaffold, approaches her, a basket in his hand.

She stares at it for some moments, kneels, places the bundle preciously inside.

Call the mothers. Let them bury their own ... Tell them to take comfort. In time we may come to see these are the lucky ones.

Chatterjee nods. The two heavies sent to drive her away arrive on the hulk; glare balefully at the problem woman. They part as she begins to leave, to let her through; follow her. O'Toole stands. Sniffs, face satanic in the bloodied light. Ryder edges towards the basket in Chatterjee's hands. A siren sounds, five miles away east.

RYDER: (*To whomever*) What we gonna do about this, then?

Silence. Ismael turns quietly, face deathly, pistol in hand.

ISMAEL: (*Deliberate*) You put it back. Is what you do. You put it back. Major's orders.

RYDER: (*Slow*) Hey, hang on a minute, friend ...

O'TOOLE: (*In time*) Here, give it here. (*He takes the basket from Chatterjee, leads them back to the wall, casually replaces the basket inside the shrine.*) Wall party, fall in, let's go, it's time we were out of here ...

He pushes Ryder up the steps; Ryder's legs have gone, Chatterjee has to help from above. O'Toole begins swinging blocks up to the platform.

Distant explosions, five miles east.

Another siren sets up, a mile closer.

O'Toole and Ismael check watches, as one. Ismael moves up to the rubble ridge, face blank, eyes bleak.

RYDER: (*Finding trowel; a sleepwalker*) I'm gonna make it. On my own, thank you. I've got a ticket, I've got a visa ...

O'TOOLE: (*Casual, as he works*) Finish, leave, OK? The time for finesse is long past. Stay well away from miladdo, it's possible he's reached the end of his elastic ...

RYDER: (*Laying*) I'm all right, I'm all right ... Ticket, passport, visa.

O'TOOLE: OK. (*He dips into his bag, comes out with spray-can and lens-crown.*) Let's see if I can remember how this goes ...

RYDER: You won't see me for dust ... Ticket, pass ...

O'TOOLE: Billy.

RYDER: Fuck off.

O'TOOLE: The papers, Billy.

RYDER: What about 'em?

O'TOOLE: (*Patient*) They're not. Chat'll tell you. Tell him, Chat.

He pads off towards the pool.

RYDER: (*After him*) 'S he gonna do, drop me a line, he's a dummy, right ...? (*To Chatterjee, over shoulder*) Sorry, no offence intended ...

CHATTERJEE: (*Own voice, Chapeltown*) None taken, don't mention it.

RYDER: (*After O'Toole*) Prick. (*He swivels suddenly to look at Chatterjee, who's removing Ryder's papers from the envelope. He gropes in his pocket.*) Wait a minute …

CHATTERJEE: Bad news, friend.

RYDER: (*Snatching it*) Joke over, sunbeam.

CHATTERJEE: (*Resuming work*) Not if you try an' use that lot, pal. Your ticket'll get you in half-price at the Museum of the Arab on Hakawati, an' your visa's a menu from the Desert Bloom, a local chophouse … (*Ryder lays grimly on, trying not to listen.*) I've bin a coupla times, s'quite good.

RYDER: (*A mutter*) Two of a fuckin' kind, eh, a Paddy 'n' a Paki, just my luck …

A siren sets up, a mile closer.

O'Toole has knelt at the pool to wash: feet, torso, face and head. The washing is thorough, measured, flecks of ritual here and there about his process, focus inward throughout.

The Ancients rise up on the far side of the ridge, stand in silence to watch the sun sinking beyond the city. On the siren, just setup, they make a long, slow, unflurried exit.

Ismael stands suddenly, calls down to the men's perimeter; no answer. He tries the women's; someone replies, voice edgy. Ismael summons him up to the site. Truck doors slam, ignition, the 5-tonner grinds away from the men's perimeter.

O'TOOLE: (*Quiet; drying himself*) Exit the Guards.

He turns his head, gazes over at the scaffold. Chatterjee's trowel glints a signal: two rows.

The summoned guard appears at the hulk. He's fifteen; scared. Explosions, a mile closer. The boy flinches.

ISMAEL: (*In Arabic*) Who's left?

BOY: (*In Arabic*) Just me, sir.

Ismael nods gravely, takes the boy's Sten, orders him to the shelters. Turns. Scans the site. Ryder and Chatterjee press on in silence, rhythm found again. O'Toole has put on his lens-crown, fitted a fine-air nozzle to a paint can, begun test work on a patch of masonry amid the rubble. Ismael moves silently up behind him to watch.

Siren sounds, the other side of the city. Cuts. Deep silence.

ISMAEL: O'Toole.

O'TOOLE: (*Absorbed*) Ismael.

ISMAEL: I phone my Major.

O'TOOLE: (*Working on*) What's he say?

ISMAEL: He say you know too much.

O'TOOLE: Ahunh.

Ismael looks across at the shrine.

ISMAEL: He say I have to kill you.

Silence. O'Toole works on, deep in process.

O'TOOLE: Did he say. Who he'd told. To kill you? (*Explosions, far side of the city, intense, intermittent. Pricks of light pierce the gloom of the site. O'Toole stands, wipes his hands, stares out. Distant fires begin to ruddy their faces. A final deadly barrage. Silence.*) Rumours. Dreams. Superstitions. Tattle. Women's talk. A hawk hovering above the shrine, dogs braying like donkeys, headless horses in the souk, an empty school bus being pushed into the river this morning, a driver shot, military using the crèche at night, a mute who sang at sunset …

Chatterjee's voice floats out across the site, grave, slow, pure:

'Here we go, here we go, here we go …'

The two men stare at each other in the near-dark.

O'TOOLE: (*The wall*) All done, son.

Ismael frowns, peers across at the finished wall. The men have gone. Ismael smiles, oddly.

ISMAEL: You fulla tricks, Gilderman.

O'TOOLE: We're all fulla someat. With you it's shit. You didn't even know the babs were in there, did you, your Major told you they'd been washed away in the river, he had you execute the poor bloody driver for falling asleep at the wheel, he fed you the cover story, you couldn't swallow it fast enough, you took his lies for truth and now you're down to die for it, you poor ignorant bastard … (*Siren, sudden, loud, their sector. Neither moves. Siren cuts. Silence. Eventually; a whisper*) Let's go.

Silence. Ismael unslings the Sten from his shoulder. Stares at it. Drops it into the pool. Draws his revolver carefully; it follows the Sten. Stares up at the sky.

ISMAEL: I die is my business. Fuck off.

O'Toole smiles faintly, holds his hand out, palm up. Opens the hand. Shows Ismael his bullets. They follow the weapons.

O'TOOLE: Go home, eh?

ISMAEL: You wanna go? Bye bye. Sure thing. I stay.

O'Toole shakes his head, gathers spray-can, walks slowly over towards the shrine.

O'TOOLE: I'll go when I'm done.

O'Toole clambers up the scaffold, begins to work unseen on the breezeblock wall.

Ismael watches him. Begins to laugh. Finds the ball. Flicks it from foot to foot for a moment, then belts it into the blackness.

ISMAEL: (*Released; laughing; sobs*) You think you big man, O'Toole? Tough guy, hunh? You think you better than Ismael, eh? FUCK YOU, MISTER. (*Gathers bag, crosses to shrine.*) DID ISMAEL DO THIS? EH? YOU THINK ISMAEL DID THIS? YOU THINK MY MAJOR DID IT? YOU. YOU DID IT. YOU NO GOOD. YOU NEVER NO GOOD. EVIL. EVIL. (*He's wrenched the Man United shirt out, scrunches it to a ball, throws it at the scaffold. O'Toole works on.*) You take. I don't want this. You not fit to kiss my Major's arseholes, my Major's a good man, three wars, an eye gone to the Jews, an arm left in Persia, EVERY WEEK HE GIVE ME FREE TIME FOR TRAINING ... (*Sobs, fury, pain*) You people did this thing ... I not speak your words no more. (*His fingers tear at his tongue.*) YOU DON'T JUDGE ISMAEL. NOT YOU PEOPLE. NOT YOU PEOPLE ...

O'Toole's finished, lowers himself carefully down. Ismael hurls himself up the ridge, falls to his knees, repeats fragments of the outburst in Arabic. O'Toole moves some paces towards him. Watches his hopeless weeping misery.

Bombs and missiles hit the sector with deafening abruptness, close enough to feel the breath. Ismael looks up at the sky, arms lifted as if in prayer.

(*In Arabic*) Ismael, son of Akram, brother of Said, spits in your face, you Mongols, you hear me? You hear me? Mongols ...

Sound cuts. An extraordinary explosive light rips across the site. Invisible cluster-bomb fragments follow its path, rip Ismael along with them like a shirt on a line.

The blast passes. What's left of the young minder flops on its back on the rubble slope. Smoke rises from a heap of clothing by the shrine, all that's left of O'Toole.

Distant rumbles. Silence.

Chatterjee appears under the roof awning. He scans the gloom, listens, swings lithely down, crosses to the ridge, gazes mutely on Ismael's remains, then goes to stand over O'Toole's mounded garb, lips pursed.

Sniffs. Gathers O'Toole's grip and instrument case, finds the lens-crown, puts it carefully on his head, takes a fallen lamp, pads forward, gradually assumes the full O'Toole gesture.

CHATTERJEE: (*Lamp to face*) Now praise and glory be to Him who sits throned in eternity above the shifts of time; who ...

RYDER: (*Off, close; slow, soft, sung*) 'I've got a ticket to ride and I'm OK.' (*Chatterjee looks around him. Siren sets up: all clear. Ryder emerges from shrine-side canvas, hands and knees.*) I'm fine. I'm fine. Thanks. (*The siren cuts. He stands. Pats breast pocket.*) I'd like to go home now. If that could be arranged. I have the necessary ... (*Holds up envelope.*) Ticket visa passport. A prile of priles. 138,000 quid in bank loans, me house, wife and business down the Swanee ... Last time I vote bloody whatsit ... (*Scans the site.*) Where's erm? (*Long silence.*) What are you, RAF? Pilot, yes? Half a million a year t'train you, 'course they're gonna send someone in. Brilliant. A mute called Chatty. Brilliant, both o' you. (*Silence.*) I was so scared. I was so ... (*He shakes his head, turns, begins to leave.*) Bus station.

CHATTERJEE: (*Soft*) Billy.

RYDER: Can't hear you, sorry.

CHATTERJEE: Just wait by the corner, I'll take you down to the river, Persian steamer, gotta tidy up, I'll see you right. OK ...?

RYDER: (*Turning*) Your oppo, what's-his-name, he could've had us all dead.

CHATTERJEE: Some of us are, Billy.

He swings his lamp across the dead Ismael. Ryder peers at it across the site.

RYDER: I meant us. I meant me.

He leaves. Chatterjee watches. Resumes.

CHATTERJEE: (*Lamp to face, master again*) ... who, changing all things, remains himself unchanged; who alone is the paragon of all perfection ...

A waking groan cuts him off. O'Toole stretches upward to sit on the crest of the rubble ridge. Blinks across at the Indian. Chatterjee shakes his head in disbelief.

O'TOOLE: You woke me up with your yammering. I was takin' a nap. (*He looks around him, slowly reconnects, draws himself to his feet, sees the lens-crown.*) Hey, don't get ahead o' yourself, you're a cheeky bugger ... Where's er ...?

CHATTERJEE: Standin' by ...

O'TOOLE: Best get after him, he'll be climbin' lamp-posts ... I'll see you down there, gotta tidy up ... Java, here we come, eh?

CHATTERJEE: (*Laying crown in O'Toole's bag*) Sod Java. Sod you. I'm off back 'ome, look for someat on me own.

O'TOOLE: I got you out, didn't I? Some thanks.

CHATTERJEE: You got me bloody in too, O'Toole. Was you did the gold tooth, when they came for you, you bloody shopped me.

O'TOOLE: Grow up, boy. How in God's name were you gonna get me out? Mm? You haven't the wit, son. When I took you on, you were nobbut a scruffy lad labouring for a brickie at the Harrogate Pump Room, I've shown you a true craft, I've shown you the world according to O'Toole ...

CHATTERJEE: Christ, what a clown. A legend in your own three-ring circus ... Come on, you bollox, let's go.

O'TOOLE: (*Sudden, hard*) I'm not done. Get off.

CHATTERJEE: (*Soft; unafraid*) I'll wait down the hill. You'll not find your way else.

A final flurry of bombs and missiles rips into the city, a mile away.

Chatterjee leaves.

O'Toole picks up his grip, slings instrument case, scans the site. Takes in the dead Ismael. Gathers the Man United shirt from the scaffolding. Carries it to the body. Crouches to gaze on the stilled face.

O'TOOLE: Lord, hear my tale, and let my tale come unto thee. Concerning young Ismael, the life to the death, a tragedy, if you'll pardon the expression. Who, acting on orders, almost single-handed, for a whole day kept the site of heinous and hydra-headed infanticide under wraps until the evidence could be buried and a covering account set in place by his commander. Who failed to return from the brothel one afternoon, and was not on hand when the crèche supervisor rang in to say the bus had not arrived to take the kids over the river. Who were simply left there, forgotten. In a building the military had begun using, with some sort of command 'n' control gear in the roof, a known target of enemy guided-fire since Day One. What a pickle. I pass over the part taken by the enemy, Lord, I know you're a sceptic on the matter. Save to ask whatever happened to proportion, doesn't this sort of thing stretch the credulity a touch, even yours, they could see it was being used for military purposes but managed to overlook – or at least overcome – the fact that it was in regular use as a nursery, oh come on, Lord, these men know exactly what they're doing, the rest is teasing. This boy, our hero, Lord, met death from a surfeit of orders and choked on his own obedience, for he was a good soldier …

He lays the shirt across the young man's face and body. MAN UNITED gleams up out of the gloom.

He stands with effort. Looks up at the sky, out front.

    Finished?

No answer.

What light's left begins to die. O'Toole treads along the rubble ridge, fades into the dark.

The gilder's lamp shines down on the face of the patched wall. The gilder's work shimmers strangely in the air, in front of rather than upon it. It reads, in English and Arabic, GOD IS GOOD, under the image of a child's hand.

Slow fade.

Dog breath.

The tent falls away; the building within shimmers in the dark. Points of fire begin to light the distant horizon. Hell reinvents itself. The world burns.

Western voices move in, out, on the fade, recounting the war they had.

The Ancients rise up from the rubble ridge. Stand, immutable, inerasable, staring out at the city.

END

THATCHER'S CHILDREN

Thatcher's Children was first performed at the Old Vic, Bristol, on 19th May 1993.

The cast was as follows:

Mona Patterson   Marva Alexander

Tom Clare   Ian Driver

Gurvinder Singh Kuthani   Kulvinder Ghir

Hester Patterson   Heather Imani

Daisy Jay   Miranda Pleasence

Sandra Cope   Cassie Stuart

Wayne Richards   Giles Thomas

Musicians   James Woodrow, Howard Gay

Director   Andrew Hay

Designer   Mick Bearwish

Lighting   Tim Streader

Music composition and direction   John O'Hara

Thatcher's Children

ACT ONE

Changing room, Leighley Juniors, lit from corridor. Evening. Buzz and clack of parents arriving in adjacent Assembly Hall; sounds of pop medley of Christmas carols on bad relay.

Gurvinder *arrives, clicks on the lights, moves gravely into the room. He's ten; two years in Britain, in Yorkshire one term.*

He wears a floor-length overcoat, a makeshift wool turban, a stove-pipe hat atop it; carries a long brush-stale and a Safeways plastic bag. He stands facing out, lips quivering, close to tears. Sits. Removes hat and turban, reveals a beautifully wrought head of Sikh braids. Takes out a draw-string marble-bag from his pocket, fishes out a pair of scissors, slowly begins to cut the braids. On the final snip, the, lights suddenly dim, flutter, surge back, as the grid heads for overload. The boy looks fearfully up, sensing judgement.

Voices from corridor. Laughter. Teachers' shushes. The lights bobble again, appear to steady; abruptly cut.

Hubbub from hall, corridors. The Headmistress's voice rises above the din to announce contingency plans involving storm lamps, should the power cut persist. Some ironic parent applause.

Class teacher's voice in corridor, detailing 4H to take lamps with them. Children appear, lamps in hand, nattering and giggling as they go, move in to occupy the now empty room.

CLASS TEACHER: (*Off; after them*) Has anybody Seen Sandra? Hester …

They fall silent, attentive, as if she were in the room.

HESTER: (*Black; eleven; dressed as Wise Man*) No, Miss. Don't think she's come yet, Miss.

TEACHER: (*Off*) Oh my God, that's all we need … What is she …?

HESTER: First Virgin Mary, Miss.

MONA: (*Her sister, ten; a heavily pillow-pregnant black Virgin Mary*) Second.

HESTER: First, you're second …

TEACHER: All right, all right. Mona, you can do both, all right?

MONA: I can't, I don't know t'words, Miss …

HESTER: I know them, Miss, I'll teach her them …

Mona pulls a face.

TEACHER: Thank you, Hester. (*To another group across the way; seamlessly.*) Shepherds! Stop talking! Yes that does mean you, Darren Claypole! (*To them again.*) Right, go over your lines with each other and be ready when you're called.

DAISY: (*Angel Gabriel as the Good Fairy*) Miss, Gurvinder's not here either, Miss …

TEACHER: (*Off*) Jesus Ch … Wouldn't you just know it … Has anyone seen him?

WAYNE: (*Minimal Innkeeper; a large ten, from Pontypridd; one term up from Wales*) I seen him, Miss.

TEACHER: (*Off*) When was that, Wayne?

WAYNE: (*Giggling*) This mornin', Miss.

Laughter, which they try to sit on.

TEACHER: (*Off; to corridor; loud*) Have any of you children seen Gurvinder Kurthani … ?

GURVINDER: (*Hidden in room; tiny voice*) Here, Miss …

TEACHER: (*Off*) Gurvinder, are you there … ?

GURVINDER: (*Crawling out*) Yes, Miss.

The children hold up their lamps to light his passage.

TEACHER: (*Off*) You're going to have to speak up, Gurvinder, you're in Yorkshire now, no one hears you in Yorkshire unless you shout … Good, go over your lines, please, and stay put … (*Seamless segue, to the clatter of feet in corridor*) Walk, Roman Soldiers … How many more times …

She's gone. The group stare at the young re-turbanned Sikh, who lies face down on the floor sobbing.

MONA: What's the matter with him? What's a matter with ye, Girlie?

WAYNE: Er, he's skrikin', Girlie's skrikin', mardy bugger …

DAISY: Oh *do* shut up, Wayne …

MONA: He's always sayin' right stupid things, 'im …

Daisy and Mona move in to comfort the Sikh. **Tom's** *already there, in Joseph costume, a wire coat-hanger in his hand which he's been struggling to fit around his tea-towel kuffiah since arriving.*

TOM: (*Squatting; ten; pale, shy, well-spoken*) Come on, Girlie, it's all right, you don't need to cry …

DAISY: (*Elbowing Tom*) … It's all right, I'll look after him …

MONA: (*Close in*) Come on, Girlie, we've gotta do it in a minute … You're gonna ruin everythin'.

DAISY: Poor Gurvinder.

TOM: He might be sick.

WAYNE: (*Fiddling with his 'Pontypridd Baths' towel in his waistband*) Er, don't touch 'im, yell catch the lurgi …

The girls tell him to shut up. Daisy whacks at him with her wand. He backs off, well pleased. The girls close in, concern rising. Even Hester, who's been running her lines, draws in to look.

TOM: Shall I tell Miss?

DAISY: Gurvinder. What's happened? Are you poorly? Mm? What's up?

The boy rolls suddenly over onto his back, laughter pouring from him. The girls recover, begin punching and joshing him. **Sandra** *has appeared unseen from the Hall side. Stands in darkness watching the mêlée: she's ten, sad-faced, a perfect white Virgin Mary.*

MONA: (*As the weird laughter drains away*) ... Tell us wharrappened, will ye, ye're goin' ruin everythin' ...

GURVINDER: (*Grave, sullen*) I cut me hair.

HESTER: You didn't.

GURVINDER: I did ...

DAISY: What did your dad say?

GURVINDER: He 'an't seen it.

MONA: Ye kiddin' again, aren't ye?

GURVINDER: Not.

DAISY: (*Arms around him*) Oh Gurvinder.

WAYNE: Er, Daisy Jay's snoggin' Girlie ...

MONA: 'E's kiddin' us.

TOM: Are you?

The boy shakes his head.

DAISY: Are you?

He sits up. Removes his turban. They stare at the shorn head. Tom's hand wavers towards it, hovers, trapped between want and don't. Wayne moves in to have a look.

Feeling the head; fearless

Oh, it's really soft.

WAYNE: (*Smirky*) Like 'is 'ead.

Mona feels it.

DAISY: (*To Tom*) Feel it.

MONA: Are you gonna tell us why ye cut it, Girlie?

HESTER: (*To Mona*) Come on, I've got to teach you Sandra's lines ...

MONA: You're not my mother, ye know …

HESTER: You heard what Miss said …

MONA: (*Defiant*) Come on, Girlie, tell us why you cut it.

GURVINDER: (*Standing*) So's they wunt call us Girlie.

Silence.

The lights plunge up abruptly, bobble, hold, to ironic cheers and clapping from the audience in the Hall; cut again, to groans off. The Headmistress's voice rears again: they'll begin at seven, come what may. Applause.

In the brief illumination, the group becomes aware of Sandra at the back of the room. Her face has creased and grown wet with anguish.

WAYNE: Oh God, not another skriker.

Sandra blubs on, immersed in the pain of things.

DAISY: What is it? Where've you been? What's happened?

SANDRA: Miss told Mona to learn my words

WAYNE: 'Cos you weren't 'ere, stupid.

SANDRA: I was …

DAISY: Poor Sandra.

WAYNE: Boo boo.

SANDRA: … I was lookin' t'see if me mam'd come …

DAISY: Has she?

SANDRA: (*Worse*) No …

DAISY: Listen, don't cry, it'll ruin your face …

HESTER: (*Decisive*) What's the problem? She's here now, she can do her part …

SANDRA: She doesn't like me, Miss Hutchison …

WAYNE: Nobody bloody likes you, girl … S'cos you stink, see, boohoohoo …

Sandra's wails grow worse, Wayne sniggers, pleased with himself. Gurvinder brings him a wholly unlooked-for clout over the head with his broom-stale, Wayne yelps, doubles over, head in hands.

Aah aah aah, you stupid bugger, what d'you do that for …? (*Gurvinder puts a finger to his lips: say no more.*) I'll bloody get you for that, you little sod … You're bloody barmy, d'you know that?

He makes an unconvincing show of retaliating.

GURVINDER: (*Stick raised again*) I'm a king, me.

HESTER: Gurvinder. Put that down and get ready. Come on, I'll help you …

GURVINDER: All friends, all friends.

He returns to sit meekly between Hester's legs to have his turban tied. Daisy and Mona begin repairing Sandra's face. Wayne worries at the bump on his head, checking for blood. Tom can't get the wire coat-hanger to fit on his head. Bits and bobs of lines get rehearsed throughout.

TOM: Can someone help me with this, please?

MONA: Come 'ere.

He sits by her, hands her the hanger, she sizes up the job. Gurvinder fiddles a thermos from his plastic bag.

HESTER: (*Finishing touches*) What you brought that for?

GURVINDER: Miss told me to.

HESTER: What for?

GURVINDER: 'S for me myrrh.

HESTER: Do you know your words?

GURVINDER: Is it a star? Is it a sign? I must follow it as far as Leeds, me.

HESTER: As far as it leads me.

GURVINDER: Yes.

TOM: What's your dad going to say when he sees your hair?

GURVINDER: Nothing.

SANDRA: Have you cut your hair?

GURVINDER: No

SANDRA: Y'ave,

GURVINDER: Haven't,

MONA: He'll kill ye, won't 'e?

GURVINDER: He won't.

MONA: You'll get the belt.

GURVINDER: I won't.

TOM: I bet he won't take you to Gotscam Chairs this weekend.

GURVINDER: He will.

DAISY: Is he coming tonight?

GURVINDER: I don't know.

DAISY: He is, isn't he?

GURVINDER: He might be.

SANDRA: Have ye kept it?

The Sikh shows them the marble-bag.

GURVINDER: 'S in there,

MONA: Ye can sell it, ye know. I saw it on t'tele.

WAYNE: Gerroff.

MONA: I did.

WAYNE: Who'd wanna buy that?

HESTER: (*Setting stove-pipe hat on Gurvinder's head*) Where's your glass,
   Wayne?

WAYNE: 'S on the stage where I left it.

HESTER: What about the pretend cigarette Miss gave you ...?

WAYNE: Oh shit, I knew there was something ...

He searches his roll-bag, muttering.

TOM: Shall I help you look for it?

MONA: (*Still at work on the hanger*) Sit still, you.

WAYNE: Bloody 'ell, 'ow'll they know I'm an innkeeper if I don't 'ave a fag ...?

Daisy whispers something in Mona's ear. Mona giggles.

SANDRA: Me dad always has a fag.

WAYNE: Aw, 'e bloody would, wouldn'e ... ?

SANDRA: Behind his ear. 'Cos he's an innkeeper.

WAYNE: (*Searching pockets*) That's not an inn, that's a pub ...

DAISY: (*Fumbling a ten-pack of Craven A from her knickers*) You can borrow one
   of these if you like.

WAYNE: (*Crossing*) 'S 'ave a look. (*She opens the packet. He takes one gingerly.*)
   Where'd you get 'em?

DAISY: My mum left them on the Welsh dresser.

Wayne gains confidence. Pretends to smoke it. Tries tucking it behind his ear.

MONA: It dunt look right, that.

WAYNE: Course it does.

DAISY: Mona's right, it's the cork tip, it's wrong.

WAYNE: How d'ye mean?

DAISY: They didn't have cork tips in those days.

TOM: (*Quiet*) They didn't actually have cigarettes.

Silence. They all stare at him, he colours up.

DAISY: Here. Try one of her roll-ups. She always does a couple before she goes out. See. No tip.

Wayne takes the roll-up; frowns at it. Daisy holds a lighter out, clicks on the flame.

WAYNE: 'S that for?

DAISY: You have to smoke it a bit, then dimp it and put it behind your ear, like Sandra's dad.

WAYNE: 'E 'as a *pub* ...

MONA: Er, look at 'im, mardy bugger ...

WAYNE: I aren't mard ...

MONA: 'Ere y'are, give it 'ere, smoke it ...

HESTER: Don't you dare ...

WAYNE: No, you won't ...

He ducks down for the light. Comes up puffing. Splutters a bit. Applause, laughter from the group. Hester turns away, disgusted.

MONA: 'Ey, ye look right good wi' that, Wayne.

WAYNE: Course I do.

He smokes on, posing and strutting.

MONA: (*Leaning back, clutching her pillow*) Aagh, aagh ...

TOM: What's wrong?

MONA: I'm pregnant. I think me waters're bursting ... Feel it. (*Tom very delicately lays a hand on her huge middle. Mona slaps it.*) Not too hard ...

SANDRA: (*To Wayne*) Save some for behind your ear. (*Finger and thumb.*) About that much ...

The piano strikes up by the stage, a buzz and applause as the first and second years troop out to sing the Shepherds' song. The kids tingle into readiness, little hums of nerves from the girls, exaggerated gesturing from the lads.

CLASS TEACHER: (*Hall side now; low; distinct*) ... Hester, Gurvinder, Daisy, stand by please, you're on when the song ends, all right, just as we did in rehearsal, Daisy first ...

HESTER/DAISY/GURVINDER: Yes, Miss.

GURVINDER: Miss?

CLASS TEACHER: (*Off*) What is it, Gurvinder?

GURVINDER: (*Worried sick*) Has me dad come, Miss ... ?

CLASS TEACHER: (*Off*) Gurvinder, how would I know ... ?

GURVINDER: He wears a turban, Miss ...

WAYNE: (*Another puff*) And a skirt.

CLASS TEACHER: (*Off*) Thank you for sharing that with us, Wayne. Now *shut* up, the lot of you, and stand by ...

Wayne giggles, out of control. Others join in; Hester and Daisy try to quiet them. The Shepherds' song draws to a ragged close. Vast parent applause. Third Year Roman Soldiers thud on and disperse the Shepherds with shows and blows.

Daisy walks out, calm and straight, her wand aloft. We follow her.

DAISY: Beebeebeebee. I am the Angel Gabriel ...

She stops suddenly. Gurvinder has followed her. Hester whispers him back, off; too late.

GURVINDER: Is it a star? Is it a sign?

They stare at each other. Gurvinder realizes something's wrong, makes as if to leave.

DAISY: (*To him*) I am the Angel Gabriel. Pray tell me who you might be?

Silence. The boy has no lines. Hester appears suddenly.

HESTER: We are two Wise Persons following that bright star in the East.

Silence.

GURVINDER: (*Suddenly*) I am a king, me.

They look at him.

HESTER: We bring gifts, gold, frankincense and myrrh (*Gurvinder holds up his thermos flask*) ... for the child about to be born.

Gurvinder turns to leave. Hester grabs his arm to stop him. The top hat falls from his head. As he stoops to collect it the turban follows.

Gurvinder freezes, on the edge of tears. Hester stoops, tries to set the hat on his head.

GURVINDER: l must follow it as far as Leeds, me ...

DAISY: Good. Beebeebeebeebee.

She disappears. Hester leads Gurvinder off.

GURVINDER: (*Distraught mutters*) I lost me turban, me dad saw me hair, he won't tek me to God's Armchair now ...

Tom appears, drawing a stool behind him on a piece of rope. Mona trots after him, straddles the stool with difficulty, follows him at a crouch around the stage.

MONA: Joseph. Joseph, we must find a place to stay, I'm almost ready to have the baby …

TOM: I'll try this inn, shall I?

MONA: Yes, yes, try that inn.

Tom knocks. Steps back. They wait. Mona gestures him to knock again. Tom steps forward, knuckles ready.

WAYNE: (*Off*) Hello? Who is it?

TOM: Mary and Joseph.

Long silence. Wayne appears, glass in hand, roll-up dimped and wedged behind ear.

WAYNE: What do you want?

MONA: We have travelled a long way and I'm tired and I'm pregnant. Do you have a room?

Long pause. Wayne gazes upward, as if in another dimension.

WAYNE: Yes.

Silence. Mona and Tom look at each other, aghast. Wayne smiles fondly at them, well pleased.

TOM: (*Finally*) Miss!

The stage lights suddenly come on, flooding them with dawn light. They freeze.

Hester, Gurvinder, Sandra and Daisy appear from the wings, propelled by the desperate Class Teacher, join the others at front of the stage.

Piano. Guitar. They sing

ALL: Hello, Mr Sunnyman,
          Lift your sleepy head,
          All night you've kept us waiting
          While you've been in your bed.

          Come along, Mr Sunnyman,
          Spread your lovely light,
          Fill the world with goodness
          And love and peace, all right?

Slow fade to black.

Image of green roller-blackboard. On it, chalked up in teacher's hand:

'FOR ME, THE HEART OF POLITICS IS NOT POLITICAL THEORY, IT IS PEOPLE AND HOW THEY WANT TO LIVE THEIR LIVES.'

Copy out two hundred times and hand in to the Headmaster's Office not earlier than 5 pm.

The image holds, dies.

*Bring up: Sandra, in spot, facing out, copying out in exercise book, voicing each
slow word she writes. She lifts her head to check the board (out front now); she
carries an ugly bruise on her left cheek.*

*Bring up: class room, comprehensive school; late afternoon, late spring. Wayne,
Mona and Sandra spread around the room, copy out their lines. They're Fifth
Year, C stream.*

SANDRA: ... people and how they want to live their lives full stop (*checks board*)
for me comma ...

GURVINDER: (*In at speed from corridor*) I don't believe it. I just seen Tom an' DJ.
Who busted ye ... ?

They shush him, gesture the stock-room out front.

WAYNE: (*Sotto*) Ratface.

GURVINDER: Fuck this, I'm gonna 'ave a word ...

SANDRA: Don't, you'll mek things worse ...

GURVINDER: (*At stock-room door; downstage; the teacher invisible and unheard
throughout*) 'Scuse me, sir, could I 'ave a word ...? Well, it's just couldn't ye
let 'em go, sir? We're goin' campin' this weekend up the Dales an' we got train
tickets 'n' stuff, ye know (*Listens to Ratface.*) No. I'm not sayin' that, sir, ye
could keep 'em in next Monday, its just it's Sandra's birthday an' it's all
arranged ... (*listens again.*) Aw, go on, sir ... Why not? Ye gonna ruin
everythin' ... Ye could. Course ye could. Why not? Give us one good reason
... Y'aven't got one, that's why ... (*low.*) Oh fuck off, ye little shit (*Moves
back into room. Returns to answer him.*) I said fuck off, ye little shit!

He heads back towards his desk, searches angrily for his gear.

MONA: (*Chewing gum*) Ey, cool it, Girlie, ye know Ratface ...

Eyes swivel to the stock-room door.

GURVINDER: (*Still searching*) Sod him. (*Looks up as Ratface speaks.*) I'm looking for
me gear. No. I won't, it's me dad's, I left it here ... (*Listens, eyes hardening*) Ye
put it *where*, what ye put it there for? I'm askin' you a question ... Junk? Ye
callin' it junk, ye ... racist pig? I'll bloody junk you, if that gear's damaged you're
in trouble, mate. Serious. (*He's heading out. Ratface says something.*) ... I'm out
of 'ere in four weeks, chum, you can't do nothin' ... I'll be back ... Serious.

*Silence. The three watch; return as one to their chore as the teacher turns to look
at them.*

ALL: (*Responding as he follows after Gurvinder*) Yes, sir.

*He's gone. Wayne's on his feet, follows to the corridor door, chunner and double
V-signs, pissed off. Mona lights up, hands it to Sandra, who puffs at it nervously,
worried she'll be caught.*

MONA: We could just go.

WAYNE: No way. They'll just sling us out, look what they did to Darren Thingie …

MONA: Let 'em. I don't mind. What ye think?

SANDRA: No. I couldn't. Me dad'd kill us …

MONA: He'd kill ye if 'e knew you were goin' campin' up Malham, too, what's the diff … ?

SANDRA: 'S different, that's all.

Wayne takes the cigarette from her, draws deep.

WAYNE: I gotta get my exams, see. But I tell you what: if I ever get into uniform, I'll have that little fucker for this, see if I don't …

Hester appears, books in hand, not privy to the planned weekend.

MONA: What do you want?

HESTER: Are you still spending the weekend at Carmen Johnson's?

Wayne and Sandra give Mona a look.

MONA: Yeah, why?

HESTER: No reason. (*Takes in blackboard.*) Who busted you?

WAYNE: Bloody Ratcliffe.

HESTER: What for?

WAYNE: Nowt.

HESTER: (*To Mona again*) So Mum'll be able to call you there if she needs to, will she?

MONA: Aye, if she can find a phone that works in Harehills …

HESTER: If she needs to, she'll find one.

MONA: What's it to you, anyway?

HESTER: Not much. Only I just saw Carmen getting on the Field Trip bus to the Lakes.

MONA: So?

HESTER: So what're you playing at?

MONA: Mind your own bloody business, will ye …

HESTER: You'd better tell me, our Mona …

MONA: Mind your own business, will ye, I can look after meself, thank you, what are you, bloody KGB … ?

Daisy arrives, Tom in her wake, both keenly got out for camping. Each carries a huge backpack, bedrolls, tentrolls, pans, tin mugs hanging neatly down from them.

DAISY: (*Glancing at stock-room, low-voiced*) ... Hopeless, I rang the station, it's the last train ...

WAYNE: Fuck.

DAISY: So. Another great idea bites the dust ...

MONA: 'S all right, he's not there, Girlie threw a moody, he's legged it after 'im ...

HESTER: Last train to where?

TOM: Craven, We were meant to be camping out at Gotscam Chairs ...

DAISY: Sandra's birthday. Bugger. (*She puts her hand on Sandra's shoulder.*) Never mind, you can stay at my Mum's, we'll have a party ...

SANDRA: Doesn't matter. Honest.

DAISY: (*The bruise*) How'd you get that?

SANDRA: 'S nothing. (*Beat*) I ran into a lamp-post comin' t'school ...

Daisy gives Tom a look. Hester has fixed a withering glare on Mona. Mona gets up, lights another cigarette, crosses to the doorway, stares out down the corridor.

TOM: (*From nowhere*) We could go. (*Daisy turns, looks at him.*) There's time.

DAISY: Tom. There are times you are just ... so selfish, it's Sandra's birthday present, she's the whole point of it ...

TOM: Yes, I know ...

DAISY: Well, then.

MONA: Right on.

WAYNE: Hellfire, listen 'em. That's women all over for you, one down the toilet, all down the toilet. I understand, Thomas boy. All you're seeing's a golden opportunity to get your little end away goin' up in smoke, right boyo?

Tom blushes and laughs, stranded between the two. Sandra laughs too.

SANDRA: You're a dirty beggar, Wayne Richards.

WAYNE: (*Leering*) Aren't I just.

He makes for her, pretending to undo his fly as he goes. Sandra purrs behind her pretend shrieks.

MONA: Ratface!

Rapid adjustments in the room.

'S OK. He's turned into t'Staff Room.

WAYNE: I wish 'e'd turn into a corpse. Little prick,

DAISY: You wouldn't have a word with him, would you, Hes? If he lets 'em go now, we could still make it ... Come on, you know he fancies you ...

HESTER: Do me a favour,

MONA: She won't help.

TOM: 'S worth a try, Hes.

HESTER: What are you supposed to have done?

WAYNE: Nowt. I told you.

SANDRA: It was, it was nowt, he was tekin' us for social studies an' he was dronin' on an' on about what a good thing the election was for this country, we're gonna see some changes, unions and workers and us lot are in for a rude awakenin', on an' on like, oh yeah an' like last winter they couldn't bury the dead an' that an' then Wayne said ... (*giggling*) What did ye say ... ? Go on ...

WAYNE: Nowt. I just told 'im we couldn't get anyone to bury my grandad an' he said, 'cos o' the strike, right? An' I said, no, 'cos 'e wasn't dead ...

Sandra and Mona start laughing. Daisy joins in. Tom follows. Hester waits.

HESTER: And what about you?

SANDRA: I laughed.

MONA: Me too.

HESTER: And Gurvinder?

WAYNE: Girlie was over doin' someat wi' their lot in Multicultural Studies ...

DAISY: Yeah, he was brill ...

TOM: Brought his dad's gear – the five Ks – told us what it all meant, amazing ...

DAISY: Come on, Hes.

HESTER: (*Leaving*) I'll see what I can do. But whatever happens, she's not going, not unless she asks our mum first ...

MONA: (*After her*) ... Ye make me sick, you ...

HESTER: Mutual.

She's gone. Daisy holds up crossed fingers. Sandra smiles palely. Mona dimps her fag, still on watch.

WAYNE: (*Examining Tom*) Nice gear.

TOM: It's my brother's.

WAYNE: Bet that cost a packet.

TOM: I don't know.

MONA: Right, she's collared him.

They listen. Mona peeps out occasionally, as Hester tackles Ratface. Her voice gets closer, as she trails him up the corridor. Mona legs it back to her desk as he returns.

DAISY: (*To his question*) We're just waiting for our friends, sir.

She pulls a face, reluctantly heads for the corridor, pushing Tom ahead of her, to wait outside.

HESTER: (*From doorway*) ... Excuse me, sir, I don't think you have the right to do this, they're going to lose a lot of money on rail tickets and things ... (*She cuts as he shouts at her.*) Sir, threats are no substitute for argument ... (*He says something else.*) Fine, I'll see if the Headmaster'll deal with it ...

She walks off, calm and tough. Daisy and Tom push out into the corridor.

WAYNE/MONA/SANDRA: (*Replying*) Yes, sir.

They watch him into his lair. Relax. Wayne gives him the double V-sign.

SANDRA: I really like your sister.

MONA: Ye can 'ave 'er.

Suppressed giggles, which cut as the teacher reappears in the stock-room doorway.

MONA: (*Replying, eyes down*) Yes, sir.

They work under his gaze for some moments.

WAYNE: Sir, who wrote this, was it Mrs Thatcher, sir ... ?

A roaring rumpus down the corridor, heading their way.

TOM: (*From corridor*) Hey up, Girlie, what're you ... ?

Heads swivel. Gurvinder appears at speed through the door, dressed in his dad's gear [turban, keche, kara] a solid steel kirpan in his hands. Dives straight far Ratcliffe, scimitar outstretched. Stops a foot or two from his face, eyes burning.

GURVINDER: (*In Punjabi*) 'One for all and all for one. Praise the Lord.' (*He motions him with the sword to leave the room. Follows him with his eyes to the door. After him, responding*) Yeah, sure. Go an' get the cavalry you don't scare me, Ratface ...

WAYNE: Wow, fuckin' Bruce Lee ...

Laughter released, anxiety too; it was heavy, for a while. Gurvinder laughs, a kid again.

DAISY: That was brill, Girlie, but maybe you should scarper ...

MONA: Right. He's a mean bugger, is Ratface ...

TOM: Yeah.

GURVINDER: (*Fast*) No. No no no. (*Sword outstretched again.*) All friends, all friends, hands please. (*He gestures them to place their palms on the blade. Frowns, giggles.*) We will do it. We will do it.

TOM: Do what, Girlie?

GURVINDER: Hands, please. I show you ...

WAYNE: (*Offering hand*) Don't cut the bugger off, will you ...

Other hands follow, cover the blade. Some laughter, joshing, dying away. Hester returns, watches from the doorway.

GURVINDER: (*In Punjabi, then translates*) All for one, one for all, praise the Lord. (*In Punjabi again, then translates.*) We swear by this holy weapon to make our way together one day, some time, to the place called God's Armchair.

DAISY: Gotscam Chairs.

GURVINDER: Yes. All swear.

They swear, somewhere between embarrassment and fascination.

HESTER: On your bike, Girlie, Ratcliffe's called the pigs ...

GURVINDER: No. You too. Hand, please ...

SANDRA: You've gotta split, Girlie...

GURVINDER: Hand. Please.

HESTER: Me? Why?

GURVINDER: Because I love you.

HESTER: What?

MONA: Do it. He's gonna get busted ...

He holds out the sword. She moves in.

HESTER: I swear.

GURVINDER: All right. Fuck 'em.

Fast black. Bring up:

THATCHER'S VOICE: (*Tape; echoic*)
> Where there is discord, may we bring harmony.
> Where there is error, may we bring truth.
> Where there is doubt, may we bring faith.
> Where there is despair, may we bring hope.

Bring up: image of Thatcher. It stays for some time, presiding over what follows. Mona, Tesco check-out, the work unrelenting.

MONA: (*Out; speaking around the process*) What d'ye think? Great, eh? YOP scheme. Youth Opportunity. I should be so lucky. Still, it's better than waxin' chickens for Plumleys Plumptious. Not a lot, mind ... (*To customer*) D'you want a bag for them? (*Hands her one. Moves on.*) £32.50 a week for 48 hours. Good, eh? Never mind, I'm off out tonight. Clubbin'. See what's 'appenin'. (*Checks her queue*) God, look at 'em. They've all been lookin' for the '500 items and over' till and fetched up wi' me. Ah well. Only one thing for it. (*Takes out a hairpin, carefully jams it in her till. Several tings, the till goes down. Presses buzzer. Calls.*) Supervisor, please! Till 15.

She crosses her legs, swivels in her seat, rubs an emery board across her nails, flashes us a smile.

Her light cuts. Sound of doorknocker.

Bring up: Gurvinder, briefcase, jacket, spruced up.

GURVINDER: (*As door opens*) Good morning, madam, I wonder if I can interest you in my company's revolutionary range of herbal health products ... ? (*The door closes in his face, He turns, gazes out; perfect Tommy Cooper*) just like that.

Light out.

Bring up: Sandra, in long blonde wig, bedroom above rowdy pub. She's deep in thought, dressing up in her mother's clothes before a mirror. Mumbles to herself as she becomes a notional glamorous other.

SANDRA: That's not right, She needs to be more ... (*She works on.*) That's more like it, if ye've gorrit, flaunt it.

Hears sound on landing, swivels, freezes.

DAD'S VOICE: You asleep, girl?

SANDRA: (*Sleepy.*) Yes, dad.

All clear. She clips on bits of Ratners' here and there, poses this way, that. Hunts for something. Comes up with a red garter, puts it on, begins reworking cheekbones, eyes. Pouts, sticks her bum out in the tight dress: Marilyn. Fits a cigarette butt into a long plastic holder, checks for danger below, lights it; soignée.

What d'ye think, Mum?

She stares at herself for a long time in silence. Air slowly leaves her; form and face crumple. She removes the wig, revealing her spiked mouse beneath. Picks up the lipstick again. Draws a raw vertical slash down her face: forehead, nose, mouth, chin. Stares on. The light shrinks to the face.

Bring up: Daisy, night, self-chained by the wrist to flower-decked MOD wire fence, in People's Right to Work campaign T-shirt, jeans and Docs, a No to Cruise placard propped beside her. Women call each other along the perimeter, locating, encouraging, supporting. Sirens, car, men's voices, MOD police boots on gravel. A searchlight up, scanning fence. It picks up Daisy. She's scared, firm.

DAISY: (*Calling*) Mum. You OK? (*Indistinct reply.*) Yeah sure, I'm fine.

Men's voices, raised. Sounds of boots on the trot. The lights shrink down to her face. Sound of doorknocker. Cut light. Bring up:

GURVINDER: Good morning, madam. I'm doing a survey on behalf of the local council regarding house contents insurance ... (*Door closes, he swivels into follow-spot to face out, mike in hand, to laughter from working men's club audience*) ... Ye've gorra laugh, 'aven't ye ... Anyone 'ere got a job? (*Someone puts his hand up.*) Mine's a pint. I'm down the dole office, right, the

Black Hole, bottom of Eastgate, run by really lovely people. I reach the counter, this clerk says, Oh Christ not another bloody nigger, I says, I beg your pardon! He leans forward, takes another look, he says I'm sorry, Paki, I said, I should think so too. Guy next to me's on crutches, one leg, he's complainin' he's had his disability allowance cut, the clerk says he can't help, there's too much dependency, he says, people've gotta learn to stand on their own two feet ... I thought, that's a good idea, I'll go out and sell what I don't need ... So I sold all me pockets ... Anyroad, walkin' 'ome, mindin' me own business ...

The follow-spot dies. Flames begin to burn out the image of Thatcher. Bring up: sounds of inner city riots: burning buildings, voices at full pitch, the pop and smash of petrol bombs.

Something lands at Gurvinder's feet, he stoops to pick it up, it's a milk bottle, half-filled with petrol, the top stuffed with a charred rag. A sharp siren close by, cars screech in, doors slam, hurled voices, boots at the double. Gurvinder backs away, searches for escape: nowhere to run.

Fast cut to black.

Visits Room, Borstal, packed with visitors. Tom sits at a table, throwing covert glances around him as he waits. A door's unlocked, instruction issued, door locked again.

Gurvinder appears, uniform, shaven head, a still healing slash, ear to mouth, down the side of his face.

GURVINDER: (*Sitting; contained; scarcely there*) Hey up, Tom.

TOM: (*Dealing with the face.*) How're you doing?

GURVINDER: OK.

Laughter from nearby table. Tom takes a look, returns his eyes to the damaged face.

TOM: So what happened?

GURVINDER: This? (*Face*) Or this? (*Place*)

TOM: Both. I've been in London doing job interviews, Hester called me ...

GURVINDER: Yeah, she's bin out t'see us a coupla times, good lass ...

TOM: She said something about arson ...

GURVINDER: Yeah. Night o' the Chapeltown riots, two cops swore on a bible they saw me throwin' petrol bombs ... (*Fingers the cut.*) This was a welcoming present from a couple of NFers, Stanley knife, just after I got 'ere ... Think it suits?

TOM: Christ. This is ... Did you report it?

GURVINDER: (*A dry laugh*) Oh sure. (*Sounds of a woman sobbing. Gurvinder flicks a look. More laughter, nearby table. Tom studies the new Gurvinder.*) D'ye get the job?

TOM: (*Uncertain*) Erm. Matter of fact, I did, yes.

GURVINDER: Good.

TOM: It's … erm … abroad. Working for the British Council.

GURVINDER: What's that?

TOM: It's to … promote the idea of Britain in other countries …

GURVINDER: Oh.

TOM: It's just for a year. Before I go up to university or whatever …

GURVINDER: Oh. (*Silence.*) I thought your dad had ye down for the Army or someat.

TOM: My dad's abroad, overseas tour. I'll deal with that when I have to. It's just for a year or so …

GURVINDER: Right.

TOM: Listen, Mona asked me to tell you she's planning a visit next month. Sandra might come with her

GURVINDER: That'll be nice.

TOM: Wayne I haven't seen. (*Pause*) Or Daisy. She got her A levels.

GURVINDER: Did she?

TOM: When d'you get out?

GURVINDER: Christmas.

TOM: Will you be all right?

GURVINDER: Oh yeah.

TOM: I left a package of stuff for you at the gate, bits and bobs …

GURVINDER: Ta.

TOM: If there's anything else …

GURVINDER: I don't think so. (*Pause. Tom glances at his watch.*) Time is it?

TOM: Quarter to four.

GURVINDER: Is it? (*Pause.*) So.

TOM: Yeah. (*Pause.*)

GURVINDER: Eh, guess what?

TOM: What?

GURVINDER: In the van comin', guess what I saw through the window?

TOM: What?

GURVINDER: God's Armchair, five miles.

TOM: Right. Gotscam Chairs ...

GURVINDER: Yeah.

TOM: Ha.

GURVINDER: Aye. We will do it. When we need to. (*A voice lifts, is shushed to stillness. Eventually*) Where ye gonna be workin?

TOM: (*Refocussing*) ... Jerusalem.

Long pause. Tom scans the Sikh's blank-eyed face.

Bleed in:

INSTRUCTOR'S VOICE: Punch, kick, punch. Punch, punch, kick, punch ...

Slow fade to black.

Bring up: mug-shot image of Peter Sutcliffe.

Bring up: Hester, judo gear, at Tai-Kwando class. The Instructor calls out small patterns, the class perform them (sound effects).

INSTRUCTOR: (*Finally*) ... Punch, punch, kick, kick, punch, punch. Rest.

Hester stands, draws breath, moves to neutral space, bows to instructor. Fade Ripper image, bring up black gospel singing, a capella opening.

Bring up: Image of black Christ on the cross.

Hester steps into the singing, joins it, swinging and clapping with the rest as the song gathers momentum.

The singing returns to a capella; underpins what follows on the fade.

HESTER: (*Jamaican*) I speak for myself, seen? I don't know about anybody else. But I don't know how to be British, God knows I try and try, but it's not easy and nobody helps. Me nah complain – I state the fact. Here is where I'm born, here is where I live, here is where I learn, here is where I work, here is where I pay my taxes and National Insurance, here is where I get my A levels at night school, here is where I study accountancy ditto, here is where I'm just another black bastard scrounging on the great white British state ... But make no mistake, we Jamaican women strong, we got a sisterhood all we own, we nah go nowhere but forward and we all go do it together, mek the men them shake them locks and sing of Abyssinia, we ah go do the work and make the progress, watch we ... (*Received Standard English*) You see how difficult it is? In Jamaica, no matter how many sentences you start with an 'I' you always fetch up with a 'We'. Maybe it was the same here once, I don't know. But I try. I try to keep to I. I am. I do. I will. I want, I have. I own, I hope. (*Jamaican again.*) But you know, it's a poor tongue you teach we. And a poor tongue pauperizes its people. But see it deh. Peace.

She fades.

Bring up: image of Thatcher.

Bring up: Strobe light image:

LASSIE FAIR

SAUNA

MASSAGE

USUAL FACILITIES

Bring up: Mona washes her hands in cubicle, dries them, presses her buzzer. She wears underwear under a short medical-looking white nylon coat.

MONA: (*Out*) ... Be with you in a minute. (*Turns to deal with arriving client.*) Massage is it, sir? Just lie down, if you would, there we are ... (*Pours oil on her hands.*) Right, just relax, that's it ... (*Begins.*) ... I'm sorry? A menu, yes, I do, what would you like ... ? Well, one hand £10, two hands 15, leather glove 20, topless add 10, tit sandwich 30 ... No, I don't do that, unhunh, no, you have the list ... 20? Fine. No, ye pay now. That's right. (*She pockets the money, puts on a leather glove.*) Ye wanna turn over, that's it ... (*She climbs up on the table, straddles him, sits on his chest, her back to him, facing out. Begins.*) My, look at that, who's a hungry boy then. (*Out, as she does the business.*) What d'ye think? Great, eh? Well, let me tell ye, where I come from it's all 'ands to the pump, if ye'll pardon the expression. All right, first thing, me dad's job goes up in smoke, he's on the dole for the first time since he got here, starts drinkin', can't 'andle it ... Me brother, right? Steward on the cross-channel boats, gets sent out t'Falklands, does what 'e 'as ter, comes back, two weeks later no job, puff ... Me mum? Kitchens. General Infirmary, right? Fifteen years, come hail or come shine. She's off work, angina, she gets a letter tellin' 'er the kitchens've bin contracted out, she can apply for 'er old job with the new lot, but it's fifteen quid less an' more hours ... (*To the punter, calm, over her shoulder.*) Don't do that, all right? (*Goes on with the business.*) Then this nationality law thing they bring in, suddenly everyone's wonderin' if they've a right to be 'ere, I was born in fuckin' *Sheffield*, even *I'm* askin', right? I mean ... I took two hundred quid nearly last week. Someone's gotta pay the bills ... (*She jerks backwards as the client comes, still takes some of it on her torso.*) There you go. Very nice ... (*She dismounts, hands him towel, wipes herself with another, peels the glove, presses her buzzer. To client*) ... Sorry, I'd like to, downstairs don't like us chattin' when there's a queue. Thank you. Come again. (*Turns out again, washing hands.*) Still, she got back in, didn't she? So she must be good for someone, right? (*Thinks, shakes her head.*) You know someat? I find that really scary ... (*Turns to new client.*) Massage is it, sir? Just lie down if you would, that's it.

The cubicle slowly fades, Mona with it, The Thatcher image endures.

Bring in:

THATCHER'S VOICE: (*Echoic, over.*) In the last four years, Britain has recovered her confidence and self-respect. We have regained the regard and admiration of other nations. We are seen today as a people with integrity, resolve and the will to succeed ...

A sudden downspot lights a large man in Special Response Unit gear, long perspex shield, long baton, helmet, visor, boots. He stands motionless, ready to move.

Instructor's voice (outdoor acoustic, some distance away) calls the Advance.

The man, in sync with three dozen or so others on the gravel training ground, takes a ritual step forward, bangs shield with baton. Another call, another identical step forward, until he arrives, large and menacing, front of stage.

Another call from the Instructor, the men begin rhythmic banging, batons on shields, voicing victory sounds, yips and hollers.

A call to stand down, the man relaxes, removes helmet and visor, laughing and joshing with his mates. It's Wayne.

Bring up: The Clash: 'London Calling'. Wayne slowly fades.

Bring up: Phonographique, city centre club, throbbing to Strummer. A mirrored post throws light across the dancers. The four women out there, dancing it up. Daisy wears jeans, good boots, man's straw hat, 'Coal not Dole' T-shirt; Mona wears short white mini, gold rings and chains; Hester has a mans jacket, cord tie and collar, trousers, cuban heels; Sandra is full Goth, white face, black spiked hair, black eye make-up, purple lipstick, chains and crosses.

They fade.

Bring up: Michael Jackson: 'Thriller'.

Bring up: downstairs urinal, the music above now perspectived. Wayne, Tom and Gurvinder stand side by side pissing. Gurvinder wears black leather blouson, thick gold necklace, rings, Armani jeans, baseball shoes; Tom's in lightweight suit, a black and white kuffiah around his neck; Wayne wears pale slacks and navy blue gold-button blazer, shirt and tie, a police social club badge sewn on the top pocket.

WAYNE: (*Eventually; sodden*) ... Oh God, I'm fucked.

GURVINDER: Ye will be, come tomorrer, eh, honeymoon boy?

WAYNE: 'Er? Forget it, she's four month pregnant, she don't wan' it and I don't fancy it ... No, I mean that last pint's done my 'ead in ... Musta bin off.

TOM: (*Deadpan*) Couldn't have been the three Johnny Walkers you poured in it, could it?

Wayne gives him a leaden look.

GURVINDER: (*Climbing stairs to landing payphone*) Up the spout, eh? Got it.

WAYNE: (*Looking for him*) Whaddya think, ye twat? 'S only fuckin' reason I'm marryin' 'er ...

TOM: Does she know that?

Wayne looks at him, uncomprehending.

WAYNE: I don't bloody know, do I?

TOM: Just asking.

Wayne zips up, backs out of his stall, Gurvinder's on the phone ordering something.

GURVINDER: ... That's right, the Nouveau, nine o'clock, Richards. Yeah ... and it'll be Miss Patterson, right? And you've got the message ... Ta ...

WAYNE: This is my third stag night this week. Come on; I've 'ad enougha this place... where we goin' next ... ?

GURVINDER: (*Checking Rolex*) Hang on, Duke. We can't leave just yet, got someat lined up for ye ...

WAYNE: Oh aye? What's that, ye sly bastard? Hope it's a tart ...

GURVINDER: No fishin', 's a surprise.

TOM: Where've *they* gone, by the way?

WAYNE: (*Staring at him*) What is that, anyway?

TOM: (*Checking Wayne's eyeline*) It's a kuffiah.

WAYNE: Bit puffy, innit? (*To Gurvinder*) You're not thinkin' o' comin' to t'Registry tomorrow in your dad's skirt, are ye ... ?

He laughs. He takes himself in in the mirror, begins exaggerated efforts to smarten himself up.

TOM: The women, Wayne.

WAYNE: (*Focussing*) They've gone to the bloody Phonographique, haven't they.

Bring up: Siouxsie and the Banshees. Urinal fades.

Bring up: Phonographique, bar, Daisy and Sandra sit on stools facing out, their backs to the bar counter, surveying the dance scene in the adjoining room.

Hester looms downstage, jacket and shirt discarded, dancing with style in a thin wool crop top.

DAISY: God, Hester's great, isn't she.

SANDRA: Solid. I always wanted to be like her, you know, I don't mean ... black, I mean solid.

She dumps a couple of pills down her throat, chases them with bottled Pils. Daisy watches.

SANDRA: Ye want?

DAISY: What are they?

SANDRA: Speed. Get you up.

DAISY: I'm fine.

SANDRA: I'm really glad you could come, Daise.

DAISY: Me too, man. You OK?

SANDRA: How d'ye mean?

DAISY: It's what you want … ?

SANDRA: Yeah. Dunt everyone?

Daisy laughs, orders more Pils, Mona arrives, coat on.

SANDRA: Oh no, what'd they say, flower?

MONA: Gotta go, job on. I'll see ye back there later, and don't forget the time, we said we'd get fish suppers in for t'lads …

SANDRA: 'S all right, said I'd show 'em me dress before *he* gets back …

MONA: Yeah, well I've gotta show somebody mine in 'alf an hour, I 'aven't even put it on, I'd best get me skates on … Where's Miss Goodness?

DAISY: (*Indicating*) Doin' her stuff. What d'ye think? Great, eh?

Mona stares at her sister.

MONA: If ye like Meccano, (*To Sandra.*) Tell 'er I 'ad t'see a man about a dog. If she notices …

A look between the two. Sandra kisses her cheek. Mona leaves. The music surges, cuts. Takes up again: Sisters of Mercy.

Hester cuts out, walks to the bar, sinks her large orange juice.

DAISY: Where d'ya learn to dance like that, Hes?

HESTER: 'S in the genes. Didn't ye hear? We got rhythm …

DAISY: (*Laughing*) Come here, bitch … (*She takes her in her arms, kisses and hugs her off her feet.*) I'm really glad you came, lovely.

SANDRA: Me too.

HESTER: That makes three of us. But I don't think it gets our Mona's vote … (*Looking.*) She still phoning?

SANDRA: No, she's 'ad to go, she'll see us back at her place, she said she was on call tonight … (*Hester frowns a question.*) … Pizza Palace. Deliveries.

DAISY: Who was that woman you danced with … ? Tall, big eyes …

HESTER: Dolly Wardle. She was in 5G …

SANDRA: Was that Doris Wardle? Bugger me, I thought it were a dyke in on t'wrong night ... Dyke Night's Thursdays ...

Pause.

DAISY: ... Don't look unless you're interested, sweetie, but there's a guy making signals at you over there ...

SANDRA: (*Swinging at once to look.*) Oh God, it's Geoffrey Marsden. I owe him fifty quid ... I'd better go. I'll be back. I hope.

She moves off. They sit to watch her. Make giggly signals to her, as she talks and poses.

DAISY: Who'd have thought it?

HESTER: What?

DAISY: Sandra a Goth.

HESTER: Oh. Right.

A beat or two. They !augh, ridiculously, spilling slightly onto each other on their stools.

DAISY: And Tom's back.

HESTER: Yes.

DAISY: Be lovely to see him. And Girlie. San said he's been in Manchester ...

HESTER: Yeah. His folks threw him out, after the Borstal thing.

DAISY: Oh God, really?

SANDRA: (*Arriving*) Is my bag there? (*Finds it.*) I've just got to nip outside a minute, don't go away ...

DAISY: D'you need anything?

SANDRA: Get us a snakebite, will ye ... ?

DAISY: ?

SANDRA: Cider and lager... I'll definitely be in need o' someat after this ...

She leaves. They watch her go.

DAISY: Oh dear. I hope she's not going to do anything *very* foolish.

HESTER: Sandra? No no. Not in her nature. Want to dance?

A moment. They laugh again. Move off onto the floor. Dance.

They fade. Nouveau, bar. The men sit at a table, watching the scene.

WAYNE: ... I fuckin' love it, boy. I fuckin' love it. I tell you, it's not like a job, it's more like a vocation ...

GURVINDER: What, like a holiday ... ?

WAYNE: V*o*-cation, twat. (*Gurvinder winks at Tom.*) S'like, S'like bein' a priest or a doctor or a ...

TOM: Estate agent.

WAYNE: Aye, that kinda thing. Ye know, ye walk down the street, people look at you different, automatically give way ... Finest company of men you'd find anywhere in the land, nothin's too much for a brother officer. Like family, it is. God, look at that pillock there wi' the fuckin' 'air, did ye ever see anythin' like it in your life ... ? (*Sups his lager.*) Bein' in the force, you know what it's like? It's like playin' for Wales.

GURVINDER: (*Deadpan*) Wow, that good, eh?

WAYNE: That good.

Tom looks at his watch. Gurvinder gestures to hang on.

GURVINDER: How about the women, Duke?

WAYNE: 'Opeless, boy. Can't do the job. Not up to it. Man's work. Good for only one thing, are the women ...

TOM: What's that, Duke?

WAYNE: You 'avin' me on?

TOM: How'd you mean?

Wayne turns to see who's called him, waves.

WAYNE: Ey up. Mark, 'ow's it goin' ... ? (*Watches him move off, waves.*) There's one, salt o' the earth, shoulder to shoulder at Orgreave we were, me an' Mark, oh aye. You don't forget stuff like that ... (*He dwells on the memory, begins cackling with the pleasure of it.*) Fuckin' Orgreave. Oh boy. I need another piss. When's that bloody surprise comin', our kid, I'm gettin' itchy ...

GURVINDER: All in good time. What're ye having?

WAYNE: Pint.

He lumbers away. Tom watches him go. Looks back at Gurvinder.

TOM: He's out of his tree, right?

GURVINDER: How d'ye mean?

They laugh. Gurvinder strokes the tight bristles of his head, fingers the face.

GURVINDER: What d'ye think to it?

TOM: Yeah. Great job.

GURVINDER: Two 'n' half grandsworth.

TOM: On the Health?

GURVINDER: Where've *you* bin? Cash.

TOM: How did you find it?

GURVINDER: I found it. Nuff said.

TOM: So what is it you do?

GURVINDER: This 'n' that. Whatever comes along.

TOM: I thought you wanted to do stand-up ...

GURVINDER: Did that. Moved on. What about you, how was wheresitsname ... ?

TOM: Jerusalem.

GURVINDER: Right.

TOM: Extraordinary.

Silence.

GURVINDER: What? Y'ad a good time?

TOM: Loved it. Loved it.

GURVINDER: Yeah?

Silence.

WOMAN'S VOICE: (*Off*) Telegram for Mr Richards ...

GURVINDER: (*Calling off*) Duke, over 'ere. Surprise time.

Wayne shambles back on.

WOMAN'S VOICE: (*Off*) Telegram for Mr Richards, Mr Richards ...

GURVINDER: (*Calling*) He's 'ere.

Mona appears, in abbreviated version of WPC costume, plus stockings, suspenders, boots. Gurvinder, huge grin, feeds her on with pointed finger to Wayne. She takes him in. Doesn't find it funny. Tom stands, frowns, not party. The buzz of the room has stilled a little as nearby people ritually watch for the kissogram to unfold.

WAYNE: Fuck me, Mona Patterson, as I give a heave ...

MONA: This your idea of a joke, Girlie?

GURVINDER: Aught for a laugh, kid, you know me.

She looks at Tom, who shakes his head.

WAYNE: Come on then, cariad, show us yer kecks ...

Mona takes out her greetingsgram and a pair of toy handcuffs.

MONA: 'I come to wish you all the best.
                         Tomorrow is your Marriage Test
                         And so that Sandra gets some rest
                         I hereby place you under arrest.'

(*She steps forward, snaps a cuff on Wayne's wrist, the other onto the crossbar of his stool. Laughter, applause from the encircling crowd, as Mona holds up the key.*) Anyone want it?

She hurls it into the crowd. Leaves.

WAYNE: Hey. Hey. Ye pillock, what game on … ?

He tries to get up, stumbles, falls over the stool. Thrashes around like a fish in sand. Sound dies.

Bring up: BBC 9 o'clock News *intro, music. Lights cut abruptly. Fast plunge up to: Daisy, crosslegged on floor, face lit by TV, builds a joint in the flickering gleam of the screen.*

NEWSCASTER: (*Calm, measured*) In the last hour …

He delivers a three-minute headline history of the last five years: tax cuts, unemployment, recession, riots, famine, disaster, privatization, deregulation, growing wealth and poverty, homelessness, urban decay, war, AIDS, law and order, ecology, family values, crime … A relentless misericordia, seeding the future, ends of sentences blurring into beginnings, the whole unrelentingly punctuated by reports of the trivial, the frivolous and the mundane (i.e. the Good News). It ends on the September '84 day in question, with news of new hopes of a settlement of the six-month-old Miners' Strike. The last headline begins to fade. Daisy lights the joint, a WC flushes, lights up on the room, TV out, low hi-fi up.

Hester in from toilet. Joins Daisy. Declines joint.

HESTER: God, they're going to be all night in there.

DAISY: (*Calling*) Hey, come on, people, we're waiting for the show here.

MONA: (*Off, calling*) Hold your horses, it's got to be right, right?

Daisy crawls forward to turn up the music a fraction. Pulls a face as she recognises Joan Armatrading.

DAISY: Who put this on?

HESTER: I did.

DAISY: Joan Armatrading did a *Showbiz for Thatcher* concert.

HESTER: Doesn't make her a bad singer.

DAISY: Come on, she *voted* for the bugger …

HESTER: I know. A lot of us did.

DAISY: Get outa here. (*Stares at her.*) You pulling my plonker?

HESTER: (*Giggling*) Maybe. (*Daisy grabs her, pushes her down, begins tickling her. Ecstasy*) Oh no, oh don't, don't do that …

They roll around on the floor, end up with Daisy kneeling astride the pinned Hester.

DAISY: Come on, I want to know, did you or didn't you … I'll not let you up.

Mona in, looking for something.

MONA: … I 'ad some pins, somewhere … (*Takes them in as she swoops on the discarded joint.*) Hey, you two. Who put this on?

DAISY: Your sister,

MONA: Right. (*Takes her pins. Leaving.*) Nearly there, ladies.

She's gone. Daisy looks down at Hester's face, stands, legs astride her.

DAISY: You know something? (*Hester shakes her head.*) I could really fancy you.

HESTER: (*Eventually.*) Yeah? What? Are you. A … ?

DAISY: Uhunh. I'm overwhelmingly men. You?

Hester gets to her feet, uncertain, dealing with stuff.

HESTER: (*Soft*) Get outa here. You having me on?

DAISY: (*Laughing suddenly*) Maybe.

Daisy laughs on. Hester eventually joins her, but mutedly. Mona in, beating an African drum.

MONA: Deda. Right. Ladies and gentlemen, please raise your glasses and be upstanding for … The Bride, right?

Sandra enters on cue, weirdly wonderful in full length hand-made black velvet dress with half-bustle, bows and matching accessories. They stare at her, stunned.

DAISY: (*Coming to*) Wow.

HESTER: Ditto.

MONA: Dunt she look great?

SANDRA: Do you like it?

DAISY: It's

HESTER: Wonderful.

SANDRA: I made it myself.

HESTER: 'S brilliant.

MONA: I did the bows.

DAISY: What does Wayne …

SANDRA: Hasn't seen it. He'll have to wait till tomorrer.

MONA: Don't want bad luck, right?

DAISY: Right.

SANDRA: (*Speed and love in difficult alliance.*) Listen. While we're here. I wanta, I'm really glad you could all, because you're my best friends in all the world and it means a lot to me and because you are my best friends I'm goin' to let you into a secret, well, two secrets really, the first bein' I'm pregnant. I told 'em both on the same day, me dad threw me out and Wayne said 'e'd marry me, two birds with one stone, an' the second bein' I 'ad me fingers crossed all the time 'cos I'm not pregnant at all an' I wanted you to be the first to know ... (*She smiles, shy, radiant. The three hug and kiss her in turn.*) I'm so happy. Aiee. (*She winces as Daisy, last, squeezes her upper arms.*) 'S all right, 's just a bit sore ... (*The three focus on the heavy bruising on her pale upper arm*) ... I musta bumped into a door or somethin' ...

A clatter on the stairs, Wayne's voice singing 'Fish and Chips' to the tune of 'Here We Go'.

MONA: Goon squad's back, let's be havin' you, San.

She ushers her back into the bedroom.

DAISY: Bumped into a door?

HESTER: Out of the frying pan ...

Another huge clatter, Wayne curses, Tom and Gurvinder struggle in with Wayne supported between them, the toy cuffs dangling from a wrist.

GURVINDER: Ladies and gentlemen ... pray silence for the Groom.

They stand him carefully up. Wayne sways, focusses, loses it.

WAYNE: (*Weird Orville*) I wish I could fly right up to the sky, I wish I could fly. But I can't ...

GURVINDER: Come on, old son, we'll get your fish 'n' chips ...

WAYNE: ... Where's my lovely lady then, my wife-to-be, where's my Sandra gone, are you there mam, dad's 'ome, dada's 'ome, my love ...

He stumbles across the room and exits for the bedroom, ignoring the women's attempts to dissuade him.

GURVINDER: Hey. Look at these two, then.

TOM: Ahunh.

GURVINDER: Don't fancy yours.

DAISY: (*Grinning*) Piss off. Come here.

A crash, a shriek, moans from the bedroom.

MONA: (*Lifting*) Wayne! WAYNE! Stop it. Jesus Christ ...

A heavy heaving sound, Sandra calls out, a long tortured yowl. Mona tries to comfort her.

HESTER: (*Calling*) Need any help in there?

MONA: (*Off*) No. It's under control.

DAISY: Listen. Somebody should tell them this is a bad idea.

GURVINDER: Good old Daisy.

DAISY: Girlie, I'm serious ...

Tom begins to giggle, the booze hitting him suddenly.

HESTER: What?

TOM: Nothing. I'm supposed to be Best Man, what the hell am I going to *say*? (*He sits on the floor, gazes up at the others.*) It's hardly a marriage made in heaven now is it? Or Devon, as my grandmother used to say. My deaf grandmother ...

GURVINDER: I'll feed ye a few jokes, son, ye'll be fine. (*Seeing Mona arrive.*) D'ye get the chips in, petal?

Mona ignores him, pours herself a glass of wine, lights a cigarette.

DAISY: What?

MONA: (*Sitting back*) Oh God, I don't know. Nothin's ever. Right in this world.

Silence.

GURVINDER: Are they in the oven?

MONA: He walks in, right? She's just took her dress off, he spews up all over it ... She's heartbroke. He's fast asleep.

Silence.

GURVINDER: Have ye got any bread, I could murder a chip butty?

DAISY: Oh fuck.

HESTER: All right, so we'll clean it up, what's the problem?

MONA: It's not right. 'S just not right.

DAISY: If I'm her friend I should tell her.

MONA: Tell her what?

DAISY: It's a bad idea. Marrying Wayne.

MONA: Gerroff with ye. She's nuts about 'im.

DAISY: They're wrecks, Mona, both of 'em.

MONA: Who isn't? Nothin' t'do with it.

Silence. Gurvinder makes a discreet rumbling noise behind his hand.

GURVINDER: 'Scuse me. That's my stomach, does that when I'm hungry ...

MONA: (*Standing, glass in hand*) Right, who wants?

All hands go up, She makes to leave.

GURVINDER: (*Chuckling*) Eh, you shoulda seen your face down there at the club, our Mona … Made Wayne's evenin', did that … (*Leans forward to tell the story.*) Ask Tom, he'll tell ye …

Mona's reached the wine bottle behind Gurvinder. Fills her glass as he rattles on. Slowly pours it over his head. He blinks, splutters, astonished.

MONA: (*To group*) Fish 'n' chips?

Lights out.

Music: bring up: the room, the seven, sitting or lying around it, each in separate spots. Wayne lies on his face in the centre of the floor, contributes little beyond the occasional groan.

SANDRA: Stupid Sandra. Poor old Sandra. Can't help being stupid, that's the way she was born. A victim. A born victim. See it in their eyes, I don't have to look, Daisy, Hester, even Mona. How can they understand? I love me dad. Yes, he's always knocked us around, me mam too 'fore she went to Nottingham, so what, 's how men are, the one's I know anyway. Someat, someat makes men so angry, I don't know what it is, is it me, is it the world? I haven't a clue. Wayne? Most 'o the time he's like a big baby, needs mothering, that's all. That's all right. I quite enjoy it. He's gonna buy us a house, the money he earns, specially this year wi' the strike 'n' all. My own house. My own house …

HESTER: … I go into the vault to reset the timers, he follows me, every morning …

SANDRA: I've planned every room. Every one. Furniture. Fabrics. Walls …

Her light goes out.

HESTER: … This is the Assistant Bank Manager we're talking about. Sometimes he'll stand really close, behind me in the vault, I'm working, he's breathing through his nose, sorta smelling me. Then he'll go and stand in one of the bays where he thinks I can't see him and he'll watch me and there'll be this moaning, (*Wayne moans*) low funny sounds coming from him, like a little animal trapped, he thinks I can't see him, his hand's deep in his pocket, deep … I mean, this is nine o'clock in the morning, for God's sake …

DAISY: Nobody ever grows up nowadays. It's like a collective arrested development …

HESTER: … I'm this thing. I'm this … rubbing post thing he can't quite reach …

DAISY: I have this dream. We're on a cliff, a rock, hundreds of feet up, waiting for something …

HESTER: Respect.

TOM: Respect?

HESTER: There's no respect there. I'm this … Every morning. In the vault.   Thing …

Her light goes out.

DAISY: ... It's night. And we're all in kids' clothes, waiting for something, the bell, the teacher, I don't know. Holding hands, waiting ...

MONA: Waitin', right.

Wayne moans again.

DAISY: And then. The sun rises. And I wake up. But only in the dream. I look at the others and they're still asleep, eyes open, but. Sleeping. Arrested. (*Wayne stirs, lifts his head, stares out, lost, returns to oblivion.*) Nothing signifies any longer. Our eyes never close, we see everything, but nothing ever means. Menu-time. The post-modernist rules OK. In a land where everything is something and nothing is anything. Constructed innocence. True false rich poor first third winner loser now never me all fuck wank pick choose be do ... Menu-time.

GURVINDER: I'm havin' a good time, me ...

DAISY: I do miss my mum, though.

GURVINDER: I'm doin' all right ...

DAISY: Before she left – she couldn't stand it here after Greenham went and ... (*Long pause*) ... yeah, and her mum was ill she left me this note, card, she'd copied out something her mother had written her years back when she was coming here ... (*In Hebrew, then English*) 'Your life is the only truth you have. And the only truth you need.' Oh God, my grandmother. She came over to visit once when I was little: (*Her voice, in heavily accented English*) 'You gotta look in the pool, Daisy, you understand me, look deep in the pool, what you see? You see things movin' about, you see things floatin', mm? Awright. Truth swims. Lies float, awright. Now you know the difference ...'

TOM: 'But oh, the difference to me.'

DAISY: So my mum went home. To Israel. Yes, I know. And I'm on my way up to Sellafield to do a piece for *The Guardian* on leukaemia-clusters among children living around the plant. And every time I look in the pool I see only me there. Floating.

MONA: Kiting.

DAISY: Not swimming.

MONA: Kiting's what you do like when you've liberated somebody's credit cards, right?

Daisy's light out.

WAYNE: They wanna lock the bastards up 'n' throw away the key ...

MONA: Ask Sandra, she's the expert, she kites for Yorkshire, her ... She's furnished most of her new home by kitin' ...

TOM: ... Just please, just let me say, will you, what I have to say and then ... we can talk.

MONA: I met this bloke, right? I really like 'im. Talkin' to 'im as well. He can talk about all sorts, he can. Anyway, he says what sense is there making a lotta poor people poorer ... I mean, what d'ye prove by it? Ye can do it? We know that. And get away with it? Do it an' get away with it? Forget it. Ye'll pay. One way or another. Scammin', thievin', kitin', smack, sex, porn. Whatever works. Hands up those'd do different. Try it. Whatever's necessary ...

TOM: (*Slowly*) I found something there ... Dad. Mum. That ... Not ... how to ...

MONA: That's what *he* says, anyway. Trouble is, 'e's a fuckin' Rasta. 'E'd want to call the girl baby Ethiopia or someat. Meself, I like Tamsin. What d'ye think to Tamsin? Tamsin Patterson. Tamsin Patterson. Tamsin. (*She pats her stomach: an echo.*) Tamsin? (*Whispers.*) Can you hear me? Tamsin? (*Giggles.*) It's your mum ...

TOM: Dad ...

MONA: (*Whisper, light fading*) It's your mother, Tamsin.

She's gone.

TOM: Oh fuck it, I'll write. I can't tell them, there's no language, they think I'm nuts as it is, gone native or too much sun or something. I start talking about history and ... culture and language and people, they'll send for a doctor. Jesus, I'm not even sure I can explain it to myself, I've had my name down for Sandhurst since I was three. I learnt to salute before I learnt to shake hands. My country, right or wrong. Mean and cunty. Cadet-speak ... (*Takes off his kuffiah.*) The child who gave me this. In Ramallah. On the West Bank. Under military occupation and ruled by decree. In violation of international law. Who lost the whole of his immediate family in the massacre at Sabra el-Shatila, Father, mother, two sisters, four brothers. Where three thousand-odd Palestinians, men, women, kids, babies, ancients, were systematically shot and clubbed to death street by street and shack by shack by Christian militiamen. While the Israeli military sealed the camps up against escape or rescue. Showed me, the boy who gave me this, more affection, more respect, more grace, more of what it is to be human than anything in my life here has ever prepared me for. At home. Or anywhere else ...

WAYNE: (*Unbudging*) Talk about the enemy within! Oh boy!

TOM: Do not teach me what to feel.
      Until you are able first to teach me how.
      When you weave me into your life
      Do not tie off the thread.
      You have travelled the world
      And seen only England there.
      I have been among old souls
      For whom two hundred years is like
      A single day and two thousand miles
      A single stride ...

GURVINDER: Fuck 'em.

TOM: Listen, fuck it. I'll write.

Light out, Gurvinder sits, blowing gently on steepled fingers, lips moving darkly towards meaning.

GURVINDER: Fuck 'em. I'm a king, me. (*He looks around the room.*) Wayne, you awake? Wayne? (*Toes him in the ribs. He moans.*) The package, Wayne, ye got it?

WAYNE: (*Not moving; tapping the blazer he's wearing.*) Jacket.

Gurvinder kneels into Wayne's downlight, feels the blazer, fishes a brown manila envelope from inside pocket, examines contents, opens and studies a typewritten invoice, sorts it into his coat, takes out a roll of fifties, peels eight, folds them, fixes them to the back of Wayne's jacket collar with a paper clip. Sits back in his chair. Broods.

Light out.

Silence.

Wayne slowly struggles up to hands and knees, the notes on his neck. Stares out.

ACT TWO

Wayne, in summer uniform, smokes a fag and chews gum in a corridor. Sounds of trial in nearby courtroom.

WAYNE: (*Out*) You won't want to know about Orgreave Coking Plant, will you? No no. A squeamish people, we are. We act ashamed of some of our greatest triumphs. Well let me tell you, the war was won because the battle of Orgreave was won. And Orgreave was won because the High Command – I don't mean policemen either, I mean Upstairs – because the High Command decided that's where we'd stand and fight, got it? (*Deliberately.*) By any means necessary. That was the words used. Nearly five thousand of us mustered down there, from all over the place, I'd no idea where some of 'em came from, Hampshire, where's Hampshire ...? Two hundred horses, a hundred dogs, four hundred long shields, five hundred short shields, protective gear from visored helmets to steel-cap boots, oh yes, planned and executed with military precision, we 'ad a hundred and fifty paras in unmarked police boiler suits, two buses filled with fuckin' CS gas, that's how serious they were Upstairs ... We were there to beat the shit out of 'em that day an' by God that's what we did. Hey, I watched one o' the mounted boys chase a gang o' pickets into the fuckin' Asda down the village, followed 'em inside ... (*Laughs*) An' the fuckin' Met, oh boy, my mate Mark saw the boys from the Met charging down the High Street smashin' in every car windscreen with an NUM sticker, hundreds of 'em, with a couple o' lads followin' up with a little printed card for the wiper, Mark showed me one: 'Congratulations. You have met the Met.' There's pride, is it. The really comical thing is, the poor bastard pickets 'adn't come for a bundle at all, they thought it was gonna be business as usual, you know, shove an' heave when the lorries moved the coke out an' a bit of a laugh ... Most of 'em were in T-shirts 'n' daps, you know, trainers ... Didn't know what hit 'em. We followed through, too. Oh yes. We had men scourin' the hospitals all night, draggin' the wounded out 'n' bangin' 'em up, we did. An' a brand new charge to throw at the buggers too, them we arrested: riot. Carries a life sentence, see. Exemplary. Upstairs again. Oh yes. (*His name's called. He drops the fag, treads it out.*) We've been months stitchin' this lot up – I didn't write a fuckin' word o' my statement, I don't think anybody did, 's all bin taken care of, see ... (*Points: Upstairs. Grins. His name's called again.*) A riot, eh?

He saunters forward to the witness box. Chews on as he takes the oath.

DEFENCE COUNSEL: (*Off*) ... I appear for the defendant Ian Clayton. Now, Constable Richards, since you have made your Statement to this Court as Arresting Officer all those many months ago – you have a copy of your statement ... ?

WAYNE: Yep.

COUNSEL: (*Off*) ... As I say, since last ... December, when you signed your Statement of Evidence, we have had the good fortune to learn of the existence of a continuous video record of the day's events taken by the Police Authorities themselves. And the court in its wisdom has allowed the defence to have the whole of that recording admitted as evidence in this trial. Now, what I'd like to do, Constable Richards, as I have done with your colleagues from the Assistant Chief Constable down, is to take you through your sworn statement, step by step, in the light of what the objective police record of those same events has to tell us ...

A monitor throws garish light on Wayne's face. He turns a little to stare at it.

COUNSEL: (*Off*) Are you chewing gum, Constable?

WAYNE: I am. (*Takes it out.*) Musta forgot it.

COUNSEL VOICE: (*Off, on the fade*) You'll see, top right corner, the time code. We'll begin at 12 noon, the time at which, according to your statement, the short shields moved out to clear the men on the bridge ...

WAYNE: (*Out again: screen still bright*) Can you imagine? We've got the buggers stitched up fair 'n' square 'n' then we let 'em see a police recording of what actually went *down* ... ? Dear God, what a cock-up eh? ... Dear dear dear ...

Trail car radio news: UN says 19 million Africans face famine; Poll Tax to start in 1990; Water to be privatized; 278 AIDS-related deaths in Britain; hole in the ozone layer above the Arctic ...

Bring up: Gurvinder, lancing down M62 in big car, tapping out number on phone. Radio out as he connects.

GURVINDER: Sidney? Mr K. You got your pad? OK, the six houses in Peckham, yes? Buy 'em, I'll send you the names for the mortgages. Ahunh. No. I think it's right, ye can smell it a mile off ... (*Listens*) Listen, I'm off to Manchester about that other thing ... peashooters, right. (*Laughs*) I'll let you know. There's a market, don't worry. They demand, I supply. I rest my case ...

He laughs, listens a moment, hangs up, drives on.

Bring up: underneath.

MONA: You're not.

SANDRA: I am.

Lights up on the women, both on the phone.

MONA: You're not.

SANDRA: I am.

MONA: 'S amazin'. So am I.

SANDRA: You're not.

MONA: I am.

SANDRA: You're not.

They laugh.

It's not ... ?

MONA: I think so, yeah. Hey, what did Wayne say?

SANDRA: He said: Oh aye? Where've I 'eard that one before?

MONA: (*On the fade*) He didn't? Bastard.

SANDRA: (*On the fade*) He bloody did.

Lights out.

Bring up: Daisy, rehearsing piece to camera from autocue; invisible Make-Up bobs in and out, doing her eyes in breaks.

DAISY: 'Whatever bland reassurances are to come out of the Ministry of Agriculture, the facts are bleak and inescapable: the world's worst nuclear disaster has sent a huge wave of radioactive contamination across the farmlands of North Yorkshire and the cost to the lives of the people who work them will be enormously high'... (*Peers at autocue*) ... Is that it? Where's the link passage for the Kirkstall piece? (*Puts cans on.*) Anyone there? Charles, is Charles there ... ? (*To Make-Up*) Easy with that one, I've an infected follicle ... (*Back to mike again*) Charles, the link to the Kirkstall piece ... it's what? Wait a minute, are you telling me ... Listen, fuck the Head of Local Programmes, fuck ITN, we have a stream in the middle of Leeds registering a bequerel-count of several squillions and you're telling me they don't want it ... ? So it was a CND group took the reading, you think they're less reliable than the Ministry of Agriculture for God's sake? ... So it's out. I see.

Long pause. She stands there a long time dealing with it. Removes the cans. Angles for the make-up again.

Cross fade to Mona, watching TV, swaddled infant asleep at her tit. Neighbours *end titles. She clicks sound off, looks at kid. Gently eases mouth from nipple. Lays kid down to sleep, at her side. Returns to her exercise book and pencil. The kid stirs.*

MONA: (*Jamaican; the first time*) This is for you, all right? When you is old enough to read, like a diary, but not all the days, 'bout all the things that did happen while you was still inside me, seen? Like ahhmm … (*Flicks pages*) … You wahn me read you some eh? Hear dis. 'Friday June 26ᵗʰ. Me did get the results dis morning and you is a girl. I been really happy all day, knowing. What you think of Jojo for a name? Or Marva? Me no sure. I gwahne work extra hard you see so that we can have a chance of being happy together and not down in poverty an' … (*Screws up nose*) Is that how ye spell poverty … ? (*She's not sure, works on it. Phone rings. She picks up. In English.*) Hello. Oh, hello, Bluesie. What? Oh no, I'm feedin' the bab. (*Listens.*) Yeah, an' what does 'e want? Ahunmh. No, it'd need to be twenty. OK, put 'im on. (*She checks the bab. The guy comes through.*) Miss Birch here, I understand you've been a very naughty boy … Well, you'd better tell me about it and then we'll decide what we're going to do with you. Ahunh. Speak up, speak up …

She lays the phone down, gathers the babe, lays her in carrycot. The client burbles on. Fade.

Bring up: effects, a number being dialled.

Bring up: a Flight-Simulator (screen). Tom, in RAF drabs, at game control-panel, landing a plane as he waits for the phone to pick up. Gets engaged signal. Lights up.

Bring up: Gurvinder, car phone, on the road again, speaking with his money manager.

GURVINDER: TSB, I can do twenty thou, British Gas fifty. Thou, twat. I'll get you the names, don't worry, it's a big family … (*Laughs*) No, but I know a guy who does. Sidney, the houses in Streatham, make it eight, I'm tekin' a bundle over in Manchester and I need somewhere to put it … Fine, call me back. (*Phone down. He drives, palming his cropped head with one hand. Phone. Tom's light up as Gurvinder collects it.*) Mr K. Tom, ye bugger, how've ye bin, are ye back … ?

TOM: Yeah, I'm in London. Girl –

GURVINDER: Yeah? What're ye doin'?

TOM: This 'n' that. Thinking of getting into hi-tech … Listen Girlie, I just got off the phone from Hester …

GURVINDER: Haven't seen her in months, how is she …

TOM: … There's bad news, Girlie …

GURVINDER: ... Hang on, Tom, porkers ...

Tom's light out.

Gurvinder pulls into the middle lane, the chasing police Rover whooshes by at 120. He watches them a moment, takes out an imaginary pistol, aims, fire, the gun bucks in his hand, he mouths the sounds of the Rover screaming out of control and careering off the motorway: a chill moment. Returns to call.

... OK, Thomas, you give me the bad news. I'll give ye the good ... (*Listens*) You're kiddin'. Dead? I don't ... I was over there a coupla weeks back ... (*Hears worse*) Oh, fuck, no ... No.

He deals with it in silence, listening on. Lights out.

Bring up: Sandra in down spot, kneeling, blissed out, a baby-bundle in her aims.

SANDRA: (*Singing*)   ... A kiss for the baby
                        The newly born baby
                        A kiss for the baby
                        Now giv'n to the Lady ...

She repeats it, on and on, as if singing a round, bleaching it of meaning. Stops suddenly. Stares at the bundle. Loses interest. Lets it drop from her arms.

I wanted to call him Timothy but Wayne said it 'ad to be Arfon after his dad. I like Timothy, I don't know why. Anyway. Eleven months, I don't think he didn't cry more than two nights, used to break my heart, leave him, let him learn, says Wayne. How can you? How can you? Anyway. I used to wait until Wayne was asleep and then go in and lift him till he stopped. Anyway, this night he just cries and cries, I took him down in the kitchen to give him some pobs, Wayne comes chargin' down an' tells me to put 'im back in his cot an' I won't an' he tries to take 'im from me an' I won't let go an' he just goes crazy, just goes crazy, drags the boy away from me and just throws him. Just throws him. (*Silence.*) Everyone's bin really nice. I've bin stoppin' at Mona's an' Girlie's looked after a lotta things an' I 'ad a really nice card from Hester an' Daisy came an' ... (*Silence.*) I don't really blame Wayne, he'd 'ad a lot on 'is plate they'd just passed 'im over for promotion an' Wales'd lost again ... Four years, they gave him, manslaughter. (*Silence.*) I don't know who I do blame. I don't. (*Sings.*) A kiss for the baby (*Long pause.*) The newly born baby (*Long pause.*) A kiss for the baby.

Slow fade to black.

Bring up: Sounds of breakfast TV spraying headlines for '87; Zeebrugge, King's Cross, October hurricane, Bangladesh floods, Black Thursday, Enniskillen, end of Wapping, Hungerford, ten million HIV-positive world-wide, 90 per cent ozone layer depletion over Antarctica.

Bring up: Hester, in spot, at doorway of Mum's bedroom. She's fastening a short Crimplene housecoat over her dove-grey business suit and white silk shirt.

HESTER: ... Now you sleep on, Mama. Doctor'll be here at twelve, no need for you to stir, Hester's home. (*She peers in, smiles at the already dozing mother. Soft.*) That's right. (*Looks out again. Quoting, mother's voice.*) 'When Mona want help, she call Mama. When Mama want help, she call Hester. That's the way it is, child. I know my girls ...' I know my girls, mm? The girls we were, maybe. Not the women we are. Sometimes I ache to tell her. When she says; you got a boyfriend yet, Hester girl? Sure I got a boyfriend, mama, she called Joan, we livin' in sin in Peckham ... It's all right, nobody knows, you're the first to be told. I'm not ready for the world to know my business just yet. Imagine. (*Thinks.*) You know, I wonder sometimes how Mona explained Jojo and ... (*Dwells, blanking the rest out.*) ... the rest. Whatever it is. OK. Let's get this deregulated dream of a day on the road.

Bring up lights, as she moves into the Patterson living room, gathers a plastic basket of washing for the washroom.

MONA: (*Off*) Hi. It's me, mama ... (*Appearing*) Ye there, mama?

Sees Hester. Mona has Jojo's carrycott in her hands. They stare at each other.

HESTER: She's having a lie-in.

MONA: What're you doin' up 'ere?

HESTER: I got a few days off ... (*Mona lays carrycot on sofa, shakes rain from hat. Lays basket down*) ... Drove up last night.

MONA: Ye got a car, have ye? (*Hester nods.*) Is Mum OK?

HESTER: She's just tired. Called me yesterday.

MONA: Why the hell she call you in London, I'm quarter of an hour away?

HESTER: 'When Mama need help, she call Hester ...' You want coffee?

Mona shakes her head. Hester crouches over the cot to take a look at Jojo.

MONA: An' who does Hester call?

HESTER: God, she's grown. (*Stands.*) Hester stands on her own two feet.

MONA: Lucky Hester. I'll look in on Mum ...

HESTER: Don't wake her.

MONA: Look. I've arranged to leave the kid, I'm tekin' Sandra over to Hull to see Wayne ...

HESTER: It's in hand. I'll look after her. (*Mona frowns, uncertain.*) How's she coping? Sandra.

MONA: She's all right. She's waitin' in t'car.

HESTER: You've got a car?

MONA: Some 'opes. Girlie laid it on. (*Hands her the carrier bag.*) That's her grub an' nappies 'n' stuff. I'll just tek a look ...

She leaves for the bedroom. Hester methodically unpacks the bag, checks and organizes the gear: food; nappies; books and toys.

Sandra wanders in. She's pale, pinched, nervy beneath the supinity. Watches a moment, as Hester turns to study the sleeping Jojo.

SANDRA: She's lovely, in't she?

HESTER: (*Seeing her*) Hello, San. How are you?

SANDRA: I'm fine thanks.

Hester hugs her to her. Sandra begins to flake, though not to tears.

HESTER: Oh love, what a nightmare, what a ...

SANDRA: Can't be 'elped. God musta wanted it. We're gonna see Wayne, ye know about ... ?

HESTER: Yes I do.

SANDRA: He's havin' a horrible time, him bein' a copper ... ex ... an' what 'e did, like ... they've 'ad to put 'im in with all the perverts 'n' that.

Silence. She shivers, rubs her arms.

I came in for a wee.

HESTER: (*Indicating*) Help yourself. Mona's in with mum. (*Sandra heads off, returns for her handbag, leaves. Hester makes to go to the bedroom, stops as she becomes aware of Mona and mother in low-toned chat. Removing housecoat*) Mona, don't you tire her now. (*The phone rings. She searches the room for it, unearths it from inside her mother's wicker sewing-basket. Phone*) Hester Patterson ... Hello, beauty ... Of course I'm up, I just couldn't find the phone, mother hates it, she hides the damn thing ... You get my note? Yes. I'm sorry too. No, she's just a bit fragile, she'll be OK ... (*Mona returns to the room. Listens, unseen, to the call, though wholly without guile, stroking the discarded housecoat as she does so. Phone*) ... Three or four days. I've got a business to run ... well, we have. (*Laughs at the response.*) It's true, man. Time, tide and Financial Services wait for no girl ... Hey, don't start talking dirty, it's early morning, I have a child to tend and people all over the flat ... (*Laughter. Answer*) I'm wearing my power suit, that's what I'm wearing ... (*Answer*) Never mind ... (*Straight*) Yeah, you too. Mmm. Mmmmm. Call you later. Yeah.

Phone down. She stands a moment, deep in it, turns, sees Mona.

MONA: Fuck me.

HESTER: What?

MONA: Ye could do that for a livin', ye know that? (*Laughs, a touch brittle.*) I guess ye don't 'ave to.

HESTER: Does anybody?

Silence.

MONA: What's this about you inviting our mum to go 'n' live with ye down south?

HESTER: What's your problem, Mona?

MONA: What d'ye mean?

HESTER: I am not an outsider here, OK? And I don't have to answer to you or anyone else for what I say or don't say to my mother ...

MONA: ... I didn't say ye did ...

HESTER: Don't worry, you're not going to lose your childminder and general factotum, Mum's too daft about Jojo to even consider it ...

MONA: God, you're a stuck-up bitch, though ... With your fucking car and your 'power suit' an' your own fuckin' business, a real little Tory, a real little black Brit, right?

HESTER: What I do is my affair, child ...

MONA: Don't child me, sweetheart ...

HESTER: You need to take a look at yourself one of these days ...

MONA: Oh do I? 'S all comin' out, is it? Come on then, let's have it.

HESTER: Oh, go on about your business, will you. Another time.

MONA: Fine. Anytime's fine by me. (*A short fume of unreleased anger hovers between them. Hester turns to the stack of kid's stuff on the table, needing process.*) D'ye know what to do?

HESTER: Yes, I know what to do.

MONA: Ask mama if ye're stuck. I'd best get off. Sandra'll be ...

HESTER: (*Bathroom*) Sandra's in there.

Silence.

MONA: She's what?

HESTER: Yes, she came in earlier, while you ...

Mona rushes past her. Bangs on bathroom door, off.

MONA: (*Off*) Sandra! Sandra, you all right? Sandra ...

Sounds of lavatory flushing. Sandra wanders back into the room, smiling, blissed out.

SANDRA: I needed a wee ...

MONA: (*Still off.*) Oh God, Sandra, what are you doing to yourself, girl? (*She returns to the room, Sandra's bliss gear in her hands.*) How in God's name are you gonna tell Wayne ye're leavin' 'im wi' this lot inside ye?

SANDRA: I'm fine. I'm fine. Feelin' mmm fine.

MONA: Here, tek your bag, get in the car.

SANDRA: (*Perching*) Tek me home. I don't want to go to Hull. He just makes me depressed.

MONA: Oh San, we've bin thro' all this, love, ye said ye'd tell 'im …

SANDRA: I'll tell 'im. I'll tell 'im. (*She gets up, begins leaving.*) Thanks for your card, Hes. It was very kind.

HESTER: I'll call and see you before I go.

Sandra floats out.

MONA: Why didn't ye tell me she was in there?

HESTER: I didn't *know* … Jesus.

MONA: No. I bet ye didn't. Not your business to, is it? (*She crosses to look at Jojo, adjusts a blanket, rises.*) Feed 'er soon as she wakes, will ye? … Beef 'n' carrot.

She leaves. Hester follows to the window, watches her leave the building for the car.

Mrs Patterson starts to sing in the bedroom; 'How Great Thou Art', low, rhythmic, though the breathing's difficult, Hester listens, still watching. Her hips slowly sway with the song.

HESTER: Not my business. I am. I do. I have. I own. I win. I lose. (*The hips stop.*) My business. How great thou art.

Lights out.

Bring up: Radio One gunge, shot through with pop radio news headlines driving through '88: Salmonella, Lockerbie, Piper Alpha, Clapham junction, GCHQ sackings, Lawson budget [four top tax rates abolished], charges for eye tests, dental treatment, Clause 28 …

Beneath, lifting towards the end, a car-phone beeps out a number, waits for pick-up.

Fade up: Gurvinder, parked, staring intently out at something as he waits, phone to ear.

Radio out. Ringing tone continues.

Bring up: sounds of Dales countryside; a bright day. The phone's answered.

MAN'S VOICE: (*Phone; in Punjabi*) Hello, who's speaking please?

GURVINDER: Dad, it's Gurvinder. (*Silence. In English.*) Can we talk, please … ? I need to talk, Dad …

Receiver goes down. Gurvinder deals with it. Eventually buttons Redial. Ringing tone for some while.

WOMAN'S VOICE: (*Punjabi*) Hello, who is it, please?

Gurvinder bites his lip, unable to speak. She repeats the question twice; he hangs up.

Gurvinder stares out again. Birds sing. He finds he's weeping. Sniffs. Wipes his eyes. Pads out a number.

GURVINDER: (*Phone*) Sidney. Mr K. Mr K. I'm OK, I've got a cold. The houses, Sidney. Sell 'em. No, all of 'em. I smell the end, kid, the rising curve has risen, enough's enough, kill or be killed, winners and losers, there is no alternative, markets maketh man, you hearing me? (*Sniffs*) The Club Opening, Sidney. No, the one in Leeds. I've had an idea. Midsummer Night. June sometime, look in a fuckin' calendar, how would *I* know? And listen, clear your diary for it. I may need you up here hosting, I've other plans for the night. I'll let ye know …

Hangs up. Stares out again, eyes intent on something in the distance. Behind him, the distant shimmering image of Malham Cove slowly registers on the screen.

Lights down. The image and Gurvinder's rapt face persist for some moments. Fade.

Bring up: Exterior flashing neon sign: The Shining Path. *Music: Betty Boo, or worse, from inside, half drowned in the din of the opening night rave.*

Bring up: Daisy, forecourt, speaking on cordless. She wears shorts, trainers, T-shirt with Vote Donald *on the front,* Democracy is a Dead Duck *on the back.*

DAISY: (*Through*) … Hey, Girlie, it's Daisy, what's going on, where's everyone … ? No, I'm outside, waiting. No, I don't want to come in, ye've seen one club opened, ye've seen 'em all … (*To comment from passing peckerhead.*) You never seen legs before, arsehole? Yeah, up yours too. (*Back to phone.*) No, some passing peckerhead. So how long you gonna be? And Tom and Hester's train's when? Ahunh. Ahunh.

Gurvinder appears from club, phone to ear, talking quietly.

He wears shades, lightweight silk suit, Shining Path *pitcher's cap. Fetches up next to her, a couple of strides away.*

… Hang on, you're breaking up, I can't hear a fucking word you're saying …

GURVINDER: Can you hear me? Hello. Hello. (*She angles the phone, eventually sees him.*)

DAISY: You twat.

GURVINDER: (*Pulling her in to him*) Hey, Dais, look at you. You look great, wow, mm.

DAISY: Enough, I came already. What's this, your second million?

GURVINDER: Who's countin'? Shall we go?

DAISY: Go where? What is this Magical Mystery Tour crap?

GURVINDER: First we collect Tom and Hester. After which, in the fullness of time, all will be revealed …

DAISY: No way. I need at least a clue.

GURVINDER: A clue? Ten years.

DAISY: That's a clue?

GURVINDER: Trust me. When did I ever let you down?

DAISY: What, apart from the rave-up down the drift-mine, the balloon trip, the …

GURVINDER: (*Taking her arm*) Ye're growing old, chick. Trust me. First the station, next the world …

Daisy swings a kick at his arse as they leave for the car. Music surges. Segues into Talking Heads: 'We're on the Road to Nowhere'.

Lights out.

Bring up: car sounds, on the move in the dark. [All voices off]

DAISY: A *Bent*ley, Girlie. Gross.

HESTER: Really.

GURVINDER: (*Chuckle*) I know.

Car slowing, feeling its way.

TOM: So where the hell are we?

GURVINDER: Almost there.

HESTER: Almost where?

GURVINDER: Trust me.

TOM: Midsummer madness, Hes.

DAISY: Urgh, A drinks cabinet.

Brake. Silence. Sounds of deep country.

HESTER: What?

Car door.

GURVINDER: Base camp. Let's get the gear …

Car doors.

DAISY: Gear? What gear?

Bring up: Improvised camp-site, moonlit, deep in the country, a canvas awning, picnic table, hampers of food, booze, sleeping rolls, linen basket, lamps slung around the space.

Gurvinder sits crosslegged in the mouth of the awning, checking and setting an old-fashioned alarm clock.

Tom is carrying brushwood; begins lighting the fire he's been preparing. He wears an ancient leather flying jacket, a funky Biggles leather helmet.

TOM: 'S that?

GURVINDER: Just in case.

TOM: Right.

GURVINDER: Be a night to remember, will this,

TOM: I can't say I've forgotten the night of the drift mine. Partying in four feet of flood water with the 1ˢᵗ Squadron Hell's Angels tends to stick in the mind

GURVINDER: Yeah yeah. Ye'll see.

He stands, joins Tom at the fire. Gazes up at the sky. Tom stands, wipes his hands.

TOM: So where are we exactly?

GURVINDER: Close.

They look at each other. Gurvinder's eyes rage in the darkness.

TOM: (*Quiet, drawn*) You're really wired, aren't you?

GURVINDER: Na. You know me. (*He grins*) So how ye bin?

TOM: Fine.

GURVINDER: (*Eyes strong again*) Have ye? (*Tom turns away, uneasy, jabs at the fire.*) Still in ... what was it? hi-tech?

TOM: Yeah. Still in hi-tech.

GURVINDER: So that thing abroad was just er ...

TOM: Filling in, yeah.

Gurvinder crouches at the fire.

GURVINDER: Shame. (*Beats*) You're not *with* Hester, are ye?

TOM: (*Refocussing*) Hester? No. Why?

GURVINDER: I'm thinkin' of asking 'er to marry me.

TOM: What? (*Gurvinder grins, points a teasing finger at him.*) Fuck off.

GURVINDER: Come on, I'ad ye goin', right? 'S right, innit?

TOM: (*Pleased*) Same old Girlie.

Hester and Daisy in, wet from tarn, borrowed swimsuits, towels.

HESTER: (*To Tom*) The man wasn't lying, Tom. He's only laid on a mountain lake ...

DAISY: (*Crouching behind him on his shoulders.*) Come on, Biggles, tell us what you know, what's he up to?

TOM: (*Gurvinder's sounds.*) He's sayin' nowt, 'im.

DAISY: (*Pushing him*) All men together, eh?

TOM: (*Falling, laughing*) It's true, it's true ...

HESTER: Will somebody at least put me out of my misery? Is our Mona coming ...?

GURVINDER: 'S possible.

HESTER: Oh great.

DAISY: How about San?

GURVINDER: San's movin' around. On the road. Took off in spring. She knows, though. I'm in touch.

TOM: What about Wayne, anyone been to visit ... ? (*Hester and Daisy shake heads.*) Me neither ...

GURVINDER: (*Sudden, in the silence*) I 'ave.

They look at him. His eyes burn a little.

TOM: How is he?

GURVINDER: He's missed ye.

HESTER: (*After thought*) I'm sorry, I can't deal with Wayne, not after ...

DAISY: (*Scanning him*) What're you up to, King ... ? You gonna let us in on ... ?

Gurvinder swings suddenly away, scents the air, a night animal.

GURVINDER: (*Fast*) Sh.

They listen. Bleed in sound of distant motor-bike.

DAISY: What? What?

GURVINDER: (*Slow uncoil*) 'S OK, 's on the top road.

DAISY: Jesus, you looked like James Cagney there for a minute ...

GURVINDER: (*Perfect James Stewart*) Wa, tha's the way it is, sweetheart.

HESTER/DAISY: (*As one*) That's James Stewart.

DAISY: (*Lighting joint*) Wanker (*Through held breath.*) Listen, can we at least eat, please? I'm famished ...

GURVINDER: There's some nibbles, salmon mousse 'n' shit.

HESTER: Hey, you froze just then, man. Is any of this illegal, I mean you're not expecting the police or anything? It'd be nice to know.

DAISY: (*Half-hearing*) The cops? Where? (*Gurvinder swings round again to look out at the dark. Sounds of car approaching, slowing, headlamps scoring their space as it stops. Finding tin in her bag*) Oh shit. It's the cops.

Silence. Gurvinder moves forward carefully, eyes on the car. Behind him, Daisy's busy emptying contents of tin into a party bag of crisps, The headlamps suddenly dip, flood back, dip again, die.

GURVINDER: (*Five, flicking fingers*) All right! (*He moves back towards the awning.*)

DAISY: Fuck, That's all my mushrooms gone …

GURVINDER: We don't need 'em, Dais. Trust me.

MONA: (*On the approach*) … I'm in a field full o' cowshit in the middle of nowhere at midnight, right, this better be good, Gurvinder. I've come straight from work for this … (*She struggles in, tight mini, heels, sleeveless white vest and African shawl.*) Thank God, I thought I'd got the wrong mountain for a minute … (*They crowd round, greetings, hugs, sprays of chat, a surge of new energy.*) Hey, guess who picked me up in Girlie's limo? (*To Gurvinder*) Have ye told 'em …? (*Gurvinder shakes his head.*) You'll never guess.

TOM: Nigel Mansell.

MONA: I'm serious.

DAISY: Oh right. Prince Charles, Teddy Kennedy?

MONA: Listen, I'm serious ...

Wayne appears behind her, in blue chauffeur's jacket, peaked cap; stops on the edge of their space.

HESTER: (*Disbelieving*) Wayne?

Mona frowns, follows their eyes, sees him.

WAYNE: (*Uncertain; small*) Hiya. (*Beat.*) Nice to see you all again. (*No one speaks. He looks at the Gladstone bag in his hand, scans the site for signs of Gurvinder.*) Just brought this up for the Chief. I'll not stop if …

MONA: (*Aware of the group*) I don't mind, Wayne.

HESTER: (*Low*) Speak for yourself.

MONA: I do.

Tom gets up, comes towards him.

TOM: How've you been, Duke?

WAYNE: Oh, so so, you know. You?

TOM: Much the same really,

DAISY: Hello, Wayne.

WAYNE: Hiya, Daise.

MONA: I thought 'e were comin' out next month.

WAYNE: No, this.

He looks at Hester. She moves in.

HESTER: I've got a lot of bad feelings towards you, Wayne, sorry. Stuff I've got to deal with …

WAYNE: I know. Me too.

Silence, unease still hovering.

MONA: Oh, this is gonna be fuckin' great, I shoulda gone to me bed …

A high, amplified sound from the awning swivels them upstage. They focus eventually on the ghetto-blaster, through which Gurvinder's original oath in Punjabi is being relayed. Silence, as oath finishes.

TOM: Jesus.

GURVINDER: (*Off; relayed*) Ten years. All friends, all friends. An oath. A pact.

He appears in the opening of the makeshift tent in a version of his classroom Sikh gear, the kirpan sheathed, a trail-mike in hand.

WAYNE: (*Tranced; back there*) Wow. Fuckin' Bruce Lee.

GURVINDER: (*Relay*) God's Armchair.

DAISY: Gotscam Chairs? What about it … ?

He draws the sword points upwards, Their eyes follow, climbing rock to sky.

TOM: God's Armchair. Got it. Ha.

MONA: Hey, hang on, I'm not climbin' that bugger in the dark, not in this skirt I'm not …

GURVINDER: When it's time. We walk up. There's a path.

DAISY: And when's that, pray, O King?

GURVINDER: 4.42, accordin' to t'Evenin' Post. (*Sword again.*) That's east. It's all laid on.

MONA: Wow.

They absorb it. Check reactions.

HESTER: Why?

Screech-owls; silence.

DAISY: Sandra's birthday,

WAYNE: Is it?

TOM: Ratface.

MONA: Yeah.

GURVINDER: (*Small smile, eyes fixed on her*) Because I love you.

HESTER: What?

GURVINDER: Because you are my friend. (*A country clock begins to strike in the distance.*) We have a mountain, a lake, a fire, food, drink …

DAISY: Ganga …

GURVINDER: … And each other.

MONA: (*Soft*) It's never ten years, is it?

GURVINDER: Life is good.

Black.

Bring Up: a fat gold moon. Then, in three pools of half-light:

Tom, sitting; Daisy, prone, torching water beneath on a ledge of rock a foot or two above the tarn; Hester and Gurvinder by the fire, his head in her lap; Wayne upright, his back to the base of the limestone stand; Mona crosslegged on a rock above him.

WAYNE: You know what's ironic? I spent six years breaking the law of the land on a regular basis as a policeman an' I get four years for an accident, there was no intention there, I was drunk and in a foul mood and she was holdin' 'im so tight I thought she'd crush him or something. So I … (*Shakes his head: a cul-de-sac*) When I say a life of total crime I'm merely being factual, you understand, I don't claim anything outa the ordinary, monthly sweeteners, the blind eye, the odd word, a bit of recycling, you know, dope 'n' stuff, beating up on awkward buggers in the cells, bending witnesses, lying in court. Nothing outside the generality of things, I was never a rotten apple … You know it really, but you don't want to know, right? Mm. Anyway. The bubble burst. The lights went out. I thought it'd last forever. Pop (*Beat.*) Click.

Lights cut to half; Tom's and Daisy's up to full. Silence. Daisy stares hard into the torched water, her face wobbled by light. Tom carefully builds and rebuilds a delicate mound of small stones and pebbles.

DAISY: Here's the thing. I've just spent three months living rough with the homeless, OK? Manchester, Liverpool, Glasgow, Birmingham. We've put a mind-crushing film together. I mean … wow … special. Says it all. Only problem is: they won't put the bugger out. Too political. Lacks balance. They've put someone in to re-edit. Put the other point of view. Whatever that is … The poor are always with us? The homeless have only themselves to blame? It's pathetic. We sleepwalk into silence. The four Ms rule, OK. Murdoch, Maxwell, Marmaduke and Margaret. Got it all sewn up. Oh God, I met some beautiful people, too. Beautiful. (*Sudden.*) Fish.

TOM: (*Peering*) Where?

DAISY: (*Frowning*) Gone.

Lights to half; Hester's and Gurvinder's to full.

HESTER: (*Stroking his head*) For myself I give you no argument, they've been good years, you know, I buckled down when I left school, played by the rules, winners and losers, good pickings, clean nose, capital city, my own company at twenty-five. Miss Enterprise Culture. I won't say I've ever really been taken in by it all, I'm black and a woman and that'll always give them problems, you know ... But there were times I could even imagine myself being One of Us, my personal preferences a question of choice, not different from a car or a meal or a flat ...Then, out of the blue, last year, they come up with this Clause 28 and ... they meant it. They meant me. They meant me. So then I see I'm not One of Us at all. Just 'one of them'. (*Laughs.*) Clears the head. Oh yes.

GURVINDER: So. Is that a yes or a no?

HESTER: Come on, Gurvinder, I can smell your teases a mile off ...

GURVINDER: I want to marry you. Yes or no?

HESTER: Gurvinder, I just told you, Clause 28, the Bill against Gays and Lesbians: I don't get off on guys, OK? Feel honoured I tell you. OK?

GURVINDER: You're telling me you're a dyke?

HESTER: I'm telling you I'm a dyke.

GURVINDER: Oh. I can see that'd be a problem. (*She strokes his head; loves him.*) I suppose a quick knee-trembler's completely out of the question ... ?

Mona laughs. Their lights to half, Mona's and Wayne's to full.

MONA: 'S funny what they do to ye, parents. I was always the pretty one, me. Our kid was the brainy one. Upstairs an' downstairs, right? (*Thinks.*) But I tell ye, there's gotta be better than's happenin' to me. An' not just me, either, by God. It's not right. It's not. How I look's my business, I shouldn't 'ave to make a business of it. (*Thinks.*) I'm glad Sandra gorraway, I am. I'da gone with 'er, I would, I mighta fancied a bit o' travellin', meetin' folk. But I've got the kid to think of now. Gorra gerrit right for her, no danger. So. (*Thinks.*) Ye do what ye can. Ye do what you 'ave to. Ye do what they let ye.

WAYNE: Funny how like the world a prison is. Hull was a bloody nightmare, o' course, they put me in with the puffs an' the other warped buggers 'cos o' my 'crime' so-called. (*Shudders.*) Sick every night for a month, I was. Thorp Arch though – the open prison – that was a dream, I tell you. All the drugs 'n' booze ye could handle an' sex to order (*Taps his nose*) when you learnt the ropes. Better class a' people, too, white collar, see, managers, executives, entrepreneurs, solicitors, financial advisors, the cream you might say, O and A levels, degrees, the lot, good crowd, you know, unlucky to be caught, the stuff that's goin' down out here ... Doin' business is what it's called out here, in court they call it fraud, see. Felt sorry for 'em, I did. Oh yes, (*Long pause.*) I don't blame Sandra leavin' me. (*His face reddens. Eyes moisten.*) I just don't understand why she left it till I was comin' out to tell me ...

Slow fade to half-light. Bring up Tom's and Daisy's light to full. Tom's upright, staring out across the tarn. Daisy's on her back watching him.

TOM: I went back, signed on for another tour, wrote my folks. Really felt I'd had it with this place. And. My pa got sick, retired from the service, '86? '86 ... I flew home, he popped it a couple of days later. But we did get to talk a little. I told him I loved him. He reminded me of my responsibilities and I didn't go back. Palestine wasn't real, wasn't possible. Hi-tech was both.

DAISY: (*Gentle*) Cheer up, kid. At least you didn't join the bloody Army ...

TOM: Right.

DAISY: So what is it you do?

TOM: (*Long pause*) Aviation. I work with planes.

DAISY: (*Looking him up and down*) I should've guessed that.

Lights to half; bring up Hester's and Gurvinder's light to full. Gurvinder's on his feet, staring east, eyes angry; somewhere else.

HESTER: You pissed off with me?

GURVINDER: (*Returning; not turning*) What? No. Not with you.

HESTER: What then?

He shrugs, turns, pokes the fire with a stick.

DAISY: (*From half-dark*) Poor Gurvinder.

GURVINDER: Why'd'ye never call me Girlie?

HESTER: I can't bear to see men cry. I don't know. You gonna tell me what's up?

GURVINDER: We could get married. We wouldn't have to live together. I mean ... we could just be there for each other.

HESTER: Like Sandra and Wayne? Come on, big eyes, you can do better than that. (*Thinks it through a bit.*) Jesus, I don't know the first thing about you, Gurvinder. You're weird and beautiful and utterly opaque. Like, how come you're so rich, you know? What are you? What do you do?

GURVINDER: What am I? I'm a businessman. What do I do? I fuck the world.

MONA: (*Half-light*) Such a bloody waste. Everywhere ye look.

GURVINDER: Ye don't want to know.

HESTER: Try me.

GURVINDER: Open the bag. (*He hands her a key. She opens the Gladstone. Stares at the contents.*) You're looking at a hundred thousand quidsworth minimum, on the street. (*She looks up, stares at him.*) There's fifty thousand quidsworth of E in the boot o' the Bentley, another hundred thou of dope in the limo. So, what's it doing here? Well, according to extremely sweetened sources in the Drug Squad, the new club is due a raid in about ... (*Watch*) ten minutes' time. (*Smiles.*) I didn't get where I am today by not knowin' when I'm about to be busted. These've bin the good years for us folk, folk who fuck the world. The Bag-Lady's done us proud. Where there is discord, let there be profit. Where there is error, let there be profit. Where there is doubt, may we bring profit. Where there is despair ... let there be smack. Oh yes.

HESTER: (*Wide-eyed; in shock*) Gurvinder ...

GURVINDER: They put me away. They lied. They shamed my family. I cannot love these people. I cannot respect these people.

HESTER: Oh God, Gurvinder, you can't even respect yourself ...

GURVINDER: (*Tough, dark*) Who can? Who can? (*Silence.*) In Borstal, I met some brothers ... (*In their voice*) 'bahn in Barbados' ... they gave me a map of the world and a path through it, ours and theirs, us and them. The world of the Bag-Lady. And the Bag-Lady said, Let there be Wealth and there was Wealth, and a half of the people fattened on it till their bellies hung over their belts and their snouts glistened. And the Bag-Lady said Let there be Poverty and there was Poverty in spades, and anger and need stalked the land like Little and Large on Angel Dust and the folk who fuck the world cleaned up at both ends, shit and vomit, it's all one. Listen. Business is deep. Business goes all the way down. What do I do? I buy and sell. On top, above board, shares, houses, land, water, gas, oil, phones, airplanes, firms, futures. Below, underground, it's crack and smack and E and tea and speed and feed and the tools that mark out the turf (*Holds up his finger-shooter, bangs one off*). I'm doin' OK, me. Except my family won't have me in the house, won't even speak on the phone. Me dad. Me dad was the first Asian building worker in Leeds. He's still got his first wage-packet. 'S true.

He pulls away from her searching eyes, pads off to stare at the black nowhere to the east.

TOM: (*Toneless; remote*) I thought I'd write poems.

Hester closes, locks the bag, lays the key on it. Moves towards the awning, gathers the discarded trail-mike, as if to tidy it away, doesn't.

People have sifted back in, the light slowly altering to camp-site. Daisy comes to stand with Gurvinder. Rests her head on his shoulder.

Hester hums softly into the mike, finding the piece. Mona draws Tom into a slow stiff-legged dance that barely moves. Wayne picks up the kirpan, flashes at the dark with it.

HESTER: (*Sings; slow torch version*)   Hush
                                        Hush
                                        Somebody's calling my name ...
                                        O my lord
                                        O my lord
                                        What shall I do ...

Fade to black.

Bring up: moon, still fat, smaller.

Bring up: laughter, chat.

Bring up: camp-fire, down to embers. They sit or sprawl around it, sharing joints and cans of lager.

GURVINDER: (*Mid-tale*) ... So he's never bin to London, Charlie, right? Hardly bin out of Heckmondwike. Two tons o' logs on the back. Time 'e gets there it's mornin', Edgware Road, not a soul up, he's no idea where 'e is ... Sees an old feller walkin' the dog, he pulls up, he says is this London, flower? The guy says, Aye, you've made it. Charlie says, Oh that's gradely, where d'ye want the wood ... ?

Wayne arrives with a major flask of coffee and cups.

WAYNE: Coffee, chief.

People reach in for it.

GURVINDER: I've told ye, Wayne, don't keep callin' me Chief, ... people'll think I'm a fuckin' Indian ...

WAYNE: Sorry, Boss.

GURVINDER: I've told ye about that daft hat as well ...

WAYNE: 'S my uniform ...

DAISY: Oh I wondered. Thought it might be costume ...

MONA: (*Tasting coffee*) Oh God, no sugar ...

WAYNE: Couldn't find sugar.

DAISY: (*Pointing*) There's sweeteners in my bag there ...

Wayne lumbers off to find them.

MONA: Oh God, I'm knackered ...

GURVINDER: (*Checking Rolex*) Not long.

DAISY: (*Imitating him*) Not long. Not long. God, you're such a fuckin' poser, Girlie ...

GURVINDER: (*Grin*) I know.

DAISY: So what is it with you and this place, eh? Are you gonna tell us?

GURVINDER: I might.

Wayne's back with the Sweetex pills spread on a saucer, his idea of the style of things.

MONA: Oh don't. He'll just mek up more bullshit, ye know him ...

WAYNE: I know what it is, he's told me already ... (*Raises his hand, fingers extended. Glances at Gurvinder.*) Pantisabu, right?

GURVINDER: Panjisahib.

WAYNE: Right.

TOM: What about him?

WAYNE: 'S not an *im*, 's'n *it*. 'S a handprint. In a rock.

MONA: More bullshit.

TOM: Whose?

WAYNE: (*A look at Gurvinder*) Some bigwig, begins with a G ...

GURVINDER: Gurunanak.

MONA: Told ye.

WAYNE: Anyway, this guru bloke goes up on a big hill, limestone rock, to pray, see ...

GURVINDER: Meditate.

WAYNE: Right. But there's a ganga nutters livin' up there an' they don't like him movin' in on their turf, like, so they decide to get shut of 'im, and their chief hurls this bloody great boulder straight at his head, right? But the guru bloke's meditating so 'ard he's built up this kind of psychic wall around 'imself, see, so just by puttin' his 'and up like that, he stops the rock in mid-air, without even touchin' the bugger. (*Silence.*) And that rock's up there to this day. With the print of the guru bloke's hand on it.

Silence. They look at each other.

TOM: Where?

WAYNE: On the rock.

TOM: (*Indicating*) Up there?

WAYNE: No, India, I think.

DAISY: Wait a minute, what the hell has this got to do with Gotscam and Girlie?

WAYNE: Search me.

DAISY: But that was the question, Wayne.

WAYNE: Was it? Oh.

GURVINDER: (*Soft*) Me dad brought us here, when I were a kid. Told me the story, Gurunanak, Panjisahib. (*Looks up at it.*) His dad'd teken 'im to see the real thing, back home. This place reminded him of it.

Silence.

MONA: This coffee's crap. Pass us another o' them sweeteners, will ye?

Daisy holds out the saucer. Begins to examine the pills intently. Tom checks the time on his watch. Daisy goes to fetch her bag.

GURVINDER: Time is it?

TOM: Half three.

GURVINDER: Nearly there.

Hester pours more coffee. Sweeteners.

DAISY: (*Back*) Wayne, the sweeteners …

WAYNE: Oh aye, sorry, they're 'ere … (*He hands them to her. Sees the bottle of Sweetex in her hand.*) Oh, you've got two, have you … ?

DAISY: Oh shit. Who took sweeteners? (*Everyone.*) Oh shit.

HESTER: What?

DAISY: (*Handing bottle back*) What does that say, Wayne?

WAYNE: (*Squinting hard*) Mog. Mogga. Don, Mogadon. New one on me is that, aye.

Silence. Looks.

DAISY: Sorry, Girl.

GURVINDER: Duke.

WAYNE: Yes, chief?

Mona chuckles, draws sleeping bag up, rolls onto her side.

MONA: Right, that's me then.

GURVINDER: (*To Wayne*) It's OK.

Slow fade. Gurvinder goes last. He sits on cross-legged, eyes fixed, resistant. Black.

Bring up; alarm clock. It tails away.

Bring up: sound of a dozen or so bikes thundering along the bottom road towards the site.

Bring up: the camp-site. Bright day, around 9 o'clock.

The six lie like discarded dolls around the dead fire. The bikes stop by the cars; rev ominously; cut. A solitary rider continues, noses forward, appears on the edge of the site, leathers inscribed: Chapter One, *stops, takes in the scene, noses on, makes a slow searching circle of the sleepers, stops at the final figure of Wayne. Removes helmet; it's Sandra, long free bleached hair, utterly changed. She leans down to get a closer look.*

Wayne half-wakens for a moment. Stares up at her face.

WAYNE: Hello, San.

SANDRA: Hello, Wayne.

He's gone at once. Sandra takes a final look at the group, returns her helmet, revs, rumbles off. The support bikes start up, throttle up, roar away.

Bring up: music: 'Every Time We Say Goodbye'.

Slow fade to black. Screen image of Thatcher, raddled, last days, on the crossfade. The song continues, calm, felt, as Poll Tax riots slowly burn out the Thatcher face.

SONG: ... When you're near there's such an air
                         Of Spring about it ...

Begin slow mix through to image of Major.

                         ... I can hear a lark somewhere
                         Begin to sing about it
                         There's no vu more déjà
                         Than the change so strange
                         From Thatcher to Major...

The note holds, Dies. Major holds.

Bring up: Sandra, bike, leathers, bleached hair flowing below helmet, on the road.

SANDRA: (*Sound effects down*) ... I don't care if it *is* shit, it's my shit, not theirs. It's not semis and mortgages and pitbulls and Blind Date and poisoned water and salmonella and slaughter a few thousand foreigners when it all gets too much ... Fuck their shit. (*Sounds up a moment, down again.*) You should try it, friend. The Road really earths you. Puts you in charge. Drivin' your own life. Give it a go, 'is all I'm sayin', what else are you doin' ... What?

Crossing to: Tom, cockpit of Tornado, diving in for the turkey shoot (Highway 8), Gulf War, mute save for the clack and split of control-intercom.

At the end, mission complete, as he banks and peels, he's at last released into feeling, punches the air like a good 'un, tears streaming down cheeks and chin.

Fade.

The image of Major persists.

Bring up:

VOICE: Britain should approach the millennium with head and spirits high. The prize is great, the hope invigorating, the dream attainable. We want, with you, to make the dream a reality.

Major fades.

Bring up:

TOM: (*Off*) The road to Basra. Highway 8. Next day. Sent back next day. Next day.

Bring up: Tom's face, frozen on screen, mouth open. A chittering burst on fast-forward, slows to play for a moment, we hear a phrase or two: 'Sent back. Fly over it …' Freeze frame again, on midshot; he wears striped dressing gown over pyjamas, institutional setting.

Bring up:

PSYCHIATRIST: (*Off; dictating notes on to microtape*) Flight Lieutenant Thomas Peacock Clare … Post-combat stress trauma Grade VI … Trapanazene 6 grams per diem until further notice. Release date query. Await stabilization before release to community care …

Tom in, as the notes set up, directly below screen. He wears a long brown overcoat, ancient trousers, sandals, no socks. Carries a bag stuffed with his movables.

TOM: The road to Basra. Highway 8. Next day. Sent back. Fly over it. Camera. In a gunship. 200 feet. 200 feet. Smelling them. Through the skin of the ship. Smelling them. Watch out for vultures on the intercom. Thousands. In hover pattern. Waiting their turn. Our people in the sand, removing material, equipment. And for twenty miles the road to Basra black and white with birds and bones, untouched by our people in the sand. (*Touches head.*) Untouched. (*The screen image fades. He begins to shuffle off. Stops. Cocks his head, assailed by his voices.*) What? No. Ireland. Yes, What? I can't. No I can't, I don't want to, I'm going to Ireland, my mum's people, country of my mother and mother of all countries … Yes, Daisy? Don't know. Not seen. No, no one. Poems? No. Don't do poems, not real, not poss, old boy. (*Shouts.*) Ireland. (*Blinks*). The road to.

He goes.

Bring up: Wayne, at bar, talking to disinterested barman. He's in makeshift combat outfit.

WAYNE: No, so I got out of Security, loada crap, no discipline, this place is really down the tubes, right? And I landed right on my feet, all these fuckin' wars, excuse the language, course the small-arms trainin' in the Force helped, like … 800 quid a week anywhere in the world and don't have to travel to Africa to do it, 's right here on the doorstep. Great job. Oh aye. Russia last month, Greece before that … Hey, guess who I saw in Greece? D'you watch Sky News at all … ? Daisy Jay, you know, the correspondent … She was at the airport doin' an interview with some army chief, 'course I know 'er well, at school together, see, but I didn't bother 'er, I could see she was busy. (*Stares at his drink.*) Great job. Dropped lucky. Aye. (*Looks up. The guy has moved away. Looks down at his drink again. Takes a sip.*) Dropped lucky. Aye.

Crossing to: Daisy, on screen, rehearsing swishing hair from side to side as she waits for action.

DAISY: (*Running lines*) New New'n'True does it for me. All over the world …

The cameraman rehearses a pull to midshot, reveals her, in flak-gilet and silk shirt, her trademark clip-board in one hand.

VOICE: (*On-floor; off*) Ready to go, Miss Jay?

DAISY: (*To camera, can to ear*) Mark, Daisy. Just let me get it straight, you open with me covering the war in Byelorussia, mix through to the format stuff, on to this bit here (S*hakes hair*), slowed down bla-bla, and out with cabin shot me flying in to Macedonia, right? Fine. Ready when you are. Hair all right? (*Listens*) That *would* be the end of the world ... What? Remember allure? I think of little else, darling ...

VOICE: (*From floor*) Stand by now and, New New'n'True Hairways, scene two take three. Action.

Screen sound cuts. She does her piece, remembers allure. Daisy has walked on below. Watches briefly. Turns away. Approaches bare wood coffin. She wears a simple black dress, carries a single rose, a seasoned thirty-two-year old child. The Daisy on the screen mutely continues, remembering allure.

DAISY: The old trout died before I could get there. Eighty-three years of age, she was changing a front tyre on the Hebron Road when her heart went. She called me from the hospital to tell me not to come. I'll go when I'm ready, she said, and you've got work to do, my little peacenik. (*Camera fades to black on screen. She stops to lay the rose on the coffin. Lights the two candles at either end. Stands.*) Daisy Jay, Sky News, Haifa, on the road, signing off.

She goes.

Bring up: Hester and Mona singing: 'How Great Thou Art', a line each.

Bring up: screen. A faceless Tory leader, an election favour in his lapel: Minor, perhaps.

HIS VOICE: (*Off*) In the last seventeen years. The Conservative Dream. Millennium. In the last seventeen. Stuck to the road. Conservative Dream. To the. Stuck. To the road. Your dream. Safe in our hands. To the road ...

Song ends. Minor fades.

Bring up: Hester, Mona, coffin, candles. A hubbub of folk about the house, dominoes, shouts from the men, talk and reminiscence from the women, laughter from the kids: Nine Night, a Caribbean funeral custom.

The two women kneel side by side before a sea-trunk, sorting Mrs Patterson's things. Clothes and objects on the floor about them. House sounds fade to low: still there.

MONA: (*Gazing at framed photograph*) ... God, this must be the wedding party in Kingston, just before they left. (*Hester leans in to study it with her.*) Look at me dad. (*They chuckle.*) She was so beautiful.

HESTER: She was going to be a teacher.

MONA: Gerroff.

HESTER: She was.

Hester returns to sorting. Mona looks on at the picture a moment.

MONA: I never thought of her as brainy.

Hester opens up the scrunched-up Crimplene housecoat, hands it to Mona.

HESTER: Put that with throw-outs …

Mona takes the coat, studies it, feels it with her face, smells it. Stands as if to discard it; slips it on. Gradually finds her large, heavy, powerful, exhausted mother. Sits heavily on a stool by Hester, addresses her.

MONA: (*Jamaican*) Come here, Mona girl, do your hair while I've a minute …

She draws Hester to her. Begins to do her hair. Talks to her throughout; of fatigue, of the family, of meeting her father, of the hospital, of hopes for Mona; of the pretty one.

Pickney gal – come here, let me comb your hair while me a sit down. Did you nah grease you scalp this morning, me nah want no dry head pickney you know. Got to feel the comb walk the scalp. Teck your hand out your hair. You is a Virgin Mary tonight eeh - you gwhen look sweet. And Hester is a what, wise person, a not a wise person – a wise man! I don't know if I can come tonight me can't teck another night off work, perhaps your daddy gwhen come, but him going be tired. (*Finishes hair.*) Nee go set the table I gwhen lie down little while.

She relaxes slowly back into herself. Hester's crying. They hug. Stay close.

HESTER: You know something? I used to go to bed every night when I was a kid and pray for a sister.

MONA: Did ye? I used to pray for a blonde wig.

HESTER: She loved you

MONA: She loved us both. Big heart. Right?

HESTER: Big heart. Right.

They return to the trunk. Work on. House noise up a little. Factual; non-declaratory.

Name:	Elizabeth Rose Patterson
Date of Birth:	4/5/35
Country of Birth:	Jamaica
Occupation:	Hospital ancillary; various

MONA: Cause of death: coronary infarct. Related factors: racial abuse, precipitating heart failure.

HESTER: Ambulance response time: 53 minutes.

MONA: Hospitals refusing admission: three.

HESTER: Hospital admission time: 2 hours 20 minutes.

MONA: Other comments:

HESTER/MONA: Dead before diagnosed.

Their lights slowly fade,

Gurvinder appears above them, buttoned Indian jacket trousers, by the screen, a box of virtual reality cartridges in his hand. He kneels to feed them into his computers, checks each image in turn as it's fed onto the screen: Wayne, Sandra, Hester, Mona, Daisy, Tom, all in their thirties. He stands, touches a sensor, bringing up lights on the penthouse apartment below to which he now descends. A TV in an adjacent, otherwise empty room flickers greyly: a New Year's party for the millennium.

The viewing room he's reached is also empty, save for the screen and a great moulded chair facing out. He gathers a VR visor and glove from the arm of the chair, puts them on; sits; fingers console. The lights dip. Fingers it again. The screen comes to life again: the image of Gotscam. He moves the glove, the image becomes a close-up section of the ledge, the Chair itself. Midnight in the next room. Chimes. Cheers.

Lamps appear in the dark of the ledge, figures. Daisy's Angel Gabriel, Tom's Joseph, Mona and Sandra's Marys, Hester's Wise Person, Wayne's Innkeeper, Gurvinder's King. They begin speaking their lines from the nativity play, detached and not quite human voices seeking no connection. White light slowly grows on the ledge: sun rise; power restored. They abandon the lines; piano and guitar set up, leading them into 'Mr Sunnyman'.

The song ends. They stare on, as white light reaches Gurvinder in his chair.

He glares hard through the visor, staring into the light.

GURVINDER: (*Fierce; low; echoic; relayed*) I don't know if you know. Or if you care. But this place is turning. Into shit. I don't know if you know. Or if you care. But you fucked up. We. You're going to have to start again. We. Start again. (*He reaches into his jacket pocket, takes out the marble-bag, holds it out in the palm of his hand. Opens it. Draws out the scissored Sikh braids. Holds them out.*) For a start. How do I get this back on? (*Silence. The white light slowly fades, screen above and chair below.*) I don't hear you. I don't hear you.

The ungloved hand touches the console.

Fast fade to black.

END

WHO SHALL BE HAPPY …?

Who Shall Be Happy ...? is the theatre version of *Hope in the Year Two,*
which was first broadcast on 11th May 1994.

Who Shall Be Happy ...? was first presented by Mad Cow Productions at the
Old Museum Arts Centre, Belfast on 7th November 1995.
The cast was as follows:

The Prisoner   Stanley Townsend

Henry   Kulvinder Ghir

Director   Trevor Griffiths

Designer   Hayden Griffin

Lighting   Aidan Lacey

Original music by   Neil Martin

Who Shall Be Happy ...?

The play is set in the Palais de Luxembourg, Paris, in April 1794 at the height of the Great Terror.

Black up to dark.

A distressed grande salle, Palais de Luxembourg, Paris, Germinal in the Year Two; a large metal cage, framing lopsided chaise longue, chair, lamp within.

A slow spot gradually reveals the **Prisoner***, prone on the tilted divan, perhaps asleep, perhaps laid out for burial. His lips begin to move; a soundless struggle for meanings, then a slow disconnected rumble of words.*

An image large enough to frame the cage appears on the back wall, a late 20th century European cityscape, seen through glass from moving car.

The Prisoner's eyes flicker, bobbling on dream.

PRISONER: *Who ...*

> Don't read me lectures on how this tribunal shall proceed, Fouquier-Tinville. I created this bloody Tribunal, dreamed it up ...

Who shall ...

> Vadier sends Danton a message: tell that fat turbot, we'll gut him soon enough ...

Who shall be ...

> Danton answers: Tell Vadier, one step in my direction, I'll cleave his head open, suck his brains out and shit in his empty skull ...

Happy ...

> Vadier meant it. Danton didn't ...

Who shall be happy ...?

> No matter.

Who shall be happy ...?

Prison noises, sudden, resonant: locks, steps, a voice, another. The back-wall cityscape begins a slow fade. The Prisoner is up, alert; listens: nothing untoward. Approaches the bars. Stares out into the dark. The last of the cityscape seamlessly gives way to a new image, gradually readable as a mirrored reflection of the audience watching from their semi-dark.

PRISONER: ... Still there? Aye, I see ye. Little white faces in the dark. The future we are hatching here. Fell asleep. Tired. Little white faces in the dark. Waiting to be born. Where was I? Had I reached Paris yet? It doesn't matter. Touch any part you touch the whole ...

A door slams. The Prisoner turns to watch a young guard shuffle awkwardly in, musket on shoulder, Phrygian bonnet rouge, ill-fitting boots, a tray of food in his hands. He spends some time finding nowhere to put it, finally lays it down on the floor, begins to head off. Audience image slowly fades.

PRISONER: *(out into the dark; indicating guard)* As you see, we have begun upon experiments ... Henry is but the first fruiting. The new citizen, the new man ...

Henry has stopped, slowly turned to watch.

HENRY: *(finally)* What?

PRISONER: What, did I speak?

HENRY: Don't start that.

He watches on a moment, clumps off into the dark far reaches of the Salle to gather something.

PRISONER: I've got him thinking I'm the Madman. Apparently there are two of me. It seems the Committee, fearing a rescue plot, have summoned up a second Danton from a neighbouring asylum and had him caged, identically alone, in the Conciergerie down the road, to confound the plotters. I came in a sealed coach and hooded. Not even the prison governors are allowed to know who it is they hold. But, while it amuses me to play games with this ignorant youth, and might just possibly yield me some advantage, I would not lie to the future. I am Danton. It is I who will die this fifth day of April, this sixteenth day of Germinal in the Year Two. True, they like to pretend the trial has not concluded. But we know better. *(He takes out his watch, studies it)* So. We have a few hours.

Henry returns with card table and stool, lays them down, sets the tray on the table, approaches the cage, gestures the Prisoner away from the gate with his musket, keys it open, fastens a long chain to the bars, beckons the Prisoner foward, snaps the chain onto his ankle, indicates the tray, heads off down the room again.

PRISONER: The letter ...?

HENRY: *(leaving)* Eat.

The Prisoner ponders, then moves towards the food. Discovers the chain holds him a tantalizing metre or so away from it.

PRISONER: Who would be an optimist? *(Bellowing down room)* What, is the trial ended, and the sentence death by starving, doughface?

Henry returns, bowl, razor, metal mirror and towel on a tray in his hands. Sees the problem. Adjusts stool and table.

HENRY: Stay calm, citizen. That's eighty sous ...

The prisoner pays him, surveys the meal, sniffs the wine. Henry takes out a flask from his pocket, places it on the table.

On the house.

The Prisoner sniffs it, swigs, swigs again, shakes his head.

PRISONER: Jesus God. Weasel piss.

HENRY: Spanish brandy. All there is. Have you slept?

PRISONER: I don't know.

He stuffs food into his mouth without relish. Henry lights a clay pipe, taps his finger on the water bowl.

PRISONER: *(Seeing the toiletries)* Ah.

HENRY: Fifteen sous.

The Prisoner counts out coins, inspects tray.

PRISONER: Soap?

HENRY: *(from pocket)* Five.

PRISONER: We'll make a rich man of ye yet, boy.

Thumbs razor, sets metal mirror, begins lathering up. Henry puffs on his pipe, slyly eyes him, drawn to the man.

PRISONER: The letter, Henry. Did ye speak with your Gate Serjeant?

HENRY: I did.

Silence.

PRISONER: Yes?

HENRY: He's opened a book.

PRISONER: A book?

HENRY: Aye, a book. On which of us is holding the real You. Us or them down the road.

PRISONER: Has he?

HENRY: He has. An' he has you clear favourite.

PRISONER: The letter, Henry. Do ye have his price?

HENRY: A hundred. That's for him. He says I should ask the same ...

PRISONER: He has a reliable carrier, yes?

HENRY: He has a fair few, he's thinking to use the Three o'Clock Runner, he has a set deal worked out wi' most o' the Committee Runners ...

PRISONER: Henry, I said reliable, if he runs for the Government he'll be a spy for 'em too ...

HENRY: O'course he's a spy, why should that get in his way, he can't live on wages no more than the rest of us.

Long pause. The prisoner nods, takes out a draw-purse, lays coins on the table.

But ...

PRISONER: All right. *(Taps coin-pile)* His. One hundred. *(Removes gold wedding-band)* Yours. Worth three hundred, a year from now five maybe. *(Takes out a letter, lays it on the table.)* But?

HENRY: I've told ye, he thinks ye're 'im. Says it's too risky.

PRISONER: *(Lays it out for Henry)* An innocent document, he can read it, read it yourself, Henry …

HENRY: *(Looking at it, as if reading)* He says it could be in code, calling for a rising of your followers …

PRISONER: I have no followers, Henry, it's Danton has the followers … He's a huge man, big swaggerbelly, great arse, broken nose, scar on the lip, a Titan, Hero of the Republic written in blood all over him, *that's* your Danton, friend. I'm the former actor detained in a Home for the Temporarily Cracked and currently on loan to the Luxembourg. I'm the Madman.

HENRY: Are you?

PRISONER: *(Quietly)* You know I am.

HENRY: I know nothing.

Silence, eyes, locking.

PRISONER: I believe you.

HENRY: You could be anyone.

PRISONER: That's what actors *do,* Henry.

HENRY: What?

PRISONER: *Be.* Anyone. *(Silence. He reaches forward, lays his watch by the ring on Henry's side.)* Ye know what that's worth?

HENRY: D'ye know what they'll do if we're found? Carrying letters from Him?

PRISONER: Trust me, Henry. Ye won't be. It's true I have trouble on occasions knowing who I am, I'm always clear about who I'm not. Ye're in no danger. Read.

He takes the letter, stares hard at it for a long time. The Prisoner resumes shaving.

HENRY: *(Laying it down)* I haven't much reading. Ye'll have to do it.

The Prisoner smiles at the illogic, gathers the letter. Henry walks around the table, to watch over his shoulder.

PRISONER: *(Reads)* 'My dearest wife, I am transferred to the Luxembourg Prison overnight, where I am held in solitary confinement the whole time. Send money and succour post-haste, my condition worsens and I begin to entertain the morbid fear I may never be restored to freedom. Care for my sons, won't ye. I miss them so. And know I shall love you always, on whatever side of the grave. Eternally your Husband.'

He lays the paper down, moves sombrely away from the table, moved. Henry examines it.

HENRY: That's it?

PRISONER: That's it.

HENRY: What's this on the back?

PRISONER: *(Takes the page)* The back? Ah yes. 'Post scriptum. I have again petitioned the authorities to allow me to address a company of active citizens of their choosing to judge the condition of my mind and determine the question of my sanity. If ye will, a kind of convocation of my peers ... If ye will, a *convention ...*'

The back-wall has gradually come alive again, eventually establishes itself as reflected audience. Bleed in stormy sounds of a packed Convention Hall. A bright, stark downspot isolates the Prisoner, as he waits for the presidential gavelling to restore order.

PRISONER: *(echoic; intense in the silence)* ... Fellow members of the Convention, trusted representatives of the sovereign people, fathers of this proud republic, friends ... I do not appear before you because I fear for my neck. If I had feared for my neck, my friends, I should have slipped across a border and saved it. I am here before you because I fear for my country. And you cannot take your country with you on the soles of your shoes ... You will have read by now the contemptible calumnies those terrified midgets of the Committee like to call the charges against me ... corruption, malfeasance, conspiracy with foreign plotters, secret links with the monarchists, using the public purse to stuff my own, uncivic lack of Virtue ... all the ancient phantasms of rancid and envious minds dumped unevidenced like so much horseshit upon the floor of the Tribunal to steam and stink me to the Block. Well, you'll forgive me for not fouling my hands with it, gentlemen, for in Germinal Year Two, I must tell you, the chasm opened up between charge and crime has come so wide we are in danger, all of us, of falling into the void. *(The hall grows stormy, some clapping, hostile shouts, gavelling. He waits.)* Well then, what is my crime? My crime, gentlemen ... *(Outbursts, never lost, well up again above the gavel)* ... The crime I commit each day I am free is to place love of country above saving my neck ...

Hall acoustic dies. Light from below displaces the downspot. He gazes out at the dark.

PRISONER: *(Internal voice; grave, whispered)* You have given me such a hatred for the present, I find myself longing for the days when the whole of my weekly income depended on a bottle of ink ... You have filled me with such fear for the future, I spend my last hours rehearsing what will not happen as though it were already history. So much rising to be said, underneath, so much to hold down, so much to bite back, or choke on. How will I tell you what matters? How will I tell you, as I scan your tiny faces in the gloom, you are yourselves already dead, immured inside the dungeon walls of cant and lies and language this revolution has all the while and under our noses been a-building? How will I tell you I am grown mild? How will I tell you: it is April ...?

The spot dies, the salle and cage re-emerge. He sits as before, letter before him, Henry gazing at it over his shoulder.

PRISONER: *(Reads)* ... a convocation of my peers, if ye will, a convention. But whether the authorities agree or not to such a hearing, do not let Paré neglect Tiger, who needs regular exercise to get his blood running, let him begin tomorrow and every day until I'm home and can do it for myself.' *(Silence. The Prisoner dries his face on the towel. Looks up at Henry.)* Satisfied?

HENRY: *(finger poking envelope)* S'that say?

PRISONER: Mme. Louise Gèly, 22 Rue de Commerce, Cordeliers. My wife.

HENRY: *(poking letter)* S'that say?

PRISONER: Freedom.

HENRY: That?

PRISONER: The grave.

HENRY: Who's Tiger?

PRISONER: The dog.

HENRY: Sounds more like a cat, Tiger.

PRISONER: He's a dog.

HENRY: Does he look like a tiger?

PRISONER: Why would he? He's a dog.

HENRY: Who's Paré?

Silence.

PRISONER: Paré's a servant. Or, in the language of the new political correctitude, 'house assistant'. Now, what could be more innocent? Trust me.

Henry gathers the letter in his finger-tips, rounds the card table, lays it down between the coin-pile and ring and watch.

HENRY: The thing is.

PRISONER: Go on.

HENRY: I've an infirm mother and nine young brothers and sisters to keep fed. If I'm found ... Even if you're not Him.

PRISONER: It's a gamble. I see that. *(Uncaps flask, takes a pull on it)* The watch is worth six hundred livres, the ring's solid gold. What do they pay you?

HENRY: Three livres a day.

PRISONER: I'd be tempted.

HENRY: Would you?

PRISONER: I would.

HENRY: I am.

PRISONER: You should be.

He raises the brandy flask, glugs for a moment, suddenly spumes a mouthful of it into the air, showering his upturned face in the downpour. Words form in his throat.

PRISONER: Germ. Germinate. Germinal. April. Growing weather.

HENRY: *(Recoiling; musket ready)* Eh eh eh. Don't start that.

PRISONER: It's out of my hands, friend. It's why I'm detained. Will you do it?

Henry picks up the watch, puts it to his ear, smells it. Fingers the letter. Heavy sifting rain has begun outside, drizzling the blue-walled salle with rain-shadow.

HENRY: *(delivered as one thought)* I wouldn't get 'em through, there's thirteen doors between here and the Gate House, every one of 'em under special guard for as long as you're held here, I'm searched coming and going, they find this I lose my certificate of civic worthiness at the very least, I paid good bribe money for that, and no certificate no job, I wouldn't get 'em through ...

The Prisoner takes the letter, delicately winds it into a roll, leans carefully forward to place it in the barrel of the guard's musket. Smiles. Speaks as he works.

PRISONER: ... Our lives are much like the theatre, Henry, indifferently written and scandalously short of rehearsal. Like poor actors, we must learn to trust one another. And be bold together. Henry ...

HENRY: What if they look inside ...?

PRISONER: ... They won't. Would you?

HENRY: No. But if.

PRISONER: Your fingers slip on the trigger. Pouf, up in smoke.

Silence.

HENRY: If you are the Madman ...

PRISONER: If?

HENRY: ... how come you have all the answers?

Silence.

PRISONER: If I have all the answers, friend, what the fuck am I doing here ...? *(He gestures the cage, the prison, the world. Puts his chained foot up on the stool.)* Come on, do what ye will, I've had enough ...

Henry finds the key, warily releases him, follows as the Prisoner returns to the cage, begins to relock the door on him, sees the casually palmed bottle from the table in the Prisoner's hand, gently dispossesses him of it, locks the door. Dwells a moment. Watches the Prisoner squat in the straw, head in hands, morose, inturned.

HENRY: I promise nothing. I'll give it thought.

PRISONER: *(not looking)* Who shall be happy …? What? Be happy what?

Silence.

HENRY: Sleep.

Clumps to the table, collects musket and tray, stares hard at coins, ring, watch, confronted by them.

PRISONER: Take. Get the feel of 'em in your pocket.

Henry gets the feel of them. Finally pockets them. Heads for the door. Knocks to indicate he's coming through, unlocks it, stands framed in the doorway to be searched, finally bangs the door to. The Prisoner's head jerks upwards, as the slam echoes around the room. He smiles. Holds up the filched cut-throat, blade a dull glint.

PRISONER: I play this game for hope. And know I must hold myself ready for the worst. The big one we call the National Razor. Sometimes, the Hot Hand. *(He stares hard at the blade. Folds and pockets it. Town clock sounds the half. Thunder.)* Tiger? Ye heard me? Tiger's code for the people. As in: if you would master a revolution, first you must learn to ride the Tiger. If the letter's carried, Louise will know what to do. Let the Tiger stir tomorrow, Danton may yet come whole from this. *(Chuckles)* Picture it. A rising at the court-room, the old Sections armed and marching again, the folk of '89 and '91, the folk of August '92, June '93, the plain people, menu people we call 'em, whose only wish is to be included in the fucking meal … Or in the Square itself, real drama, a legendary last-minute snatch from the block … Ah. The very stuff of story-time. *(Dwells)* It won't happen. The odds are all the other way. I play this game for hope; without it, what are we if not already dead? In these few years, in this unlikely place, these people have lived and fought and died to claim hope for the human project, to make hope the inalienable right of the living. They have decreed it: to hope is to be human; to hope is to define ourselves as human. Nobody can change that now; it will be so; part of the condition. Like me tonight, you too cannot live but in hope. Liberty may wither, Fraternity evaporate, Equality rot on the vine, Hope's a survivor; and will not die. *(He looks around him: cage, salle, world. Bellows)* Long live the Free Republic! Long live the men and women who made her! Long live Danton … who did what he could!

The cries echo round the vast chamber, meld with the sudden rolling thunder, die. He chuckles.

A world of space to fill with words and not a soul to hear. Never mind. We have our roles and it's enough. Storytime. Where were we? We need some colour, I think, mm? Some people ... who d'ye want? I can give ye a whole gallery of folk. You want Marat?

He muzzes his hair, deranges his shirt, grows short, Italian, scrofulous, operatically intense; utterly transformed.

Marat you shall have ... 'Friends, fellow Jacobins. Do not be deceived when they tell you things are better now. Even if there is no poverty to be seen because the poverty's been hidden. Even if you ever got more wages and could afford to buy more of these new and useless goods which industries foist on you and even if it seems to you you've never had so much, that is only the slogan of those who still have much more than you. Do not be taken in when they pat you on the shoulder and say there's no inequality worth speaking of and no more reason to fight, because if you believe them they will be completely in charge in their marble homes and granite banks from which they rob the peoples of the world under the pretence of bringing them enlightenment. Watch out, my friends, for as soon as it pleases them they'll be sending you out to protect their gold in wars whose weapons, rapidly developed by servile Science, will become more and more deadly until they can with a flick of the finger tear a million of you to pieces ... ' *(He stops. Broods)* Dear Jean-Paul. The Apostle of Liberty, Friend of the People, Seer of the Republic and everybody's favourite lunatic. Met him first in '86, '87, in bed, as it happens, in a rather recherché brothel owned by Orleans, the King's cousin and Prince of the Blood, and run by the Comtesse de Saint-Amarinthe, I was busy excavating her daughter as I recall, while the Comtesse her mother lay beside us having her motte truffled. By, as it turned out, the aforesaid Friend of the People. Not a lot passed between us on that occasion. I may have introduced myself en passant. I believe Marat may have moaned a time or two, perhaps his name, I'm not sure. Back then he called himself de Mara, a blue blood, full wig, powder, perfume, face paint, breeched and buckled, as befits a man who had quacked himself into a lucrative practice as doctor to the nobility while shafting half the wives of fashionable Paris ... Those were the days. *(Silence. He dwells on the man; sombre.)* On, on. More colour, more life, more people. Who? Say it, say it. Ah ...

He fiddles a wig from his pocket, fastidiously reorganizes his dress, grows eerily priest-like, precise, precious, fashions a nosegay from straw to ward off the stench of humanity.

Yes, of course ... Who else? ... Maxim the Incorruptible, Maximillion Miseries ... 'What is the purpose of the Terror under revolutionary rule? I will tell you. It is to create the Republic. Under revolutionary rule, the public power has the duty to defend itself against all the factions that attack it. For it has become clear, midway through Year Two of our Republic, that faction itself is grown the chief threat to our work, faction that fattens on two deviations: weakness and rashness, moderatism and excess. Moderatism which is to moderation as impotence is to chastity ...'

Silence. He stops, tunnelled, turned in; eventually removes the wig, barely aware he does it.

PRISONER: *(little more than whispered)*

> The man who has decided I must die.
> The man who would be certain.
> Who has outlawed doubt. Doubleness.
> All blur, haze and hover.
> Wrote. One year ago. A day or so
> After.
> After.
> My Gabrielle. Birthing a dead daughter.
> Died ...

Silence

> ... And I had.
> Detained in Belgium.
> Back too late. Dug up
> Her corpse
> To gaze on her a
> Last dead
> Time ...

Silence

> Wrote. A year ago. The same man.
> A propos.

Own voice, but the man's wig in his hand

'I love thee better than ever; and till death. From this moment forward I am thee. Close not thy heart to the words of an affection that shares all thy suffering. Let us weep together for the dear wife you have lost. Embrace thy friend. Robespierre.'

Silence, save for the rain. He shivers, draws up his collar. Takes out the cut-throat. Opens it. Stares at it.

PRISONER'S VOICE: *(Internal voice)* I could never embrace him. Who have hugged hundreds. How do you embrace a vapour, an incorporeal idea ...? A system on legs ...?

He rises, carries the blade to the cage door, stoops to work on the lock. Talks as he works.

PRISONER: Come and speak with me, my 'friend till death'. I know you're not sleeping, up there in your virtuous cot. I hear you've been sick again. But who hasn't? You'll find me much as I always was, still seeking to extend the range of human possibilities ...

Click. He stops, stands, smiles. Lays a finger's weight on the cage-door. The door truckles a few decisive inches outward. He fingers it slowly open.

PRISONER: One road to freedom opened. (*Stares out into the blackness. Lays the blade to his larynx.*) And here's another.

A rip of lightning, another, across the image. Thunder, close, serious. The back-wall images water seen through trees from moving car.

PRISONER: (*Smelling her near*) Louise ...?

Bleed in sounds of birds, insects, country; then nearby swimming sounds. The Prisoner stares on into the dark. His second wife, sixteen, appears behind his eyes, naked, glistening from the swim.

PRISONER: What?

LOUISE: *Wet ...*

PRISONER: Yet?

She gestures him to feel. His hand moves gently up between her spread thighs. The fingers reach her, slowly sink into the black.

LOUISE: *Again.*

She moans, moves on her heels. He lays his face at her lower belly. Her hands draw him in.

PRISONER: When?

LOUISE: Now.

PRISONER: (*Desperate*) How?

Louise fades. The tracking shot on the back-wall slows.

PRISONER: (*Internal voice*) Kissing a son on the mouth. Knowing my mother eats. Horse sweat. Cheesecake and cider at the Procope. Wood-smoke. Swimming in the Seine. My new bride's sweet cunt in my nostrils all day. Frost. Men's laughter. (*A whisper now*) Oh Robespierre, my 'friend till death', what will you miss, when your turn comes ...? The Committee? The Podium? The Terror? The Instruments of Rule? How sad to leave this earth so ... untouched by it. How sad the man who has never embraced commonness, who has not dared to be ordinary ...

The slowed bleached back-wall image fades. The Prisoner surveys the salle beyond the cage: rubble, lumber, a shattered chandelier, scraps of earlier meanings. Finds an ancient discomfited wingchair to sit in, a leg missing.

PRISONER: *Who ...*

The future lies in an alley, its throat slit ...

Shall ...

Even as we have been new-minting the coins of hope ...

Be ...

We have been yet busier re-issuing the banknotes of despair ...

Happy ...?

Twin legacies bequeathed on all who come after ...

He gazes out at the dark, trembling at the discovery.

PRISONER: If. If. Who shall be happy if ...? *(Can't find the rest. Roars, anguished)* WHO SHALL BE HAPPY IF WHAT? WHAT?

The roar jags around the space. Thunder.

PRISONER: *(Sings, as he wanders the space)*
>A hero is honoured no longer
>Than it pays to have him about
>We reap the fruits of his labour
>And then we sling him out.
>This may not seem fair play
>But that's the people's way
>In a Re Re Re
>In a pub pub pub
>In a Re-a pub-a Republic.

A town clock sounds the quarter.

PRISONER: The song that toppled a king. We sang that song in August '92, the Champs de Mars again, this time we meant business, this time we would remake the world. Re-invent it. Year One of the Free Republic. Everyone was singing it. There was even a play included it on stage, sung by 'Danton' himself. My friend D'Eglantine wrote some of it, I believe, a group of local actors the rest. The plan was to present it at the next Festival of the Nation ... But it fell foul of the authorities. Never actually performed. There was a widespread feeling that the title had something to do with its proscription – 'Danton Saves France' – I can't think why. Never mind. There'll be others.

Reprising
>With a Dan Dan Dan
>With a Ton Ton Ton
>With a dear old, damned old Danton.

He wanders a little, begins fiddling at his breech-flap, ends up leaning face forward against the Salle doors. Sounds as of a running tap, as he peers through the door grille.

PRISONER: Four armed guards snoring like hogs at the foot of the door. *(He pisses on a moment, listening to the snores)* Historians of a sentimental cast may want to read this as that deep desire in all of us to say 'Hello, well met' to those we cannot otherwise touch ... *(He looks down towards his feet. The snoring falters, as if disturbed; stalls; pecks on.)* The rest of you will know better. The letter's already history. Ça ira. It's not ... *(He returns to the Cage; re-enters; stoops to relock the door with the cut-throat.)* ... escape I seek. It's rescue. It's not life I ask. It's meaning.

He slides the cut-throat inside his leather boot. Finds blood on his neck. Slips on his greatcoat, buttons it to the collar to hide the nick. Lies on the bier-like chaise, crosses arms on chest, eyes closed. The back-wall comes to life: sky, cloud, dreamscape.

If. If. Who shall be happy if ...

Slow fade to black. Town clock strikes: four. Prison noises, faint, approaching. The Prisoner sleeps. Voices at the door. Henry in, rainsoaked, panting for breath. He stands for a moment, checking the Prisoner's safe. Fists at the door behind him. He crosses, opens the grille, speaks out.

HENRY: ... The Prisoner is safe and under watch, Captain.

More talk, instructions from the ante-room beyond. From other parts of the huge building, the din of search parties – whistles, bells, dogs, boots – begins to feed in to the Salle. Henry lumbers into the Salle, stops at the cage to mutter 'Bastard' at the sleeping figure, returns to the table, props his musket, removes his bonnet rouge, revealing shaved, louse-ravaged head. Lays out food-kerchief and cards. The Prisoner stands, pads over to the bars, watches.

PRISONER: *(soft)* Bastard.

HENRY: *(swivelling)* What ...? Awake, are ye.

PRISONER: S'the clock?

Henry consults the Prisoner's watch at his waist.

HENRY: *(eventually)* Four. *(Lips counting)* Seven after.

Turns back to his cards, studies them. Search sounds persist, at distance.

PRISONER: What's the commotion?

HENRY: *(untying kerchiefed bundle)* S'nothin'. The usual bollox. The Committee have uncovered another plot. National Guard are sent in to foil it. Hundreds o' the buggers. Ye hungry? I'm havin' me snap while I can. *(He turns, takes in the man's headshake.)* Ye all right? Ye look like death in a dustbin ... *(He surveys the snap: black bread, a knot of cheese, a green potato, a pinch or two of oats. Pours a dab of brandy on the oats, works it in, tries it.)* A prison rising, they reckon. A Royalist gang under General Dillon, planning to kill the guards, spring the Man-in-question and set him up king or someat. S'what I'm told, anyroad.

PRISONER: Mm. Good to know the Committee's not lost its talent for comedy. So this rising ...

HENRY: *(focus on cards)* There's no rising. This place were like a graveyard till they came. Happens a lot. A week or two back, it were a plot to spring old whatsisname and the Commune crowd, none of it ever comes to aught ...

PRISONER: Hèbert ...?

HENRY: Aye, that's him. Gate Serjeant reckons they only do it to keep our toes on the line. (*He plays on. The Prisoner peels back from the bars, sits on the divan, head down, his gaze on the floor between his feet.*) Ye don't ask if I took the letter through.

PRISONER: No.

HENRY: Well I did.

PRISONER: I hoped ye would.

HENRY: Cackin' mesen I were. Thought I'd never mek it to that Gate House. But I did.

Silence. The Prisoner looks across at Henry, who appears to be deep in the game.

PRISONER: And is it sent?

HENRY: Sent? Not yet. It's waiting a carrier.

Silence.

PRISONER: I thought ye were to use the Committee's man.

HENRY: The Three o'Clock Runner? Ruled out. He's nailed here till mornin', waiting on the Governor to finish the search and report all's safe. We've had to look elsewhere. (*Silence. The Prisoner's head goes down again. Henry stands, lights his pipe, ambles over to the cage.*) It'll be took. Hard part's behind us. I've a cousin works in the kitchens, he's off at five and ready to carry it … Asks a hundred, he'll settle for half.

The Prisoner looks up at him, eyes sunk, face pale, drawn.

PRISONER: Ye took the purse, Henry, that's all I had.

HENRY: Mm. No valuables, pieces? (*The man shakes his head.*) What's the coat worth?

PRISONER: The coat?

HENRY: (*studying it*) He'd tek the coat.

Long silence.

HENRY: I shall need to send word 'fore five. To say if he's to tek the letter or not …

The Prisoner's hand moves up to the collar-buttons.

HENRY: Keep it on. Do later.

Henry watches on a moment, drawn but wary. The man stares on at the floor. Henry ambles back to the table, angles his seat to take in the cage, relights his pipe, returns to his cards.

PRISONER: (*from nowhere*) I was with my wife earlier. I was lying with Gabrielle, the night the first-born died. But it was she was the quick one, me the dead. Yet I could smell her tears on the pillow. The lavender she kept beneath.

HENRY: Dreams be weird.

The man produces a fipple-flute. Plays: Ça Ira, *low, slow, perfect. Henry listens, wholly drawn. He finishes. Stares at the flute, his fingers hovering over the stops.*

HENRY: Will ye come out for a spell?

PRISONER: *(slowly)* If ye like.

HENRY: Ye calm?

PRISONER: Aye.

HENRY: *(the chain)* Put that on. I've a bottle somewhere.

He heads down the room, finds his knapsack, draws a bottle of wine from it, finds a couple of battered tin cups, returns to the table, crosses to unlock the cage door. The Prisoner waits, chain at ankle, Henry checks it's secured, lets him through to the table.

HENRY: *(A mug)* We'll tek a drink. (*He fills the mugs with red. They look at each other.*) The Republic.

PRISONER: The Republic.

They clank, drink, eye each other again as the cups come down.

HENRY: *(decking cards)* Cards 'r chat?

PRISONER: *(deliberate)* I'm without money, Henry.

HENRY: *(Cards away)* Oh aye. Chat then.

Silence. Wine. Distant sounds of search. They look at each other across the smoke and gleam of the guard's lamp.

HENRY: Ye wanna play Last Words?

PRISONER: Last Words of the Blessed Martyrs? By the cankered cock of Christ the Worker, child, why can we not just sit?

HENRY: Thus un's just called Last Words. It can be anybody, not just martyrs. And ye don't 'ave to know what they said, y'ave to mek it up. Wanna play?

PRISONER: *How,* for God's sake. If there's no true or false, there's no way of scoring ...

HENRY: Ye get a point for a laugh. Or a shiver. Or a tear. We made it up at school. Them as couldn't read. (*The prisoner stares at him; loves his innocence.*) Like, you give me Joan of Arc, I say now ye see me, now ye don't, that's one I made up earlier, it's not usually that fast ... You say the King of England, I say ... *(He lifts a buttock, issues a great mouth-fart)* that's another one ...

Silence. A slow, contained mute laugh begins to build up in the Prisoner's chest. Splashes of it spray up his frame, to throat, to voice, mouth. Henry follows, chuckles, pleased. As the laugh reaches the face, it begins a slow agonising collapse into pain and fear and abject misery. Small sounds move about the jaw and mouth; big in the silence. Henry waits, watches, trying to read how things are; where. The spasm ends. The Prisoner sits on, as if somewhere else. Henry pushes the bottle down the table. Touches the man's elbow with it, coaxing him back. The man sees the bottle, fills up, drinks.

HENRY: Where there's life, eh?

PRISONER: Aye.

The Prisoner stands, studies the room, as if seeing it for the first time.

PRISONER: I'll sleep, I think.

HENRY: Finish your cup. I'll tell ye a story. (*The prisoner sits*) Will I? (*The prisoner shrugs*) It's not a story as such, it's someat 'appened earlier on at t'Gate House, ye might have a thought or two on it when it's told ... Tek your mind off things?

The Prisoner shrugs. Henry restocks his pipe bowl, tops up his cup.

Ye'll recall I spoke of the Three o'Clock Runner, he was to be the carrier for your ...? (*Takes the man's nod*) Now, when I get to the Gate House with the letter in my musket, my guts are in a turmoil, I wasn't ticklin' ye, I have to hot heel it to the Necessary or my trousers'll tek the lot ... Now, while I'm in there, who's in the next box but Birdie, the Three o'Clock Runner ... that's what we call him, Birdie ... he has this great ... NOSE stickin' out of his face like a ... tap, like a ... Bit of a jack-the-lad, oh yes, knows everythin', misses naught, meks his way ... So we're squattin' there next each other, he's just brought the letter in from the Committee – the plot, right? – he's cursin' an' bubblin' he's gonna lose private trade because of it, ructions and alarums are the buggeration o' folk like us, he says ... So he's lookin' to make up his losses by laying a decent dollop with the Serjeant on who's holding the Big Un ... the Man-in-Question, see. An' o' course he's pressing me for clues, I mean he's asking how ye look, how ye talk, what ye say, what ye wear ... Cos he *knows*, he's been in the same room as the Man many a time, recent as yesterday he reckons, down at the Court ...

Silence. Henry relights pipe. The Prisoner sips more wine.

PRISONER: So. Did ye tell him?

HENRY: Tell him? (*Emphatic*) No. (*Faint, pre-dawn birdsong: blackbird.*) Dull I may be, I'm no fool. He's a starling is Birdie. Chatchatchat. He'd clean the Gate Serjeant out and brag how he did it all across town, can't help it, chatchatchat ... Serjeant gets to know an' I'm *brawn*, mister. Not a man to cross, our Gate Serjeant.

Silence. Henry broods. The Prisoner takes a look. Stands again.

PRISONER: Is it over?

HENRY: What?

PRISONER: The story.

HENRY: Nearly. There's a bit more. (*The Prisoner sits. Search sounds drift in*:
shouts, barks.) I cross the yard back to the Gate House. National Guard're still
pourin' in, droves of 'em, tryin'a form ranks in two hands o' water, the Under-
Governor's out, helpin' the officers with the list o' suspects, it's time I were
back at me post, I say, better safe than sorry ... I'm passing through the Gate
House, on my way back, big old stable it were once, I see this feller at the
other end warming his arse at t'stove an' holding forth to the Gatemen, I say I
know that feller, I come a bit closer, I see it's the Three o'Clock Runner. (*Long
hold*) An' that's very strange, because ... when he first caught me eye I'd been
minded o' someone else altogether.

PRISONER: (*slow*) Ye lose me, lad.

HENRY: Hold on. Ye'll catch up. Now I could *hear*, I knew at once what were
goin' on, he were tellin' a *story*, see, an' every now an' then he'd ... do ... be
... someone in the story, someone else. Remember, ye said it yesen earlier on,
'bout acting, *bein' anyone*, remember? (*The Prisoner flicks a look, eyes
hooded.*) He was tellin' 'em about bein' down at the Tribunal building
yesterday, waitin' on a package or someat ... and poppin' in to t'Court Room
to watch Trial... So like he's the Judge one minute, then he's the Prosecutor,
he's a defendant, he's someone in t'crowd callin' someat ... Now ye see him,
now ye don't, eh? ... (*Grins*) Then he's back to t'first feller. The one as took
my eye. And it's Danton. The Man himself. (*He stands, swells a little, going
for the gesture*) An' he's goin' at the fuckers, like a bull, head down an' both
horns shinin' ... Call this *justice*, ye dribbling sack o' snot, ye festering pot
o'pigs's piss, just remember, those who drink the people's blood die of it ...
You call my witnesses, all seventeen of 'em, for tomorrow, or this pantomime
can continue without me, I refuse my consent ...

He resumes his stool, looks across at the Prisoner.

HENRY: ... Birdie's better than me, o'course ...

PRISONER: (*a nod*) Do more. What else did he say?

HENRY: What else? I don't know. I had to bring mysen back 'ere 'fore the
searching parties set up. (*Thinks*) Wasn't what he said as mattered. It were who
he were ... bein', when he said it ...

PRISONER: (*slow*) I thought ye said he was ... being Danton, am I wrong ...?

HENRY: (*looking at him*) Danton. Right.

Silence.

PRISONER: Well. However long ye live, Henry, it's unlikely ye'll ever get closer to
the Man. Poor sod. (*He stands, drinks up, waits, wanders to the cage, sits on
the divan, stares back at the watching Henry. Shakes the chain on his ankle.*) If
ye've a minute, friend ...

Begins removing his greatcoat. Henry slings his musket, approaches with his keys. Stoops to unshackle him. The Prisoner looks down at the stooped, vulnerable guard; sees the head of the cut-throat stuffed into the boot-top; casually removes it.

HENRY: Thing is. It wasn't ... Danton ... I was minded of. Because. I don't know Danton, never met, never seen him ... It wasn't Danton Birdie was ... bein' Couldn'ta bin, could it, not for me.

The town clock strikes the half.

PRISONER: *(handing him the coat)* Here. Ye'll not forget to send word to your cousin ...

HENRY: *(simply)* It was you. Everything. Voice and Walk and head and ... Everything. *(He stands, folds the coat for carrying, drags the chain to the doorway, lays it down.)* I tell ye, I'd never play Last Words wi' the Three o'Clock Runner. He can make ye shiver ... Anyroad. That's the story. *(Turns, looks at him)* Any thoughts? Now it's told.

PRISONER: *(still)* Henry. Leave me be. *(He drags his legs onto the litter, lies back, closes his eyes. Quiet, metallic)* I cannot speak on this. Too. Painful. Too. Riving. It will make me weep again. And my tears will drown the world. Do not ask. I've cracked enough. More and I will break.

Henry waits. Closes door.

HENRY: I hear ye. *(Thinks)* Mister, I've tried to be honest with ye. I'll not alter now ... I'll not let my cousin take that letter, not from Him ... you. *(He turns the key in the lock)* Not now I know what I know. *(He holds on a moment or two, turns to clump back to the table. The Prisoner remains motionless.)* There it is.

PRISONER: *(Sudden, perfect)* Call this justice, ye dribbling sack o' snot, ye festering pot o' pig's piss, just remember, those who drink the people's blood die of it ...

Henry's resumed his seat at the table, his back once more to the cage, begun laying out cards; glances back at the motionless man; resumes his play.

PRISONER: *(Internal voice)* There be times we must strut and stamp and shake our whores' heads, though dignity and self-esteem deem it beneath us ... I will turn this boy, I will not let him be the death of me, I will win him to my purpose, I will turn him, he will not immure me inside the Bastille of his ignorance, I will touch his soul, he will turn ...

The Prisoner sits up sharply, feet to floor. Glares hard at the young Guard's back. Stands. Shifts to better light. Finds the declamatory stance. Launches.

(Sudden, big; as actor) ... Citizens, patriots, builders and shakers of the world's good morrow, you are welcome here. The New Theatre for the Old Cordeliers is proud and privileged to offer you this evening an entirely novel piece – the work principally of the celebrated revolutionary and poet Fabre d'Églantine, with additional scenes by members of the Company *(indicates them behind him)*, which we respectfully entitle *Danton Saves France* ... There

falls to me, dear friends, the enduring honour, the impossible task, of seeking
to fill the boots of our eponymous hero ... Yes, my friends, like a small boy
reaching for the Pole Star, I must essay for the evening ... the Man Himself
(shifts voice) Applause applause applause, company leave stage left, climb
onto the rostrum *(steps up onto divan)*, find the light ... *(as Danton again)*
Greetings, friends. Name's Danton, for those who don't know me. Born and
reared in the country, the Champagne, but not the sleek rolling part, the
scrawny bit ... of common stock, decent honest toilers, living useful lives in
uncelebrated places, dying obscurely as if they had never lived ... So expect no
charms and graces, I am as I come ... But come, friends, come and see for
yourselves. To my village, to our plain family house, to our life some thirty
years and several millennia ago, in the region of the fifteenth Louis – Louis the
Penultimate, as I prefer to call him – when the world and I were young ...

*He's slowed to a halt, confronting the scale of the problem. Stares at Henry, who
has turned to watch him on the arrival of Danton; moves to the bars.*

How will I fetch you to understanding, friend? Henry ... Why do you imagine
the Committee had *me* put here this night? D'ye think any piece of meat would
have served? I *played* him, Henry. In a *play.* For weeks and months I followed
him, watched him, heard him ... studied how I might become him, the voice
and walk and head. Everything. *(Stops)* So hard to speak of. So hard to ...
(Stops. Henry turns, looks at him) When you stand. In another man's boots.
Until they seem your own. And your own. No longer fit you ... Do ye
understand any of this, Henry? Ye know what ye know but ye do not know the
truth and I am powerless to tell ye because my mouth and throat are so ...
filled by it I cannot breathe, it is drowning me ...

He takes out the cut-throat, opens it. Henry rises, face pale, impossible to read.

Henry, were I indeed the Man-in-Question, the Hero of the Republic, the
Champion of the Oppressed, the Saviour of the Nation, the Towering Titan of
the Revolution, the People's Voice, the Bull among men, the Fathering Spirit of
all the Republics yet to be born into peace and justice and freedom and plenty,
were I *that* Man, Henry, surely by now I would have slit your insignificant
throat and fed you to the rats. *(Silence)* Instead ... *(He draws open his collars,
baring the blooded neck. Henry stares, eyes unblinking.)* I'll not be free until
He's dead and gone. But may not kill Him without I kill myself. Only in death
is there freedom: this is the true madness of our time. *(Pause)* I'm not the
Prince, Henry. I'm the frog who swallowed him ...

*He folds the cut-throat, stoops, lays it gently down outside the cage. Draws away
from the bars, to give him safe space.*

I could not harm ye. For you are a good man.

*Henry stares at the cut-throat, moves to gather it up; looks up at him from the
stoop. The man's eyes are raw, desperate. Silence. A sudden loud banging at the
doors. Henry stands, listens. It stops briefly.*

Henry ...

*The banging sets up again. Henry collects his musket, slogs off down the room.
The Prisoner follows his progress through the side-bars; sees him slide open the
grille-cover to mutter with someone outside; turns; stares out into the dark.*

> In one month last winter, eight hundred people died of hunger and cold in the
> district of St. Antoine. In all there are forty-eight such districts in the capital.
> Preponderantly the listed dead were menu people, this sad dullard's kind of
> people. No lawyers died, no bankers, no financiers and speculators, no
> surveyors and stock-agents, no judges, journalists, restaurateurs, commodity
> dealers, generals, elected members of the Convention; in short, none of our
> kind of people. I ate well last winter. My fire never lacked wood, my table
> meat, my linen laundering, my horses exercise. Who shall be happy …? If …?
> *(He's close but still it eludes him. He feels for it.)* … Two summers back, in the
> rising I commanded from my room that overthrew King Louis the Last and
> changed our world into yours, better than three hundred gave up their lives that
> it might be so. Harness-makers, hairdressers, house-painters, carpenters,
> joiners, hatters, tailors, locksmiths, bootmakers, domestics, laundrymen,
> brickworkers, staymakers, waiters and scores upon scores of citizens below
> these whom we in our wisdom had deemed too insignificant, that is too poor,
> to have the vote. Including two women from the market in Les Halles. All,
> once again, our Henry's kind of people. Who shall be happy …? Who? … For
> three whole years, we have been at war, with others and with ourselves. Who
> does the fighting, who does the dying? Robespierre? St. Just? Danton?

*He stops abruptly. Slowly turns. Henry's back, stands the other side of the bars
watching him, dealing with it all. Silence.*

HENRY: *(finally)* It's the Serjeant's boy down from the Gate House. They wait my
word. On the letter.

PRISONER: *(quiet)* What did ye tell him?

HENRY: I told him to wait till I had answer. Ye didn't weep.

PRISONER: Weep?

HENRY: Ye said if ye told the story it'd mek ye weep. Ye didn't weep.

*Silence. They gaze at each other through the bars. Birdsong; a touch stronger,
heading for sunrise. Soundlessly, barely perceptibly, in real time, the eyes begin to
fill, brim and spill.*

HENRY: *(blinking)* I told him to wait. Till I had answer.

*The tears grease the man's cheeks, nose, lips. More birdsong. The room has
gradually lightened a little; all but dawn. Henry heads once more for the doors.
The man turns away, rests the back of his head on the bars, weeping still.*

PRISONER: *(Internal voice; detached)* I touched him. I know it. He's touched.

*Henry returns to the table. Broods. Flicks a look at the cage. Begins to spread the
greatcoat on the floor. The Prisoner's sunk to his haunches in the straw, his back
against the side bars.*

HENRY: *(eventually; a touch annoyed)* It's sent. Go to sleep.

The man sits on like a stone. Henry lies on the greatcoat, stares at the cage; finally shucks over on to his other side; lost. The salle, the cage, the still men. The dark continues to thin. Birdsong; a blackbird. The Prisoner reaches out a kerchief, begins wiping his face.

PRISONER: *(a mumble)* My last blackbird. Little fucker.

Bring up fipple-flute and kettle-drum: Ça Ira, dreamlike. Bleed in, back-wall, slowed shot of light on water. Drum, flute, slowed light on water: dreamscape.

(Dream-voice) … Fêtes, pageants, plays, children's stories, public buildings, costume, modes of address, the names of seasons, years, months and days, songs, tunes, dances, custom, practice, ritual … We must create an Empire of Images. All will be re-made. We must colonize not just the minds … but the very lives of the people. All will be remade … A new vocabulary for a new world order …

> At Nantes
> A clear crisp morning
> Two hundred men women little ones
> Bound blindfold
> In a flatbottom boat
> Poled to the middle of the Loire estuary
> And scuttled
> Without warning
> Without due process
> Political opponents
> Men women little ones
> Now enemies of the people
> Appear in the new vocabulary
> Of the Marat Company who did it as
> Vertical deportations

When I said. One year ago. When we were young. 'Let the *government* take terrible measures, so that the *people* may not have to take them themselves' … Is this what I had in mind? … Is it? The Marat Company? Obeying orders? The Empire of Images. Virtue and Terror. Hope, despair. Love, hate. Kind, vicious. Hot. Cold. This is the inheritance, pale tiny faces in the gloom. Who shall be happy if not …? Not! Not! *(He reaches for the rest: it's still not there)* … And it was decreed that the sacred Empire of Images should stretch to the world's edge and beyond. And death would be no impediment. And lo! the great and willing David, at a cost of not less than the annual earnings of all the menu people of Nantes put together, defied Nature for three whole days in high stinking summer so that the blessed Martyr Marat's assassinated bodily remains might tastefully, decently and enduringly preside in person over his own funeral rites. Nature would be bettered. The body would be emptied and stuffed, the knife-wounds decorously diminished in size and stature for art's sake, the distressing skin condition masked, the unusably battered right arm

that was to hold the telling steel pen cut off and replaced with one in fuller
working order from the mortuary, the residual stench of natural decay
perfumed to sweetness, the unheroically lolling tongue slit in four strategic
sites to hold it steady ... Never mind we fight wars on four fronts, never mind
the British blockade shrivels supplies of food, never mind the country will
soon collapse into civil and atrocious war with itself. The Empire of Images
knows no nay and will be served ...

Fipple-flute cuts; drum plays on.

   ... Did we imagine *this* would not be remembered too? And. Built upon ...?

Drum cuts.

   Did Danton do this? Did any of us? For what? To make the world a better
place for our class of people?

Back-wall and downspot slowly die. The lips mutter on.

   ... If not. Not. If not ...

Fade to black.

Fade up.

   (from black) Ye still there? Of course you are ...

*Salle, cage. Strong sunlight shafts in from above, reshaping the space. The
Prisoner stands in the cage all but naked, washing and sluicing his body with
water from a metal bowl. Fade up reflected audience on back wall.*

   Looking back's all that's left ye, you spent what was left of the future long
since, you have nowhere else to look save back, do ye, poor sods ... *(Looks out
at the dark, smiles)* For myself, and for my sins, I'm doomed to hope and
chained to the present. This sixteenth day of Germinal in the Second Year of
the Free Republic. *(Approaches the front bars, drying himself)* You are in my
hands. Here, now. I feel you. We are the same flesh. Composed of the same
atoms. Everything we have thought, everything we have tried or imagined,
everything dreamt and whispered, designed, done ... you will develop and
perfect. Such a dish of worms we've served ye and ye'll eat 'em, every one.
The free dance of capital, the human imperative. The sovereign people, the all
seeing all saying State. Owner, worker. Nation and war, people and peace. The
power of the machine, the machinery of power. Me, all. The impossible and the
necessary dream. The road to freedom, mined every step of the way ...

Henry trudges up, a tray in his hands. The reflected audience fades.

HENRY: *(muttering, angry)* This is not guards' work. Bastards.

The Prisoner's dressing; crosses to the door to be shackled.

HENRY: *(Shackling with double leg iron)* Ye done? Yer carriage's come. Ye're to
leave at the half. *(The Prisoner nods, stretches, turns to gather his things.)* I've to
cut your hair.

PRISONER: What?

HENRY: Cut your hair.

PRISONER: What for?

HENRY: Because I'm told to. I'm to lift the hair from your collar.

He removes the linen cloth: bowl, shears, combs, metal mirror. The Prisoner watches carefully.

HENRY: Them's the orders.

He gestures him to sit at the table.

PRISONER: *(slow)* I understood the Man was still in trial, witnesses to be called, evidence to be heard ...

HENRY: That was yesterday. You wanna sit, friend?

The Prisoner leaves the cage, clanks slowly to the table, sits, face pale, still. Henry combs out his back hair, sizing up the cut needed.

HENRY: Trial's declared over. Jury's asked to proceed to judgment. Verdict's expected within the hour. S'what they say, how would I know ...?

PRISONER: If ye're cutting neck-hair, somebody knows, Henry ...

HENRY: Happen.

He shears off a hand of hair, lays it on the table. The man stares at it. The shears hover for the next slice.

PRISONER: Poor sod.

HENRY: Maybe.

A second cut, another hand to the table. The Prisoner picks it up, examines it.

PRISONER: Hey.

HENRY: What?

PRISONER: Ye done this before?

HENRY: No.

PRISONER: I thought not. Don't send me out like a bloody page boy, understood?

HENRY: This is Headsman's work.

PRISONER: Nevertheless.

HENRY: It'll grow.

PRISONER: Will it?

Silence. Henry eventually resumes the cut.

PRISONER: He's dead then.

HENRY: Good as.

PRISONER: Poor sod.

HENRY: Why?

PRISONER: Why?

HENRY: Ye think he's innocent?

PRISONER: No one is innocent, friend ...

HENRY: ... Then he's guilty. Fuck him.

Silence.

PRISONER: Guilty of what?

HENRY: How should I know?

PRISONER: Guilty of what?

HENRY: Living fat off the people, how 'bout that ...?

PRISONER: That's most folk in britches, Henry.

HENRY: Ahunh. (*Silence. Henry's all but finished. Holds up angled mirror.*) Ye wanna see?

PRISONER: No.

Henry begins to clear away and ferry trays down the room. Close shot of Prisoner, hands on table, the fingers twitching as he broods.

PRISONER: Is there word from your cousin?

HENRY: None. He'll be well abed by now.

PRISONER: And the letter ...?

HENRY: No word, no problem. It's done.

Town clock strikes the half. Silence. A brief look shared.

PRISONER: Ye're an honest man, Henry. I thank ye for your trust.

Henry heads off with the ablutions tray.

PRISONER: (*flicking a glance at the dark*) So. The farce ends. Almost time for last words ... Clop across the Pont-au-Change, pass the Quai de la Mègisserie, along the Rue de la Monnaie, down the Rue Honoré to the Rue National, a wave for the terrace of the Café du Montparnasse – Gabrielle, Louise – And ... Eh voilà! . . Place de la Révolution. Where all this ... history began. Alpha and Omega. The first and the last. Full circle. I am here. Last words then. What shall they be? Be sure to show them my head, it's worth seeing ...? Let the Committee take my head, the people already have my heart ... (*Starts chuckling*) Now ye see me, now ye don't ...?

Banging at the doors again. He turns, peers at Henry talking through the grille.

PRISONER: *(still dealing with Last Words)* ... No, I should leave with a question ...

He stands, puts his hands behind his back as if tied, gazes out across the muted throng.

> WHO SHALL BE HAPPY ...?
> IF ...? WHO SHALL BE HAPPY, IF NOT ...?
> IF *NOT?*

Henry up the room sharpish, fiddling a length of rope from his pocket.

HENRY: You're to be readied, the Guards're on their way ... Your cart's stood by.

He wraps the rope around the Prisoner's wrists, still behind his back, secures them.

PRISONER: *(Carefully)* Cart. Henry?

HENRY: Cart, carriage ...

In the silence, the sound of hooves, wheels on courtyard cobble nearby.

PRISONER: So is there. A verdict through?

HENRY: *(not looking)* Guilty. All charges.

He tugs at the second anklet. Stands. Eyes meet.

HENRY: Ye right, are ye?

PRISONER: I'm searching a question, Henry. Have to find it.

HENRY: It'll have to wait. *(Draws a leather hood from his pocket)* Ye're to leave as ye came ...

Silence.

PRISONER: *(staring at it)* In our ends lie our beginnings ...?

HENRY: What?

PRISONER: Last words.

HENRY: Game's over. *(Prepares the hood)* Orders.

Silence. The Prisoner shuffles to the stool, sits, his back to the guard. Henry quietly moves in behind him.

PRISONER: I see.

Henry bags the head, draws the cords, ties them.

HENRY: Ye breathin'?

Only the lips, nostrils and chin are darkly visible, beyond the air-slit provided at the mouth. He nods. Henry leaves the table area, gathering up his gear and belongings. A tight spot frames the Prisoner's hooded face, the vent, the barely seen mouth behind it.

256   TREVOR GRIFFITHS

PRISONER: (*a whisper*) I'm sixteen. I'm in Rheims. I'm standing in a long line of
   dignitaries clutching their cards of invitation outside the Cathedral. My clothes
   are borrowed, the money for the journey stolen, I have no card but I will go
   through, I will see the young Louis anointed King, let him stop me who dare.
   The town police keep back the crowds. There are cheers for the queuing
   worthies, I find myself ... waving acknowledgement. Just ahead, a clamour of
   beggars has wormed a way through the barricades and onto the steps of the
   West Door. Worthy coins appear on cue to soothe their noise, I fumble for a
   spare ten-sous piece, heart thumping I'll be found out ...

Long silence. Remote sounds of fists on doors down the room.

> One year ago. A day or so
> After.
> After.
> My Gabrielle. Birthing a dead
> daughter ...
> Died ...

Silence

> And I had.
> Detained in Belgium.
> Back too late. Dug up
> her corpse ...
> Detained in Belgium, did ye say ...?
> Service to the Revolution the highest law implied ...?
> Pull the other
> one, my friend, it plays
> a tolerable version of
> *Ça Ira.* In Belgium ye were
> Looking out for yourself.
> Doing deals, securing
> Your loot, covering your tracks,
> Saving France of course
> And fucking
> Everything in skirts
> That moved.

Silence.

> And knew. All
> Along. She was like
> To die.
> With this one ...

*Silence. The lips move on, soundless. Henry's at the door, standing the Prisoner's
escorts by; eventually begins the trudge back towards the table.*

PRISONER: No one is innocent.

Living's a guilty business ...

HENRY: (*from distance*) Let's go.

PRISONER: (*fast, urgent*) ... A beggar reaches for my ten-sous piece, his thick hand snaps around my wrist, I cannot shake the bugger, the tocsin swells, I'll miss the King ... The man speaks: Ask him a question. Ask him a question. Come back and tell me what he says. Ask him ...

Henry's arrived. Waits, frowning, in the growing silence.

HENRY: Let's go.

PRISONER: (*simply*) Who shall be happy, if not everyone?

Silence. Henry taps the Prisoner's shoulder, helps him up.

PRISONER: Henry.

HENRY: What?

PRISONER: I'll say goodbye.

HENRY: Aye.

He leads him out; scans the room; gathers a few remaining odds and ends; places them on or by the table for off. Picks up a lamp, lays it on a stool. Sits on the other stool, takes out watch, ring and purse of money, lays them out. The greatcoat joins them. He takes out his pipe. Can't find his flint. Reaches for his musket. Removes the furled letter from the barrel. Tapers it to the lamp. Lights his pipe. Fipple flute and drum: Ça, Ira.

Salle, cage. Flute out; drum on alone.

Henry gathers his gear, trudges off. The back-wall comes to life again: the audience is left with itself,

Black.

END

CAMEL STATION

Camel Station was written in early 2001 for *The Artists Network of Refuse and Resist*, as part of an evening of staged readings of new short plays under the collective title *Imagine: Iraq*.

The event was organised by playwright Naomi Wallace, and took place on 19th November 2001 at the Cooper Union Hall in New York. Eleven hundred people came.

A version of the story told in the play, which eventually inspired the writing of the play itself, was told me in 1995 in joke form by a Palestinian film cameraman from Gaza, while I was staying in a small village on the West Bank working on a theatre project with Akram Telawe and a group of Palestinian actors.

Trevor Griffiths

This re-worked version of *Camel Station* was first performed at the Studio Theatre in the V&A Theatre Museum in Covent Garden, London on 4 April 2006. It formed part of a triple bill of short plays by Trevor Griffiths collectively titled *To The Mountain*. The cast was as follows:

Tarik   Fenar Mohammed-Ali
Suriya   Lisa Came
Director   Tamara Hinchko
Designer   Lisa Came

To The Mountain was produced by Alexander McConnell for the Little London Theatre Company.

Camel Station

Northern No-Fly Zone, Iraq. Mountain pastures near Nineveh. Hot. A small battery radio, on its last legs, relays ecstatic commentary on the Iraq-Iran world cup qualifying match from the national stadium. **Tarik**, *13, perched on a rock beside it, works on something in a notebook, voicing words and phrases as he writes. He wears traditional arab work-dress, though the kuffiah is round his neck, to make room for the NYY baseball cap shading his eyes. Across his back, an ancient Lee Enfield from the Second World War.*

TARIK: ... The sign reads: (*thinks*) alHourani – Camel Station. Is it a mirage, the tricks of the desert, the Man from Tikrit asked himself. How can this be real?

He looks up at the sky, listens. The radio sputters to nothing. He listens on. A thin wisp of sound from the stratosphere slowly asserts in the silence. He unslings the rifle. Takes aim at the pale blue sky.

TARIK: (*Sighting*) How. Can this. Be. Real? (*Fakes firing*) Boosh. Boosh. Boosh.

A girl's shout from below. Sheep bleat, men call. He looks down the hill, re-slings the rifle, returns to his notebook.

SURIYA: (*Still toiling up*) Hey! HeadinaBook. I brought you food. (*She arrives, stops by the rock, lays down a muslin-wrapped parcel and a plastic bottle of water*) Surprised to see me? By, you've grown. You're as tall as me. (*She fondles his head, he resists*) My little cousin. (*She drinks from the bottle, hands it to him*) They told me down there you were on wolf watch, your father's so rich he can afford to lose his flock ...?

She's already looking up. The dull remote groan of a plane reasserts. Tarik sneaks a shy look at her. Black robe, white scarf. Sixteen.

TARIK: My mam said you were in Baghdad. (*She scans on*) Studying medicine. (*Nothing*) Too hard, was it?

SURIYA: (*Eyes on sky*) My mother's sick, I'm looking after her. (*The sky*) There's nothing there ...

TARIK: Reconnaissance. (*She looks at him*) No pilot. (*Returns to his pad*) American.

SURIYA: How do you know that?

TARIK: It's Tuesday. Tuesday's America Day (*Turns pages; rubs out a word, writes in another*) It'll be sending back your picture. Couple of minutes they'll be here in person. (*Shy peek*) Taking a look. (*He imitates a fighter plane buzzing the hillside, head and mouth*) Zoooosh. (*Points behind him up the mountain*) And if you look up there ... you should be able to make out ...

SURIYA: ... Eat, child. Go on. (*He fiddles with a piece of cheese*) Do you want the fig? (*He shrugs, she takes it*) Should be able to make out ...?

TARIK: Three wolves. Been there all morning. (*She looks. Finds them.*) How do I know they're still there, with my head in a book? (*Sniffs*) I smell them. My father your uncle tells me to watch for wolves, he does not tell me how. You think he's so rich he can afford a fool for a son? And don't call me child …

SURIYA: (*Chuckles*) All right, I'm sorry, all right? … (*Settles beside him on the ledge, puts an arm around his shoulder, helps herself to cheese*) My mother your aunt said they were sending you to the Hakawati School in Nineveh, is that right? (*Eats on*) I'll call you Hakawati. Hakawati of Nineveh, Teller of the People's History …

TARIK: I haven't passed my entrance yet.

SURIYA: You will. Everybody knows you were born with an old soul.

TARIK: Maybe. I still have to tell them a story …

SURIYA: The scholars? (*He nods*) Is that it?

TARIK: (*Working on*) Ahunh.

SURIYA: Can I read it?

TARIK: It's not for reading. It has to be told …

He flicks back through the revised pages. Closes the book. Stands up on the rock. Gazes out across the valley, his lips moving in silence as if delivering the tale.

SURIYA: So tell it. (*She moves from the rock, sits facing him in the dirt*) I'll be the scholars … (*She reworks her scarf into a puffed up turban; sits formal, upright; plays with her beard; aged voice*) Proceed, Hourani Tarik. It is time to lay your words upon the air between us. Be sure to speak up. And while you're at it, remove that silly hat …

TARIK: You're making fun …

SURIYA: (*Laughing*) No I'm not. Honest. I'm not. (*He screws up his nose*) I really want to hear it. (*Coaxing*) Remember the poems you wrote me, before I went off to college? I still have them.

TARIK: No you don't. You tore them up in front of me and dropped them on my shoes …

SURIYA: I was only fifteen for heaven's sake. I have them in my head.

TARIK: I bet …

SURIYA: Tarik. (*He looks at her*). Send scorpions to my bed if I tell a lie. I want to hear your story. I love your stories …

Tarik sniffs, hops down from the rock, restores kuffiah to head, improvises a travel staff, walks around, seeking the zone. She claps her hands, pleased.

TARIK: I haven't started yet …

He moves out of sight behind the rock, climbs slowly into view, stares around as if at a crowd, bangs the stick ceremonially three times.

TARIK: (*Fast, fluent; the standard opening*) … Glory to the One who made the heritage of antiquity a guide for our own time, for it is from this heritage are drawn the tales of the hakawati and all that is in them of fable and adventure … (*Another bang of the stick*) One night, in time long gone, while the country languished in the grip of foreign invasion, and plague and famine swept the land like fire on the wind, it came to pass that our ruler Caliph Saddam alTikriti, beloved Father of the Nation, had a troubling dream.

He takes out his notebook, checks lines, crosses out. She watches him.

SURIYA: Tarik, you'll change his name, won't you. They'll slaughter you …

TARIK: (*On*) … In the dream his formidable relative Great Aunt Tagrid Hourani, known throughout the North as the Midwife of Tikrit, appeared at the foot of his Bed of State and bade him rise. Take off your shirt, Saddam, she croaked, and stand before the glass, that you may see what you have become. The Caliph meekly did as he was bidden. With her hand the Midwife traced the mounded fat and wasted muscle that hung upon his bones. Where is the bright boy I pulled into this world of joy and pain? How long you have strutted these prideful palace passages, how long you have gorged on rich meats and softened in priceless silks. And now the enemy is at your door, your will and your spirit have crumbled like your flesh, and neither you nor our suffering people will be saved unless you do what I instruct. First, you will leave this place of sin and selfish ease and go back to Tikrit, to the place whence you sprang, to your kin who raised you and to the common folk who taught you all a man needs to know of kindness, of courtesy and of honour. For only thus can you recover your will to do good for the people you rule. As for recovering spirit and body, which lie together like green and blue on a woodpecker's wing, you must then journey alone into the great northern desert, feel the wind on your face, the sun on your back, the sand on your lips, and be as one with yourself and with the nature that gives you life and breath and a pumping heart. And when you have done all this, only then may you return to your palace confident of winning the enduring peace your people ask for and your heart will again desire.

He checks the notebook again; makes another edit. Suriya clacks two stones together, unhappy at his drift.

TARIK: What? You're bored?

SURIYA: Not at all. I'm worried …

TARIK: It's too long, I'll cut it …

SURIYA: Don't you see …?

TARIK: Hear me out. (*Bangs the stick. On*) The next morning, while his counsellors waited for their usual meeting, the Caliph wrote a short note of instruction to his Vizier, slipped from the Palace, saddled a horse and set out for the north. Of the days and nights he spent there in Tikrit, of hard work and simple pleasure, of the truths he learned again from the common folk, of the goodness and courtesy of villagers at one with their lives, the scribes of all ages have had abundant say

and need not detain us. Enough to say, when he came to the end of his stay
there, his will once again strong and clear, he knew absolutely the dream was
real and must be followed to its end. With a camel bought from a travelling
Sudani, a tent and provisions from the tiny souk, maps of the waterholes and the
night skies, he set out alone, lit only by the moon, on the journey that would
make him a man again at one with his life and with the world of nature he had
all but forgotten. But if the dream was real, so was the camel. On the second
night it took him an hour to haul it to its feet and get it moving. On the third, he
had to walk ahead and drag it. On the fourth it collapsed in an untidy heap in
the sand as if dead. The sun rose and still it did not move, beat it all he may.
And fear trickled down into his heart like boiling fat. And questions flicked at
his brain like the tongues of lizards. What am I doing here? How can the dream
be real if I am to die alone in the wilderness? How could I buy a camel from a
bloody travelling Sudani … ? (*Suriya yelps. He grins at her*) The Man from
Tikrit scans the empty horizon, left, right, before, behind. Nothing. And yet not
quite nothing. On top of a large dune some way off something green, something
flapping in the breeze, something flapping greenly up ahead. He grabs his
waterbottle and scrambles up the slope. And slowly as he climbs, it comes into
view, a large green tent, a small green flag flapping from its roof, and on the
tent a sign which read alHourani – Camel Station. Is it a mirage, the tricks of
the desert, he asked himself? How can this be real? As if in answer, a man
dressed in faded boiler suit and wiping his hands on an oily rag appears in the
doorway. Welcome, brother, he calls. Come inside, I'll make some tea, you look
like a man with a problem. Are you … the owner? asks the Man from Tikrit.
Abdel Hourani, at your service. How can I help? We do full service, top up,
repairs and parts. You do have a camel, do you? Broke down, bottom of the hill,
says the Caliph. Right, you'll need recovery then. He whistles up his two boys
and off they go to bring in the camel. Inside the tent, while Hourani mashes
sweet green tea from Jericho, the Caliph finds his eyes drawn upwards to the
roof of the tent, where a maze of sacred and profane texts have been painted in
gold leaf on the green canvas. And at the very heart of the maze, six lines from
the great epic of Gilgamesh, first of earthly kings, builder of the first city, which
he had learned from his mother and long since forgotten. *Be what you are. Seek
not what you may not find. Let your every day be full of joy. Love the child that
holds your hand. Let your wife delight in your embrace. For these alone are the
concerns of humanity.* How can this be real? he asked aloud. How can it not?
replied Hourani, handing him the tea. Your camel's on its way, drink up, there's
work to do. At length the boys return dragging the beast behind them and
Hourani takes it into the workshop to look it over. Ahunh, he says, I can fix this,
no problem. Place him over the inspection pit. When the camel's in position, he
climbs down into the pit to take a closer look. The Man from Tikrit looks on,
amazed. Do you know whose life it is you're saving, he whispers. Uhunh,
answers Hourani, studying the job. Your Caliph's, Saddam alTikriti's, that's
whose life you're saving. Is that right, says the man. Well well well. Hand me
those two stones, will you. Saddam hands him the stones, Hourani takes one in
each palm and lines up the camel's testicles between them …

SURIYA: (*Shrieking*) Tarik! You can't. ...!

TARIK: ... and Bang!!! The camel leaps two feet into the air with a mighty bellow and shoots off to the horizon like a Saudi racehorse ...

Suriya shrieks again, her frame wracked with laughter. Tarik sniffs, turns to look across at the wolf ledge up the hill.

TARIK: The wolves! They've gone ... (*Sudden, loud*) DOWN!

He leaps to shield her, seconds before an F15 screams past, two hundred feet above their heads. Displaced air pounds around the space, the noise slowly drains to nothing. Tarik helps her to her feet. Disturbed shouts, bleats, from down the hill.

TARIK: You all right?

SURIYA: God save us.

TARIK: ... They do worse than that sometimes. Maybe he did.

He brushes hair and dust from her face with a finger. A man's call from below: Suriya! Are you all right? Get down here now. Get down here, girl. *She smiles at Tarik.*

SURIYA: (*Calling*) Coming, Baba ... (*Tarik returns to sit on his rock ledge*) I have to go ... (*He nods*) Is there much more? (*He shakes his head*) Go on then ...

Another huge shout from below.

SURIYA: (*Loud*) I'm coming, Baba. On my way.

She shrugs her shoulders, makes a rueful face, begins to thread her way down the slope. He follows to watch her go.

TARIK: (*Calling after her*) ... There you are, Caliph, says Hourani, all fixed and up and running. What do you mean, screams alTikriti, how in God's name am I going to catch him? Not a problem, says Hourani. Get over the pit ...

She erupts into laughter. He giggles, pleased. Listens to her laughter trailing back up the hill. Smiles. Frowns, hearing something.

TARIK: (*Screaming after her*) Coming BACK!!!

The plane screams back, a hundred feet further down the hill. Rafts of bullets smash into the hillside, scything through him and the entire space he's in. He twitches and twirls with the impact, like a crow caught in a wire fence. Light thickens, darkens. The din deafens, tails away.

Silence. A slow distant moan climbs the hill: men, sheep. A single bright white downspot asserts, silvering the boy's head and face. Silence finally.

TARIK: (*His voice strangely altered, as if disembodied*) Baba. Suriya. Are you all right? I'm fine. I'm OK. I'm OK. (*He stares up at the sky. Addresses it.*) How can this. Be real? Mm? You do what you will. We do what we must. Do what you will with my body, you cannot quench the spirit it bears. Burn me in your

flames, a hundred will grow in my place. With these acts you demand your
own destruction, we have no choice but to oblige. My every day will not be
full of joy. No child will hold my hand and feel my love. No wife delight in
my embrace. But as with me, so with you. Call it not revenge but justice. We
will chase you down the days until you are no longer. This you demand. This
you shall have. (*He draws the Yankees cap from his tunic.*) No more Yankees,
Yankee. (*He pitches the cap into the dark. Takes out the notebook*) No more
stories ...

*He lifts his rifle one-handed above his head. Stares his calm defiance at the dark.
Fade in Sufi love song: Biba Sada Dil Morr De by Nusrat Fateh Ali Khan.*

The spot slowly fades to black.

END